A JOURNEY THROUGH QUALITATIVE RESEARCH

To our students

A JOURNEY THROUGH QUALITATIVE RESEARCH

FROM DESIGN TO REPORTING

STÉPHANIE GAUDET

&

DOMINIQUE ROBERT

Los Angeles | London | New Delhi
Singapore | Washington DC | Melbourne

Los Angeles | London | New Delhi
Singapore | Washington DC | Melbourne

SAGE Publications Ltd
1 Oliver's Yard
55 City Road
London EC1Y 1SP

SAGE Publications Inc.
2455 Teller Road
Thousand Oaks, California 91320

SAGE Publications India Pvt Ltd
B 1/I 1 Mohan Cooperative Industrial Area
Mathura Road
New Delhi 110 044

SAGE Publications Asia-Pacific Pte Ltd
3 Church Street
#10-04 Samsung Hub
Singapore 049483

Editor: Jai Seaman
Assistant editor: Alysha Owen
Assistant editor, digital: Chloe Statham
Production editor: Katherine Haw
Copyeditor: Neville Hankins
Proofreader: Andy Baxter
Indexer: Charmain Parkin
Marketing manager: Ben Griffin-Sherwood
Cover design: Bhairvi Gudka
Typeset by: C&M Digitals (P) Ltd, Chennai, India
Printed in the UK

© Stéphanie Gaudet and Dominique Robert 2018

First published 2018

Apart from any fair dealing for the purposes of research or private study, or criticism or review, as permitted under the Copyright, Designs and Patents Act, 1988, this publication may be reproduced, stored or transmitted in any form, or by any means, only with the prior permission in writing of the publishers, or in the case of reprographic reproduction, in accordance with the terms of licences issued by the Copyright Licensing Agency. Enquiries concerning reproduction outside those terms should be sent to the publishers.

Library of Congress Control Number: 2017947699

British Library Cataloguing in Publication data

A catalogue record for this book is available from the British Library

ISBN 978-1-4462-6712-7
ISBN 978-1-4462-6713-4 (pbk)

At SAGE we take sustainability seriously. Most of our products are printed in the UK using FSC papers and boards. When we print overseas we ensure sustainable papers are used as measured by the PREPS grading system. We undertake an annual audit to monitor our sustainability.

CONTENTS

ABOUT THE AUTHORS

Stéphanie Gaudet is an Associate Professor in the School of Sociological and Anthropological Studies at the University of Ottawa, Canada. She teaches qualitative research at the undergraduate and graduate levels as well as political sociology and life course analysis. Her current research interests include civic and political involvement, sociology of youth and family, as well as life course analysis.

Dominique Robert is an Associate Professor in the Department of Criminology at the University of Ottawa, Canada. She teaches qualitative research at the under-graduate and graduate levels as well as courses on science and technology. Her current research interests include scientific and technological controversies as well as the biographies of scientific objects in behavior genetics and neurosciences.

ACKNOWLEDGMENTS

We are grateful for all the support, assistance, friendship and conversations we had during the thinking and writing of this book. We owe a lot to a Quebec tradition of qualitative researchers such as Pierre Paillé, Jean Poupart, Jean-Pierre Deslauriers, Lionel Groulx, Anne Laperrière, Robert Mayer and Alvaro Pires. They founded a tradition of inductive researchers informed by the American tradition of the sociological Chicago school and the European epistemological and theoretical tradition. This book is largely inspired by their teaching. We also owe to our students from the past 15 years at the undergraduate and graduate levels. They helped us learn and communicate qualitative research. We are indebted toward Alexis Truong for the meticulous formatting work but mostly for the enlightened comments on the previous version of the manuscript. We are very appreciative of our colleagues in the Department of Criminology and the School of Sociological and Anthropological Studies, namely Chris Bruckert, Maritza Felice-Luna and Martin Dufresne, for discussions on research, pedagogy and all the rest. We are grateful to Françoise-Moreau Johnson at the Centre for Academic Leadership at the University of Ottawa for the writing retreats and writing groups she organized. This project has been made possible with the financial participation of the Office of the Vice-President Academic and Provost, University of Ottawa. We also want to thank Uri Ben-Gal for his diligent editing and translation work as well as the reviewers whose comments made the last version better and more consistent. This book could not have come to fruition without the patience and support from our editorial and production team at SAGE, namely, Jai Seaman, Alysha Owen, Katherine Haw and Neville Hankins. Finally, qualitative research can exist because of all those people who are willing to share their life experience at length with all of us who are trying to make sense of the world we live in. Thank you to all the people who make empirical research possible, especially Michael Parenti and Jodi.

PREFACE

How do people become politically involved in their communities? Why do young adults participate in cosplay and immerse themselves in manga culture? How do senior citizens come to equate a prescription for a drug with a gesture of care on the part of their family doctor? What rationales do correctional officers use to send a prisoner to disciplinary confinement? How is neuroscience mobilized to give a new legitimacy to the controversial diagnosis of psychopathy? What are the life-trajectory commonalities among high school dropouts? How do citizens produce and publicize their own scientific knowledge in order to resist the fracking industry in their area? Asking and answering incisive questions are your tasks as students of the social world we live in. This is especially so when you undertake a formal qualitative research project as part of your studies or your job.

Research is an exciting endeavor. Having the time (but never enough) to dedicate yourself to the completion of a research project that is important to you is a treat. Reading thoroughly the research and theory pertaining to your topic; gathering or producing research material; analysing it all and proposing an interpretation – in sum, generating knowledge – is a privilege. But it does not always feel like it. Undertaking a research project is an uneasy journey with unplanned detours, necessary reappraisals of the efforts needed to continue, and quite a bit of soul searching. In our experience, there is no avoiding some discomfort in the process. However, it is easier to go through it with a guiding team. Over the course of 15 years of accompanying students through their first undergraduate qualitative research projects, their Masters theses, as well as their PhD dissertations, we have had the good fortune to be part of many successful guiding teams. And it is in this spirit of guidance that we have written this book.

There are competent prescriptive books on conducting qualitative research. There are also knowledgeable in-depth monographs relating to one school of qualitative research or another. We like both categories of books. And we will not hesitate, during the course of your journey, to refer you to some of them. However, this book does not offer you a strict recipe to conduct your qualitative research project, nor a definitive summation of qualitative research. We wrote this book as a companion to help you become the autonomous, adventurous, but rigorous qualitative researcher that you can be.

In the first part, we will provide you with solid points of reference relating to epistemology, methodology, qualitative research approaches, qualitative techniques and ethics – using detailed examples of real research in action. Knowing your options is a necessary condition for being a free and creative producer of knowledge. Our goal is for you to feel confident in designing your own path, not just following a well-laid-out map. In the second part of the book, we will focus on analysing qualitative material, a process that is too often neglected in other method books. We will demystify the multilayered approach to producing research results by providing you with the concrete example of a research project we conducted and a detailed analysis of our sources, using different analytical strategies. We will give you advice, suggest tasks for the completion of your own project, recommend guidelines for decision-making, discuss concrete interpretive challenges, and offer some ways to produce strong and convincing research results.

We want this book to accompany you from the beginning to the end of your project, like a mentor who questions, inspires, suggests options, slows you down when needed, but energizes you as well. We wish to be by your side through the transformative experience that qualitative research can be.

HOW TO USE THE ONLINE RESOURCES

A Journey Through Qualitative Research: From Design to Reporting is supported by a wealth of online resources for both students and lecturers to aid study and support teaching. These resources can be found at **https://study.sagepub.com/gaudetandrobert.**

FOR STUDENTS

Glossary **flashcards** help you get to grips with key terms and revise for exams.

A library of **SAGE Research Methods cases and SAGE journal articles** show you how methods outlined in the book can be used in the real world and give you additional advice-by-example on applying these methods to your own research.

A **consent form template** offers you a customizable, downloadable, and printable form for use in your own interview-based research.

Full transcripts from examples discussed in the book – the Michael parenti conference speech and repertoires as well as the interview with Jodi on social participation – will give you the chance to experience discourse analysis, grounded theory, and narrative analysis in action and follow along with the authors' analysis step-by-step.

Links to the two **SAGE Research Methods videos** referenced in Chapter 3 will give you more insight into netnography and observing in a milieu.

FOR LECTURERS

PowerPoint slides featuring key topics from the book can be downloaded and customized for use in your own presentations.

1
CHOOSING QUALITATIVE INQUIRY

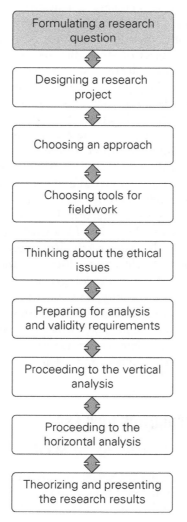

Figure 1.1 Where we are in the research process

IN THIS CHAPTER, YOU WILL LEARN:

- To define qualitative inquiry as a knowledge production process based on iteration.
- To identify the different phases of an iterative research process.
- To formulate a qualitative research question.
- To understand different epistemological stances in qualitative inquiry.

INTRODUCTION

This book is not about following recipes, but about learning the art of creating your own. As great chefs, we need skills to choose, prepare and mix our ingredients as well as knowledge transmitted by our discipline to create new recipes. The creative process is endless. Qualitative research is a never-ending journey. There are always new phenomena to learn about, new **methods** to invent and new forms of knowledge to create.

The social is your object of study. Because it is complex, dynamic and inter-subjective, we believe it calls for a specific type of **research design**. In this first chapter, our aim is to help you design your project on the foundation of an **iterative process**. That is, a research activity that continuously moves from the **empirical** basis of your study up to its theoretical apparatus and down again to the empirical basis. In short, there is a continuous dialogue between research material and theoretical aspects of the research project.

In this chapter, we will address three important elements of your qualitative research project: (1) your ontological and epistemological beliefs; (2) their connections to your research question; and (3) the iterative-driven research process of a qualitative scientific production. In more epistemological terms, we are inviting you to understand the realm of knowledge production you are most comfortable working in: **realist**, **constructionist** or **constructivist epistemology**.

You might ask yourself: why are we discussing these theoretical questions at the beginning of a book on methodology? Talking about methodology is talking about how we observe reality, how we describe it, and how we create and organize our descriptions and explanations of social phenomena. Methodology is the reflection on methods, which are tools to observe the world. Moreover, methodology contributes to the creation of **scientific knowledge**. That is why it is so important to understand what is being created while using qualitative methods.

THE KNOWLEDGE PRODUCTION PROCESS

CREATING KNOWLEDGE IS ENACTING THE SOCIAL

By questioning and explaining the social, researchers are enacting it. This is a huge responsibility and an incredible experience of creative thinking! Because of the historical and dynamic world we try to describe, understand and explain, it is very difficult (and not necessarily desirable) to create knowledge labeled as **universal**. By that, we mean producing explicit laws explaining the production of a phenomenon. For example, in natural science, we observed several times that the boiling point of water is 100°C. We can now predict, based on a universal law that water will evaporate at 100° C. It is almost impossible to find such a universally valid causal relationship in the social world among a **situation** (temperature), an element (water) and their consequence (evaporation).

> Causal relationships are established in natural science by the observation of repetitions in an experiment.

Until now, no social scientist has succeeded in identifying such universal laws because the characteristics we observe differ significantly from those of nature. It is historically situated, it is a complex object, it can take several meanings and it is based on **subjective** relationships. It doesn't mean that there is no causality in social sciences. It means that causality has a different meaning. It is not a relationship based on constant consequences between element A and B as in natural science. It means that A is part of the process by which the phenomenon is produced.

> In social sciences, a cause is an element that belongs to the constitution of the phenomenon. (Campenhoudt and Quivy, 2011)

Defining the 'social' is the cornerstone of any social science project. No one has the same answer, but many would agree that what is social is what results from relationships: relationships among humans, and among humans and non-humans. Also, social phenomena are historically situated. Thus, they remain mostly singular. They are created through relationships over time, shaped by the legacies of the generations, **institutions** and organizations that characterize particular societies. For example, the experience of being a female prisoner in a specific country is historically shaped by the laws, the prisons as architectural realities, the social policies and the training of the professionals working with that prisoner. That 'prisoner' depends on the institutional research (university and government) and the accumulated knowledge transmitted through the training and personal experience of those professionals.

The complexity of the social does not mean we cannot produce any knowledge about it. Many social scientists help us to develop a better understanding of our world. They create **localized knowledge**, knowledge that does not aspire to be universal but rather contextual to a time and a place and situated. It helps to improve society through better public policies, public programs or interventions. This localized knowledge leads us to enact the social. For example, we create social realities by naming, describing and interpreting them. Creating new understandings of social realities can sometimes help to deconstruct taboos and empower people. Sometimes new solutions come with new **interpretations** of problems.

Because we enact the social, we have a responsibility both to ensure the **validity** and to identify the limitations of the knowledge we produce. As qualitative researchers, we first need to admit that the knowledge we produce cannot explain straightforward causal relationships. Thus, the value and strength of the qualitative inquiry is to 'provide a rich understanding of complex social contexts – not its ability to provide a causal explanation of events' (Pascale, 2011: 40).

INTERPRETATION AND EXPLANATION OF SCIENTIFIC KNOWLEDGE PRODUCTION

Any scientific knowledge production implies both explanation and interpretation of a particular phenomenon. For Bourdieu, interpretation and explanation are linked and might even occur concurrently (Bourdieu et al., 1983). For a pedagogical view, we will distinguish them as two ideal objectives of knowledge production. We would define an explanation as the demonstration of relationships between things, such as patterns or recurrences. Explanations are based mostly on a **hypothetico-deductive** process of knowledge production. Explanations based on **statistical generalization** are often considered more suited to objects observed in nature and less pertinent to the analysis of historical phenomena. However, many statistical analyses are able to identify strong causal relationships between social categories such as social class, gender and race. These types of knowledge help to explain large causal relationships, and inform us about deep social trends in societies. Even if these types of research mostly explain, reliable interpretation of social situations will tend toward **theoretical generalization** – which means that the knowledge produced could explain other similar cases even if we could not statistically generalize to a universal conclusion (Pires, 1997).

Sociologists such as Dominique Schnapper (1999) insist that good social research embodies a tension between explanation and interpretation, but one has to know from which pole one is working. The research objectives and the research question will determine if the aim of the research is more likely to produce an explanation – and rely on a linear knowledge production process. Or rather to provide an interpretation – and rely on an iterative production process (Figure 1.2).

If your aim is to observe a complex phenomenon such as culture, your research design should gravitate toward the interpretation pole and develop an iterative architecture. For example, in each society, cultural boundaries exist to delineate who belongs to 'us' (as a 'community of identification') and who belongs to 'them'. In a society highly segregated by race, such as the United States, cultural groups might form around the historical black minority, the

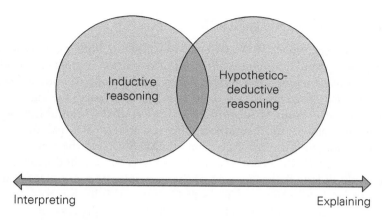

Figure 1.2 Interpreting and explaining

historical white majority and other groups (Latino, Asian, Arabic, etc.). Such boundaries can be found through interviews and historical analysis. No universal law can explain the changing cultural boundaries among the groups. In Table 1.1, we present the different aims of observation and description in iterative and linear research models. Here, we refer to observation in a general manner that covers any tool to gather or produce data (we will talk about observation in the strict sense in Chapter 4).

Table 1.1 The iterative and linear research models

	Iterative	Linear
Observations	Observations are mostly multivocal (they are mostly co-constructed by the researcher and the participant)	Observations aim to be univocal because they will be transformed into variables
	Observations are mostly qualitative but they can also be quantitative; however, they are not pre-established	Observations can be qualitative or quantitative but are generally pre-established categories applied to what we see (gender, professions, number of children)
	Researchers know the topic, want to study it but are always open to serendipity. They do not exactly know the type of information they will get from fieldwork	Researchers know exactly what type of information they want to have
		Interview grids or questionnaires are standardized
Descriptions	Search for meanings and regularities	Search for regular relationships among variables
	Researchers work with self-analysis on their research process	Researchers try to avoid interpretations
Level of generalization	Localized/theoretical generalization	Statistically generalized to a population

METHODOLOGY AND EPISTEMOLOGY

As we explained above, all knowledge is based on both explanations and interpretations, but qualitative methods are mostly aiming at producing interpretations of phenomena. What makes a valid body of knowledge is not a simple choice of methods and data. It is the coherence, the **rigor** and the transparency of a chain of scientific decisions related to the object of study, the problem related to this object, the research questions, the possible answers, the methods of data collection and analysis, and the conclusion. The hard thinking in this decision-making process is the methodology. In other words, methodology is the 'analysis of the principles or procedures of inquiry in a particular field' (*Merriam-Webster Online*, n.d.). In this book, we focus on qualitative methodology defined as an iterative process of knowledge production. Our conception of methodology is not based on a choice of data such as work or numbers, or a choice of methods, for example observation vs. questionnaire. Rather, it derives from a chain of decision-making that will help define your epistemological stance and your research design.

The first thing to do is decide whether a quantitative or qualitative methodology is the most suitable form of inquiry for the type of research problem you have. This decision is related to an epistemological and ontological position. **Ontology** is a discussion or a reflection 'about the nature of being or the kinds of things that have existence' (*Merriam-Webster Online*, n.d.) and **epistemology** is 'the study … of the nature and grounds of knowledge, especially with reference to its limits and validity' (*Merriam-Webster Online*, n.d.).

What researchers believe to be reality and what they think is possible to be known is based on beliefs. Guba and Lincoln (2004) explain very well how academic researchers can convince others of the importance of their ontological–epistemological postures, but nobody 'knows' if one posture is better than another. The most we can say is that a posture might be more relevant for one research question than another. For example, if researchers want to test the efficiency of a particular vaccine to prevent tuberculosis, they would probably position themselves in a **realist ontology**. This means that they believe that molecules, atoms and fluids are objectively real; that is, they exist outside the perceptions and beliefs of the researchers. They will also have a **positivist epistemology**, which means that they believe that the role of science is to understand laws of the natural organization of the reality they define as real. For this, they need to observe data without influencing it and analyse patterns of causality in a hypothetico-deductive way. Considering the experience of cancer patients, one would most likely prefer receiving a drug treatment tested within a positivist epistemology.

However, if we want to understand how patients interpret their recoveries from cancer, we can analyse their experiences of the different types of therapies they underwent such as meditation, yoga, acupuncture, spiritual practices. We could also investigate the support they got from loved ones, the roles they attribute to positive thoughts about their physical health, and so forth. With such questions, we are likely to believe that reality is constructed through our perception and experience of it and we will be interested in the lived experience of treatments and recovery. As cancer patients, we would prefer to be treated by practitioners open to **constructivist ontology** and epistemology in order to maximize the likelihood of our recovery.

Through these examples, we want to illustrate that one particular epistemology or methodology cannot be defined as universally better than another. There are only different types of research problems requiring different epistemologies and methodologies. In other words, certain methodological choices can be defined as better suited for certain types of research questions. In this book, we will focus on a qualitative methodology based on an iterative process that is distinct from what is recognized in a positivist epistemology. This specification has been made because some qualitative methods are used in a more positivist stance. In this book we will focus on iterative and inductive inquiries. Thus, we will focus on the realm of qualitative methodology and not expand on quantitative research design. Understanding of processes and meanings is usually the realm of qualitative methodology.

However, it is important for all researchers to understand the type of scientific culture we are living in because it influences our views on science and knowledge. Taking knowledge for granted – even **scientific paradigms** – represents a danger as it can obstruct new knowledge production. As we said before, we do not know, and it is impossible to prove whether one epistemology is better than another. In the same way, there is not one methodology better than the other. However, a methodology can be more appropriate and conducive for a certain type of knowledge. This being said, we are living in societies driven by technologies (related to economic growth) produced within a positivist epistemology and a realist ontology. There, we navigate each day within a positivist culture that influences our understanding of knowledge. This is why we need to be particularly vigilant regarding knowledge production: we need to delimitate what is scientific culture and what is research design and scientific production.

DECONSTRUCTING THE POSITIVIST SCIENTIFIC CULTURE

Positivism was the first form of scientism. That is why we often refer to it as a naive form of empiricism. Very few people adhere to it, even in natural sciences, but this epistemology is so deeply anchored in our beliefs and our modern culture that it influences our views of what can be known. That is why we began this chapter by deconstructing positivism as a 'scientific culture' and not as an epistemology per se. In the next section of this chapter, we will present the realm of different epistemologies within qualitative methodology. For now, we present positivism as a cultural artefact in order to help you choose the most appropriate research design.

Positivism was developed as a counterbalance to **metaphysics** and grand theories. In this paradigm, reality obeys laws, and the role of scientific knowledge is to link controlled and objective observations to universal laws. Thus, the aim of science is to verify or falsify theoretical claims. Positivism is poorly suited for the type of research questions and problems we are addressing in this book; we agree with the idea that science should be grounded on empirical facts. Phenomena that cannot be observed, that is apprehended somehow (even through partial indicators), cannot be a subject for scientific knowledge.

Within a positivist paradigm, the relationship between the observer and the object should be as neutral as possible in order to control for biases. For instance, objectivity is an imperative criterion to validate any positivist empirical analysis. The natural sciences widely share this stance. It has also historically dominated quantitative social research. We can readily identify it as a **hegemonic discourse** in popular and academic understandings of knowledge. Even undergraduate students often adopt this view by default in their qualitative methodology classes. They have been told that science is based on objectivity and hypothetico-deductive processes or linear processes of knowledge production as Figure 1.3 shows. However, as we have said, such understandings of knowledge production are often at odds with the research questions that interest them the most.

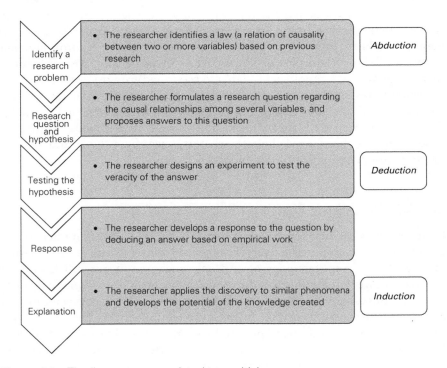

Figure 1.3 The linear process related to positivism

In the field of social sciences, students face the dominance of positivism. Recent developments in qualitative methods in the field of social sciences have articulated themselves against a backdrop of disciplines often historically rooted in positivist paradigms. The birth of social sciences, especially sociology, was facilitated by positivist thinkers such as Auguste Compte and Emile Durkheim. They both wanted to develop a scientific knowledge of social phenomena. As in natural science, they wanted to discover universal laws based on observations. For Durkheim (2013), societies operated through universal laws, the way nature did, but the role of sociology was to create inductively laws of causality based on the comparison of concomitant social phenomena. Merton (1968) reintroduced this belief but restricted the application of universality by developing the idea of middle-range theory, which is more appropriate to the purposes of social sciences.

These kinds of ontology and epistemology are derived from positivism and experimental science. It is important to understand this to establish a dialogue between researchers and also to be aware that this hegemonic discourse on science production is not necessarily legitimate in social sciences. We think that social sciences have their own ontology and epistemology because of the unique nature of the 'social' that is historically situated, complex, multifaceted and based on subjective relationships.

Thus, research questions seeking to understand a social phenomenon will be quite different from those that try to explain natural causal relationships. They will lead to iteratively driven processes throughout the inquiry and will mostly use qualitative data methods.

Qualitative research is defined by:

- the iterative process of knowledge production;
- the nature of its object of research, which is:
  - historically situated
  - complex
  - multivocal
  - based on subjective relationships.

QUALITATIVE RESEARCH DESIGN

We think that the nature of the 'social' is more easily grasped by qualitative inquiries because it is complex, historically situated and can take several meanings based on the subjects' perspectives.

Each time we argue our research question, and we explain our methodology, we go through numerous interpretations. We build mysteries, and we solve them. This process explains why it is so important to keep the coherence of our research design. Research objectives, theoretical framework, epistemological stance, research question and methods should always be 'talking' to one another.

Deduction:

> The process of deriving a statement from certain assumed statements by applying the rules of logic. (*McGraw-Hill Dictionary of Scientific & Technical Terms*, 2003)

Induction:

> A process of reasoning, used especially in science, by which a general conclusion is drawn from a set of premises, based mainly on experience or experimental evidence. The conclusion goes beyond the information contained in the premises, and does not follow necessarily from them. (*Collins Discovery Encyclopedia*, 2005)

The research question is the heart of your qualitative research design. In order to be epistemologically coherent with qualitative research, one has to ask oneself if one really wants to work in an iterative and interpretation-driven process of knowledge production. The temptation to develop a hypothetico-deductive design is always very strong. Often, while advising students in their research processes, we can see that they use qualitative data and methods, but they have learned to ask deductive questions and write as if they were describing universal social patterns. To avoid this pitfall, one must, at first, develop a question that leads to an iterative process of research. The formulation of the research question is vital to develop a good research proposal and to clarify one's methodology.

Table 1.2   Question words and research questions

Hypothetico-deductive and linear knowledge production	Inductive and iterative knowledge production
Which, what	How
Who	
Why	Some why questions lead to interpretative and comprehensive knowledge
Where	
When	

As shown in Table 1.2, question words are key in the formulation of the research question and the research design. Most of the time, qualitative design will be constructed on a 'how' question. How can we define the experience of young adults? How can we understand the political involvement process? How do researchers construct ignorance? How do costume play practices tell us about Japanese pop culture? The how questions lead to rich context-based understandings and explanations, and also lead to the understanding of social processes. This is a type of knowledge impossible to obtain with deductive types of questions. Some research questions do not use the keyword 'how' but they refer to the idea of complex process. For example, what identity transformation process do young people go through during adolescence?

ITERATIVE RESEARCH DESIGN

ABDUCTION

We would like to start with the foundation of qualitative research design, which is the coherence among an epistemological stance, a research problem, a question and a method. As a social researcher, you can be compared to a translator of social reality – you mediate your experience of social phenomena. Social researchers observe, describe, interpret and explain. As in natural science, they need to be rigorous and they need to validate the knowledge they produce. Charles Sanders Peirce, a pioneer in philosophy of sciences and inquiry methods, would say that any inquiry process begins with **abduction**, which means 'inference to the best explanation' (Dumez, 2012: 231, our translation). While writing a research proposal, a researcher needs to imagine the potential knowledge production results. The researcher also needs to imagine why the phenomenon to be studied needs explanations.

In an iterative process, the abduction period is especially important. As Alvesson and Karreman (2011) explain, the researcher builds a mystery while presenting the object of study, while in experimental science, originality can be judged based on the results of the research. For example, producing new data on breast cancer. In an iterative process, the construction of the research object is as important as the 'new results' themselves. The abduction is crucial because it is through this mental process that the researcher constructs the research object and research problem.

Based on this construction, the researcher may be able to propose new interpretations of reality. Wright Mills (1959), while talking about sociological imagination, was partly identifying this process even though he never talked about abduction. He was very critical about 'Big' theories and data-driven research. He taught that social scientists should rather propose new interpretations or 'syntheses' of what we already know rather than collect data without proposing a new interpretation of the problem itself.

Abduction is the first step of any scientific inquiry, but in qualitative methods the adduction process will often be used while interpreting the data.

INDUCTION

Induction means to create an explanation based on observations. It is a bottom-up process (data to theory). Researchers working within this induction process will observe patterns and try to establish explanations that could apply to other similar cases. Their goal is to understand and interpret in order to explain a 'localized' reality. This means that their explanation will produce 'meaning' and help to understand other similar situations, processes or **discourses**.

Qualitative methods are mostly based on induction. This does not mean that **deduction** or abduction is ignored. It means that the induction operation, or, more precisely, the abduction–induction mental operation, drives the whole process. It contrasts with the more positivist approach of science where knowledge is founded on the verification or falsification of claims mostly driven by a deductive mental operation.

DEDUCTION

Deduction is a logical operation based on universal premises from which we deduce specific information. It is a top-down process (theory to data). In this process we test our explanation: Does it make sense? Can we apply it to contrasting cases or similar situations? The classic example is the one used in Aristotle's logical lesson. The universal statement is: (1) Humans are mortals (universal law or theory to be tested); (2) Socrates is human (empirical observation); consequently, we can conclude that (3) Socrates is mortal (which is our knowledge statement) based deductively on a universal law.

Scientific claims using deduction-driven processes start with the development of a **hypothesis** based on theory, then test the veracity of their hypothesis based on the observations. Falsification and verification can mostly be supported by statistical methods using representative **samples**. The knowledge claims created by these types of explanations will be called statistical generalization, which means that regularity is observed within a sample but this regularity applies to any population having the same characteristics of the sample. For example, observations on the prostate cancer symptoms of a small group of white males in North America can be generalized to all of the Canadian and American white male population.

To sum up, the qualitative research process starts with abduction. Abductive reasoning 'begins with a puzzle, a surprise, or a tension, and then seeks to explicate it by identifying the conditions that would make that puzzle less perplexing and more "normal"' (Schwartz-Shea and Yanow, 2012: 27). Researchers imagine how their research questions can be answered based on their readings and their empirical experience. They then try to explain – through an inductive process – the meaning of their data. They will then 'test' their explanations by deduction. However, the process will not end there (see Figure 1.4). They will come back to their data, imagine new answers and begin a new cycle of abduction–induction.

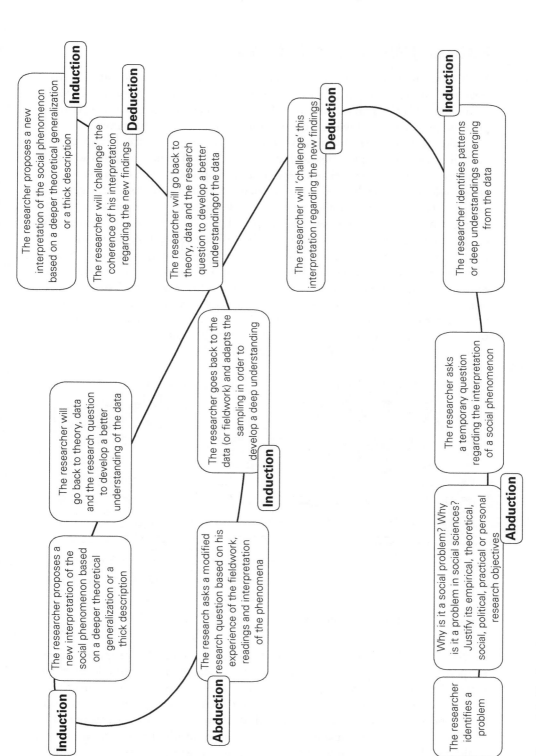

Figure 1.4 The iterative qualitative research process

REALM OF QUALITATIVE EPISTEMOLOGIES

Within qualitative methodology, the research question and its iterative formulation are at the heart of the research design. As mentioned, coherence is an unavoidable quality indicator. It is key when one needs to explain its positioning toward knowledge production, ontology and epistemology.

Before beginning research, very few researchers ask themselves epistemological/existential questions such as: am I a critical realist, a constructionist or a constructivist? However, one needs to understand the diversity of qualitative epistemologies in order to position one's research proposal. In general, experienced researchers build their research questions and designs within distinct ontological and epistemological paradigms. That is because the validity of an analysis will often depend on the coherence of the epistemological paradigm, the method and the interpretation resulting from the research process.

Within social sciences that make use of an iterative process, we count numerous ontologies, epistemologies and methodologies. Ontologies refer to what we think reality is, whereas epistemologies can be understood as what we think we can know about our world. In turn, methodologies encompass our construction of the research problem and the related tools and analysis that are used to 'apprehend' our research object.

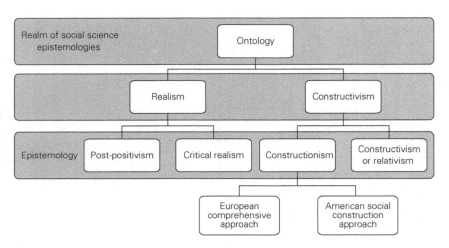

Figure 1.5　Realm of qualitative epistemologies

To clarify the differences between epistemologies, Figure 1.5 proposes a tree-shaped cartography based on ontological stance. In a very simple way, we can define two basic ontologies: realism and constructivism. The realist thesis is based on the belief that reality exists outside our perception of it. In contrast, the constructivist argument claims that reality is at least partially constructed from perceptions of it. From these ontologies, different epistemologies (beliefs regarding what can be known) are proposed. Although it could be said that many epistemologies exist because they are closely related to theories (e.g. poststructuralist epistemology, feminist epistemology), we now present one commonly used by students and academics in social sciences.

REALIST ONTOLOGY

Researchers subscribing to a realist ontology believe that reality exists outside the observer. It is based on a Cartesian ontology that differentiates the subject and the object. This ontological view has been mostly dominant since the Enlightenment in the occidental world. Realism includes very different epistemologies, from positivism to critical realism. We are more interested here in understanding the role of positivism as a scientific culture rather than as understandings of what one can know about the world. We will therefore not define it in terms of an epistemology. On the other hand, we will present post-positivist epistemology because it has an important role to play in the development of qualitative methodology, even though we will not develop this perspective any further in the book.

POST-POSITIVISM

Post-positivism is a moderate view of positivism where researchers admit that reality exists, but ways of observing and describing it are imperfect. Post-positivists might use both qualitative and quantitative methodologies. In the natural and health sciences, researchers often use this paradigm. They believe that reality can be known, but they will use probabilities to explain relationships among variables (correlations) in order to allow for the imperfection of knowledge. For example, research on the use of tobacco and breast cancer can result in this knowledge claim: smokers are more likely than non-smokers to develop breast cancer in later life. This knowledge claim is not universal – in contrast with those made by positivists, who would try to promote a universal causal law such as tobacco causes cancer.

In the social sciences, founders of qualitative research such as Glaser and Strauss (1967) are rooted in a post-positivist perspective. They believe an objective reality exists and they multiply their observations through tools such as interviews to test the ongoing analysis and theoretical explanation they develop. They have developed an inductive research process in accordance with the analytical induction methods developed by the Chicago school of sociology. An inductive process is to develop a theoretical generalization based on observations.

CRITICAL REALISM

Ontologically, critical realists believe that an objective reality exists outside of us, but the different types of apprehension of reality we have through our senses, our cognitive schemes and our knowledge are socially constructed. Epistemologically, critical realists are very close to constructionists.

Critical realists, among whom we include the materialists, defend the idea that the world exists through causal relationships, and social sciences have the task to explore this idea. Their conceptions of causal relationships are, however, quite different from those of positivists or post-positivists because causal relationships are inherent in things – they do not exist between things. Things, in the social world, are embedded in complex relationships, and they have power because they are in relations (Elder-Vass, 2012). For example, being a woman is to not an individual reality. It is related to a society's experience of sex and gender segregation. It is related to biological facts such as the fertility cycle that introduce different types of power relationships among men and women, children and adults. The British tradition of social science mostly developed this epistemological stance.

CONSTRUCTIVIST ONTOLOGY

We define two very different types of constructivist epistemology within the constructivist ontology. The first type is related to a soft ontology (constructionism) and the second to a highly critical view against realism (constructivism).

CONSTRUCTIONISM

We borrow the label 'constructionism' from Charmaz (2000). Social constructionists share the ontological belief that reality is subjectively constructed. For example, knowledge of what is a deviant depends on public discourses, culture, institutions. There is not one universal definition or existence of a social deviant. However, the ontological question is not as controversial an issue as it is for critical realists or constructivists. For example, Goffman (1961) in his well-known study of an asylum shows how interactions between patients and staff but also among patients are constructed in such a way that informal normative rules on how to behave can be identified. Even if Goffman analyses several types of interactions, some of them being influenced by power positions, he does not present a scientific problem and question informed by ontological position.

Some supporters of constructionist epistemologies have a very similar type of object of ontology. We will focus on two that have had strong influences on empirical research in social sciences: (1) a **comprehensive approach** based on a continental European tradition; and (2) social constructionism based on the American interactionist perspective.

The first is the European continental comprehensive approach. The richness of social science is foremost its capacity to 'understand', which means to interpret reality from the lived experience of subjects. Dilthey (1942) differentiated natural science from human and social sciences by the latter's aim to understand the profound meaning of human experiences. An important branch of French and German sociology is based on this epistemological perspective. In this, Weber would be the best known.

These authors do not advocate a relativistic interpretation of our social world. They believe that different types of science can exist. If we take the example of Passeron (2001), the creation of universal laws refers to one type of science. In social sciences, what is important is the comprehension of reality observable through human praxis. For instance, comprehensive researchers will consider actions as well as subjectivity. Their goal is to develop situated patterns such as typologies and the ideal typology. They are very close to critical realists, though they do not develop an ontological discourse on the nature of being. They focus on the capacity of social sciences to analyse and grasp empirical situations. They defend a scientific view of our social world based on different criteria of validity and **transferability**. In the American tradition, we would compare them to interpretivists.

The second is American social constructionism. We can identify Mead (1934/1963) and, more recently, Berger and Luckmann (1966) and their work *The Social Construction of Reality* as precursors of constructionism in social science. The latter two never developed and defended an ontological position (Andrews, 2012). Rather, they developed a pragmatic approach to social action. Their book was about knowledge and how we socially construct our relationship with reality. Their thesis, primarily inspired by the psychosocial theory of Mead, has paved the way to interactionism and a second wave of grounded theory (Charmaz, 2014).

Although they have not adopted an ontological position, we can position this tradition very closely to critical realists. Social constructionists, like critical realists, agree that their positions are very close (Andrews, 2012; Elder-Vass, 2012). For many social constructionists, reality exists both subjectively and objectively. Thus, they can be tagged as critical realists. However, we can note a slight difference between them depending on their research focus. For most social constructionists such as Goffman, the ontological issue is not the main focus. Above all, realists believe in the materiality of the social world because they think that this materiality creates power relationships; their object of focus will be on relations that include subjects as components of the material world. Their ontology leads them to position themselves relative to power while social constructionists will not put so much emphasis on this issue.

In social constructionism, importance will be given to reality (objects, bodies, places) as well as to subjective perspectives on this reality. For example, a social constructionist might be interested in how teenagers interact and how they define their interactions. The focus will be on the comprehension of teenage interactions as a phenomenon. A **critical realist** will study the evolution of these interactions and how they change in relation to power institutions (policies, institutions).

CONSTRUCTIVISM

We differentiate between constructionism and constructivism because they have very different philosophical and ontological roots. For constructivists, the ontological question is crucial, and they defend a relativist ontology. What exists, for them, is socially created. Moreover, they situate themselves outside the Cartesian subject–object dichotomy on which all the other epistemologies we have presented are based. They challenge an essentialist perspective of reality by advocating that reality is created mainly through discourses. For them, language is performative and creates social categories.

Their epistemology is based on the belief that reality is fluid and knowledge about this fluidity is possible through discourse, social scripts and visual symbolism. Thus, any research based on this epistemological frame will define symbol (language, discourse, visuals) as the object of study. Some critical researchers such as alternative accounting researchers will consider tax files as an institutional discourse to study.

CHAPTER SUMMARY

In this chapter, you learned that the first step of your research design is to clarify, for yourself, whether you prefer to interpret a singular 'concomitant' situation or to explain causal relationships using a hypothetical process. By choosing to interpret a situated social phenomenon, you are beginning your qualitative journey! In this chapter, you learned to define qualitative inquiry, to identify an iterative research question and to understand the abductive–inductive nature of the process you are embarking upon. Furthermore, you learned the different types of ontology and epistemology you are confronted with when you read qualitative research reports and articles. These foundations are necessary in order to write a research proposal (Chapter 2) and choose a qualitative approach (Chapter 3) coherent with your beliefs, your research objectives and the mystery you will build and solve.

Your project checklist

Now that you are more familiar with qualitative inquiry, you can:

- ✓   Choose a method (quantitative, mixed method, deductive–qualitative or iterative qualitative methodology) suited to your research question.

- ✓   Justify the choice of a qualitative method you have in mind.

- ✓   Draft a first version of your research question (make sure your research question is formulated with a 'how' question or a 'why' that suggests an interpretation).

- ✓   Justify your epistemological position.

- ✓   Start the design of your research project.

What you should read next

Alvesson, Mats and Dan Karreman. 2011. *Qualitative Research and Theory Development: Mystery as Method.* Thousand Oaks, CA: Sage.

- Alvesson and Karreman explain how theory development remains an obvious result of qualitative inquiry. Qualitative researchers build mysteries throughout their problem contextualization. Their role is to find new mysteries and to present new ways of solving them. As innovators, qualitative researchers need to explain through their research report how they solve mysteries with their interpretation of data collection.

Pascale, Céline-Marie. 2011. *Cartographies of Knowledge: Exploring Qualitative Epistemologies.* Thousand Oaks, CA: Sage.

- In this book, the author defines qualitative methods based on the inductive approach. She explains and maps the different epistemologies within qualitative research and she situates herself in the critical realm.

Website: http://atlasti.com/qualitative-research/

- In this website, the German qualitative research software atlas.ti offers a definition of qualitative methods and the epistemological perspective inspiring the software. A video on qualitative research and publication is embedded in the web page. A section titled 'Formulating A Qualitative Research Question' presents several examples of qualitative types of questions as a complement to this chapter.

YouTube channel: https://www.youtube.com/watch?v=lsAUNs-IoSQ

- A YouTube channel from the Center of Research Quality offers several videos on qualitative research. The one suggested here explains when and why to use qualitative methods in a research project. It gives specific information on educational research but it is relevant to any researcher. It gives a step-by-step procedure to develop a qualitative research project.

YouTube channel: https://www.youtube.com/watch?v=2X-QSU6-hPU

- Chris Flipp offers a clip on the differences between qualitative and quantitative methods which complete the information about deduction and induction in this chapter.

Want more support and inspiration? The online resources are here to help! Get to grips with key terms using **glossary flashcards**, see methods in action with a **library of SAGE cases and journal articles**, and follow analysis step-by-step with full transcripts of the sources discussed in the book.

2

DESIGNING AN ITERATIVE RESEARCH PROJECT

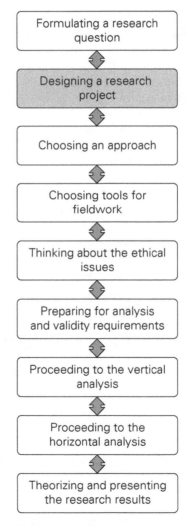

Figure 2.1   Where we are in the research process

IN THIS CHAPTER YOU WILL LEARN:

- To design a qualitative research project.
- To choose your object of research based on two decision trees.
- To document your research problem.
- To write a qualitative research proposal.

INTRODUCTION

In this chapter, we will focus on three processes that occur simultaneously when a research project is being developed: (1) the design of the project; (2) the gathering, compilation and analysis of the documentation; and (3) the writing of the project. Through this chapter, you will learn how to design a qualitative research project. You will also be informed on the literature review process in a vignette. Finally, the chapter will end on the presentation of the research design that is the research project. You will notice that the research design and the project writing are two separate processes.

The heart of a research project is its design – that is, how you develop the conceptual and empirical architecture that allows you, the researcher, to frame a problem and ask a good research question. In fact, the quality and rigor of the research depends upon the relevance of your research question and, maybe above all, upon the coherence among the different elements of the design itself.

THE DESIGN OF AN ITERATIVE RESEARCH PROJECT

Every project is rooted in a personal questioning, derived from experiences and reflections prompted by readings or observations. It is important to identify as precisely as possible the questions that fuel our curiosity. Although this task might seem simple, it can become quite complicated within an iterative research process. Indeed, the way in which we construct the problem is as important, if not more, than the results we get. It is constantly being redefined. In a linear research process conducted in a hypothetico-deductive logic, the triad of problem/question/research hypothesis will crystallize before the empirical phase of the study. In contrast, in an iterative project, the problem, the question and that which we define as the hypothetical propositions evolve over the course of data collection and analysis.

In this chapter, we will follow Maxwell's model (2013), which best illustrates the process of design: that of an iterative process where the coherence among all the parts of the project becomes the prime criterion for assessing the validity of the research. If we follow each of the ellipses in Figure 2.2, we need to understand that the research question will change in dialogue with new data analysis, new theoretical explanation and the revision of the research objectives.

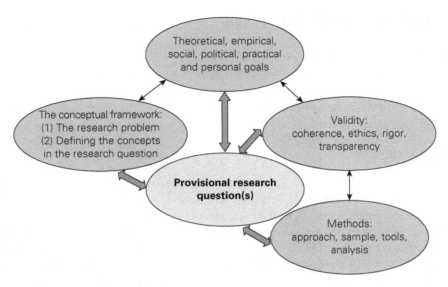

Figure 2.2   Producing an iterative research design

The research problem puts into perspective the gap between what we already know and what we desire to know. In a social science qualitative research project, research problems are often articulated from a social phenomenon that we have observed or experienced and that we would like to understand. All qualitative projects must have an empirical goal, else the field research is no longer relevant. However, even if the initial questioning often derives from empirical observations, it remains important for researchers to situate their research question well within the social science debates.

How you conceptualize your research problem will contribute to the relevance and originality of your research. Two researchers can have the same research object – for example, the life trajectories of adolescent mothers – yet conceptualize the problem in completely different ways depending on their objectives (see Table 2.1). Researchers can study this question from a public health and well-being perspective and concern themselves with risk factors that are connected to the poverty of those women. Foremost, they have empirical goals even if they test or propose new theory. Their goals will be to better identify the factors connected to the experience of poverty and to better understand this population and its life environment. Such researchers could have political goals and want to document the situation of these women in order to support the public policies that relate to them. On the other hand, other researchers might be more interested in defining the entry of contemporary young Canadians into adulthood. Studying the life trajectories of young adolescent mothers would allow them to understand marginal trajectories which cast doubt upon such a categorization of adulthood and put into perspective the life course of other young adults. In the latter example, the use of empirical research is connected to a more theoretically oriented goal: the definition of adulthood within contemporary Canadian society. An empirical goal is the objective of observing reality. A theoretical goal is the objective of defining reality.

Table 2.1 Research goals

Questions to ask for determining the goals of your project:	
What type of data do I want to collect?	Empirical goal
To which theoretical discussions do I want to contribute?	Theoretical goal
What is my personal interest in this project?	Personal goal
Is my project aimed more at an academic audience? At an audience of professionals in public policy? To the community and social organizations? At an audience of vulnerable persons?	Policy and/or practical goals

Another important step for clarifying the design of your project is to clarify your goals. The initial step is probably to choose whether the purpose of your project is first and foremost to better theorize or describe. In other words, do you want to propose a new meaning for a phenomenon? Or rather, to better identify and better describe phenomena? We could then position the research projects according to their prevailing theoretical or empirical goals as shown in Figure 2.3.

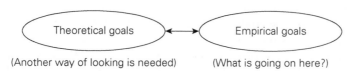

Figure 2.3   Theoretical goals versus empirical goals

Obviously, distinctions between theoretical and empirical goals are not as clear cut as it looks in the diagram, and even if the research question is primarily theoretical, the project remains empirical. A qualitative research project that is too theoretical is usually seen as disappointing. Recourse to the empirical basis of the phenomena under study is essential and must be evident at all stages of the report. The challenge for a theoretical project is to conduct a continuous and productive dialogue with the data.

Conversely, some research projects aim to describe, observe and identify phenomena. Their goal is to answer the question: what is happening here? Even if the main orientation of the project is empirical, it cannot be purely descriptive. Indeed, description that is event oriented, anecdotal or simply factual does not belong to the scientific world. It is more suited to the journalistic world. In qualitative research, description corresponds to Geertz's (1973) idea of 'thick description', that is to say, a description of a field experience wherein the researcher explicitly shows and explains recurring cultural and symbolic relationships within their contexts. Thus, a project can achieve great scientific value when researchers' descriptions carry many details and they integrate their interpretations within the descriptions.

When the theoretical goal is given precedence, researchers tend to use the data as a case, a theoretical sample, in order to better answer a question that is of a broader theoretical nature. Stake (1995) describes this type of project as being an instrumental case. The distinction between the instrumental case and the intrinsic one is quite interesting on the heuristic level, even if we do not completely endorse Stake's approach. Indeed, many researchers are interested in more global theoretical issues, such as defining social categories like 'adult', 'bisexual', 'woman', and they choose certain cases as theoretical samples in order to test their conceptualizations and further develop their analyses. For example, we can more broadly examine the transformation of relations between the state and citizens by studying the definition of the presumption of innocence inherent in the legislation pertaining to the National DNA databank (Vachon, 2008).

An overarching empirical goal responds better to empirical, practical or policy goals. Empirically, every new social phenomenon deserves to be studied, observed and described. For example, a student might carefully describe the use of a respirator in certain clinical situations to understand the issues and challenges it creates. Rich description responds primarily to an empirical goal, but research requires the use of **concepts** and may lead to more theoretical issues. Above all, we do not want to impose a model, because a researcher could very well have practical goals within a larger theoretical question. What matters is to clearly identify our own goals, support each of our choices, and be able to organize the goals within a hierarchy in order to clarify our research question as much as possible.

As noted, even a project that is predominantly theoretical must have empirical goals. These goals allow us to prepare for our future fieldwork and identify the types of data we will want to analyse.

CHOOSING THE RESEARCH QUESTION

Identifying our empirical, theoretical or practical goals can only help us specify our research question. To borrow Maxwell's model (2013), we must understand that the choice of research question is at the core of our project – it is essential. As we have said, this question often flows from a personal experience and our task is to show why this question poses a scientific problem. Since our research question is part of an iterative process rather than a hypothetico-deductive and linear one, as we saw in the first chapter, it cannot require the measurement of variances, the validation of hypotheses or the establishment of causality among variables. The question in qualitative research relates to the in-depth comprehension of a phenomenon, especially through its interpretation.

In the project, the question specifies the object of the research and the phenomenon we are trying to understand. In the design stage, the question becomes the keystone among the goals, the research problem, the theoretical framework and the methodological aspects of the project. Following Maxwell

(2013), the research question carries two essential functions within the design stage: it serves (1) to define the research object (to perceive the connections among the goals and the theoretical framework); and (2) to guide your research methods.

Formulating your research question is an important step in designing your research project, one that may require a lot of time. It is important that your question is clear, neither too vague nor too narrow. For example, consider the following question: how do changes to the setting of an urban area change the lives of the people who live in it? Such a question is too vague and would lead to imprecise results. A large number of information sources would be necessary to answer it: information documenting the impacts of changes to transportation habits, the quality of life, sociality in the neighborhood, etc.; information from children, adolescents, adults, the elderly, business people, workers, etc.; information regarding the addition of a park, the closing of a pedestrian mall, the zoning of a district, etc. On the other hand, questions that are too narrow will have the effect of reducing if not simplifying the social problem under study. One must also avoid making a value judgment within the very formulation of the question. For example: how do young Congolese immigrants deal with discrimination when they arrive in Canada? In this question, researchers assume that these young people are in fact stigmatized even though it is possible that such an experience is not shared by all members of this group.

It is also important to know whether our question has already been answered, and, if it has, to explain why we are dissatisfied with the answers provided by those researchers. For example, existing results possibly did not help us to understand the phenomenon we wanted to explain. The other reason for a literature review would be to identify the theoretical debates within which our question is situated. For example, a research question that relates to the ways that young people interact on Facebook can be situated within feminist debates, theoretical debates about the formation of social groups, or debates regarding theories of communication. Here, the literature review becomes a crucial tool and the quality of the reading notes can make all the difference between a project that is technically well designed, but of poor quality, and a thoroughly excellent project (see the vignette on reading notes).

To help you choose your question, we have prepared a decision-making tree based on your capacity to imagine what you would like to observe and explain presented in Figure 2.4 and 2.5. This capacity to imagine your data and the type of responses you think might emerge from your analysis is essential for the proper design of your project. Designing an empirical research project based on theories alone would be a very serious error, because throughout the research there would be a gap between the empirical and the theoretical levels. For example, students might be interested in the marginalization of sexual minorities in schools. They could develop a research question and a conceptual framework, but will they succeed in finding relevant people to talk to about this problem in their fieldwork? Questions chosen solely on the basis of theoretical concerns could create a split between the theoretical and the empirical levels that would be difficult to bridge. The readers would have the impression that the fieldwork has been conducted largely to justify a theoretical answer already given. For this reason, one must make sure that the design of the project is done well from the start and takes into account the empirical issues and actual empirical constraints.

To this end, we suggest a decision tree in three stages. First, decide whether the research goal is to be predominantly theoretical or empirical. Second, decide whether to observe a phenomenon **synchronistically** or **diachronically**. Finally, decide whether to observe a situation, a discourse, **practices** and **representations** or a **narrative** in the case of a diachronic phenomenon. We will now proceed to better define each of these stages.

DECIDING WHETHER THE RESEARCH GOAL IS PREDOMINANTLY THEORETICAL OR EMPIRICAL

The first issue that you must deal with relates to the connection between the research goals and the research question. It is necessary to determine whether the research goal is mostly of an empirical or theoretical nature. If it relates to an empirical goal, the question must focus very precisely on the observed phenomenon. Researchers must therefore justify the empirical relevance of their question: refer to observed facts and newspaper clippings demonstrating the importance of the gap between what we already know about the phenomenon and what we need to know in order to add to the knowledge of it. If a new social phenomenon is involved, it probably also relates to better management of interventions or public policies.

If your goal is mostly theoretical, your fieldwork will play the role of an instrumental case study in the sense meant by Stake (1995). The goal of the researcher is therefore to justify the theoretical relevance of a new interpretation of a familiar problem or to show the relevance of new definitions to help understand the phenomenon. In this context, it is especially important to identify the theoretical debates that relate to the question, because they provide the justification for a theoretical inquiry. It is essential to answer the question: 'in which theoretical debates do I want to become involved?'

Let us consider the following question: how do experiences of assuming responsibilities define adulthood? The fieldwork could likely focus on adults who have lost autonomy, but still have responsibilities – or the case of young adults who are not yet independent, but are autonomous. Here, the theoretical goal pertains to how we define the category of 'adult', certain experiences (practices and representations) of responsibility that involve the ideas of independence and autonomy of judgment used in contemporary society.

DECIDING WHETHER TO OBSERVE THE PHENOMENON SYNCHRONISTICALLY OR DIACHRONISTICALLY

In order to properly choose our question, we have to know if we are more interested in observing a phenomenon that is evolving (**diachronic**) or understanding a phenomenon situated in time (**synchronic**). This question is crucial, because the design of a project pertaining to a process is quite different from one that pertains to a synchronic phenomenon. For example, one can observe youth social engagement in an organization (diachronic) while another researcher could focus on the life course of youth in order to understand the process through which they have chosen to get involved in this organization (synchronic). Still, the research object is youth social involvement. The way the researcher constructs and analyses it is quite different. This different perspective will influence the **methodological approach** and research tools.

DECIDING TO OBSERVE SITUATIONS; DISCOURSES; PRACTICES AND REPRESENTATIONS OR NARRATIVES

In order to design the project, you must be capable of imagining what you want to observe. In general, a qualitative project addresses several of these aspects: discourses, narratives, practices and representations. However, we believe that researchers must decide which of these aspects they will focus upon or emphasize.

SITUATIONS

A situation is a social interaction embedded in time and space. Observing a situation causes us to analyse **narratives, discourses, representations** and **practices** – but the main point of our study remains the interactions in a space bound within time. Here we are referring as much to geographic spaces as non-territorial social spaces, such as networks on the Internet. For example, one could choose to analyse gendered interactions on Tinder. For example, observing a situation will lead us to choose methodological approaches such as ethnography or the case study – as we will discuss in the next chapter.

DISCOURSES

Commonly, a discourse is 'a set of statements bound together by a specific and consistent logic, made up of rules and laws which do not necessarily belong to a natural language, and which provide information about material or ideal objects' (*Dictionnaire Larousse en ligne*, n.d.). In the social sciences, discourses embrace two related phenomena. First, they refer to the socio-linguistic structures used by actors. For example, is the interviewee trying to convince his interlocutor or is he searching for a meaning to give to the phenomenon he tries to describe? Second, they refer to a consistent logic constructed by societies in a specific historical period as defined by Foucault (1971). For example, this author demonstrated how discourses on sexuality evolved over time. This type of discourse refers to a vision of the world that societies unconsciously embrace. Therefore, social discourses are not unrelated to socio-linguistic structures. For example, the use of the word 'risk' in the development of public policy over the course of the last 15 years is not unrelated to the imposition of a certain worldview. Again, it should be noted that discourses are everywhere. For example, in an interview conducted as a life story both discourses and narratives will occur. But if the project pertains to the processes, interest in the narrative will dominate that in the discourses.

NARRATIVES

In our daily lives, we formulate a coherent story explaining to ourselves and to others our experience and how events are generated. The narrative creates the temporal thread that a person uses to order a sequence of events. It must be noted that the narrative is a window into the **subjectivity** of individuals. In health sciences, education, social work, sociology narratives and standpoint perspectives, narratives are used to understand individual experience. A narrative is descriptive and explanatory at the same time. For example, it can be a relevant tool to understand experiences such as motherhood, life transitions or illness experiences. Narrative analysis will give importance to people's identity and social roles, social norms guiding performances and interactions.

PRACTICES AND REPRESENTATIONS

Analysing social practices is often linked to the study of social representations. That is why we present those two **concepts** together. Practices refer to the actions taken by people. For Bourdieu (1980), a social practice is objective and subjective. It is an action structured by social norms and constraints, and it is subjective because it is also a set of actions that a person may want to adopt to position themselves. For example, you might want to understand why young black Americans like hip hop culture and how they practice it in their daily lives. To do so, you will also need to identify their social representations of 'hip hop' and 'black American youth'. A social representation is 'a mental state or concept regarded as corresponding to a thing perceived' (*Oxford English Dictionary Online*, n.d.). Representations are not unrelated to discourse. The distinction is that a social representation indicates a particular object – for example, the social representation of alcohol – while a discourse indicates a historical process wherein a more global vision of a phenomenon develops.

In Figures 2.4 and 2.5, we present a decision tree based on: (1) the orientation of your research goal (empirical or theoretical); (2) the temporality of your research object (diachronic or synchronic); and (3) the type of phenomenon that you want to observe: stories, discourses, situations, practices and social representations. We present an example of a research question for each option.

THE THEORETICAL OR CONCEPTUAL FRAMEWORK

Until this point, we have dealt with goals, the research question and, in the diagrams, the connections between the goals and the research question. We will now discuss the connections between the research question and what we

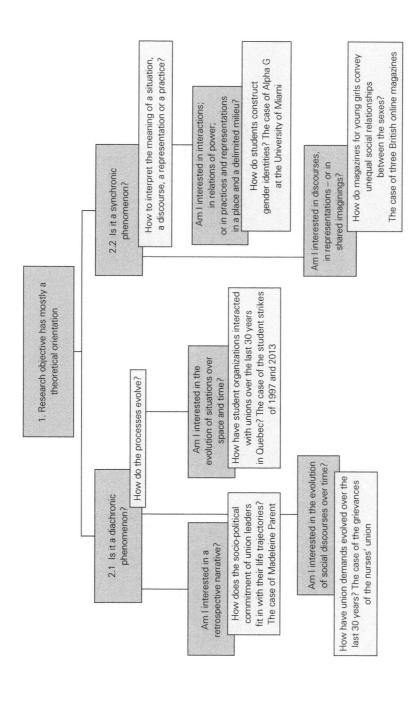

Figure 2.4 Decision tree for theoretically inclined research

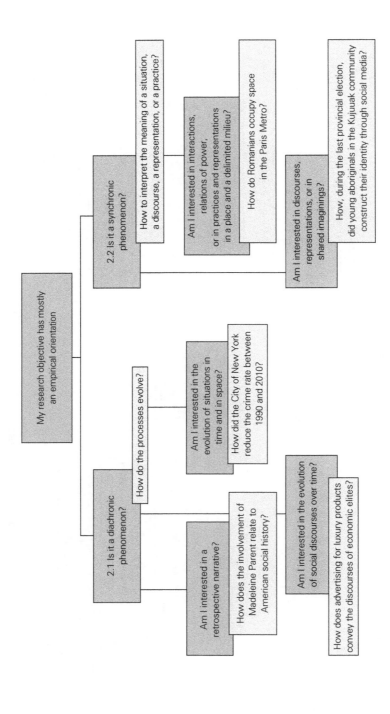

Figure 2.5 Decision tree for empirically inclined research

call the theoretical or conceptual framework. The theoretical framework includes what we know about our research object based on the literature review and the theoretical debates. Some may argue that it is impossible to make a decision about your research question before clarifying your theoretical framework. Because the research design is iterative, we argue that these two aspects of your research design will be in dialogue. If your research objectives are theoretically driven, your theoretical frame might be set before your research question but it will need to evolve all through the process.

A theoretical framework is a broad paradigm on which the researcher stands to look into a problem. For example, it could be a Marxist theoretical framework or a feminist one.

A conceptual framework is the presentation of the different concepts – as tools – that the researcher uses to observe a phenomenon. It is a step toward the operationalization of the research problem.

Indeed, the literature review has three purposes: (1) it allows you to justify the empirical, social and political relevance of your question by showing the gap between what the existing studies teach us and what we should know; (2) it allows you to situate your question within the debates in order to identify the theoretical relevance of your project (especially if your research goal has a mainly theoretical orientation); and (3) it helps you to define the concepts of your research question according to the theoretical framework you will have chosen.

VALIDATING THE EMPIRICAL, SOCIAL AND POLITICAL RELEVANCE OF YOUR QUESTION

Let us use the example of how we define adulthood. We have a lot of information about entry into adulthood. We know that the traditional markers of entry into adulthood are pushed away or displaced in contemporary society and we can support those statements relating to the texts read and discussed in our literature review. But we know little about the subjective definition of this social period in life. The empirical realization of the project would thus require that we interview people in order to understand their definitions of this life transition. Disciplines such as psychology, demography, sociology, medicine and nursing concern themselves with this period of life, but their definitions of entry into adulthood are very different. The theoretical relevance of your project might lie in more clearly defining this stage conceptually. Finally, the practical, social and/or political goals might be to analyse the consequences of this redefinition as they relate to public services and policies that are directed toward young adults.

SITUATING YOUR QUESTION WITHIN THEORETICAL DEBATES

Efforts to define adulthood are made in various disciplines. In demography, where we identify markers relating to the passages into adulthood and old age, we are concerned with the intersections between the ages and the events and consider the effects of age, cohort and generation. The issue of defining adulthood arises within the field of the psychology of human development; it arises in criminology and in law in relation to defining responsibility for certain actions; it arises in public policy in relation to life transitions that render certain people vulnerable; and it arises in sociology within debates regarding the institutionalization of the ages of life, of social scripts. These examples reflect debates that are more discipline oriented, but there are also theoretical debates in relation to ideas of autonomy, independence and responsibility.

DEFINING THE CONCEPTS OF YOUR RESEARCH QUESTION

The literature, especially the more theoretical works, will not only introduce you to the current debates relating to your subject, but also help you define the concepts embedded in your research question. Each word of your question has meaning. For example, the definition of adulthood can refer to theories which define human beings as rational entities and the idea of responsibility then becomes essential to our theoretical frame of reference. Feminist theories see human beings as being interdependent; it thus becomes necessary for us to define the adult as a being that renegotiates the bonds of interdependence with others. Behaviorist theories will see a particular stage of human development as being connected to physical and neurological changes. Of course, the way you conceptualize each term at this stage of the research will have an impact on other intertwined elements of your research design.

Your theoretical positioning is not unrelated to your epistemological orientation. Indeed, if you adopt a critical perspective, your research question will likely aim at analysing power relations between men and women, among social classes, age groups, people and institutions, people and the mass media. You will thus define the concepts of your research question using the works of authors such as Bourdieu, Luhmann, Butler, Foucault, Boltanski and Lamont. If you adopt a constructivist perspective, you will be more interested in better defining, better understanding and better describing situations, practices and actors without necessarily focusing on relations of power. The concepts of your research question could be defined by using the work of authors such as Berger and Luckman, Goffman, and Mead – to name but a few.

There is a great need for creativity in developing your conceptual framework, because a single research subject, such as the transition to adulthood, can be studied in different ways. The validity of qualitative research is dependent on the coherence of theoretical, epistemological and empirical choices. Is there a theoretical coherence in the research design? For example, if, in a project that you want based on a critical frame of reference, you define concepts based on functionalist theories, there will be a problem of coherence.

Does your frame of reference refer to current debates? Have the concepts from the research question been well defined?

THE METHOD AND VALIDITY

What do you want to observe? How do you think you will do it? Based on what criteria will you choose documents, people and situations to observe? In the following chapters, we will discuss the various choices to be made: the approach, the terrain, the techniques, the analytical strategies. We will also discuss the different ways of ensuring the validity of our research in Chapter 6.

THE WRITING OF A RESEARCH PROJECT

From the beginning of this chapter, we have discussed the different decisions that must be made during the design of the project. One has to be able to imagine the various interrelations among the goals, the research question, the theoretical framework, the method and the validity of your project. Note that this design is very organic: a change in the goal can have effects on all the other elements of the design. We must also emphasize that this design will evolve over the entire length of the research process. The qualitative research process has an iterative character.

When writing your project, it will be necessary to artificially streamline this organic model. Indeed, the writing phase will require a more linear presentation of the project. In other words, the project is a linear argumentative text that must present your choices regarding each element of the design. In more visual terms, the design requires us to perceive a three-dimensional architecture, while the writing phase requires that this information be presented in two dimensions, exactly as an architect does when drawing up plans.

In the introduction, it is a good idea to introduce the subject using a concrete example to later lay out your problem: the research question. Also, the goals would have to be quickly presented in the introduction. For example, in research on social participation, we would begin a research project in the following way:

Newspapers and politicians underline the low voting rate of young people in Canada as well as in many occidental countries. Does it mean that youth are less socially involved than before? The goal of this research is twofold. First, we aim to understand young adults' representations of social involvement and redefine its definition in the light of their social representations. Second, we would like to identify the diversity of their political and social participation with special attention to any emergent social practices.

Our research question is: how do young adults define social involvement and how do they participate through their emerging adulthood? The literature

(Continued)

review shows that social engagement often varies depending on people's social network, age, sex or social class. In this project, we will focus on the effect of time and meet twice young adults aged 18 to 25. The second interview will be held five years after in order to understand how practices change or not.

The goal of this part of your project should be to argue for the relevance of your question. Why is it important to ask your research question? Have answers to it already been suggested? With such a question, in which theoretical debates are you participating? The quality and depth of your problematization depend in part on the quality of your reading notes. For this reason, it pays to engage in effective summarization practices – producing comparative tables and systematically keeping your bibliography up to date.

Students often ask us if they need to write one section about the problematization (which frames the theoretical and empirical problem and the definition of the concepts related to our question) as well as another about the theoretical framework (the theory chosen to inspire hypothetical assertions). Our response is that anything is possible. If your epistemology is critically oriented and your theoretical goal dominates your empirical one, and your theoretical framework leads you to define your concepts in a way that is very different from the current practice in your discipline, you should create a section that presents your concepts according to your theoretical approach. The goal here is to ensure that your writing clearly reflects your position within the theoretical debates, but also within the available knowledge about your topic.

In other words, you need to justify and explain the problem that you want to solve through your research. This part of the research project is the most original in the social sciences. As Bachelard, a great philosopher of science, explains:

> Above all, one must know how to frame problems. And whatever we might say in the scientific world, problems do not come already framed. It is precisely this sense of what a problem is that defines the true scientific spirit. For a scientific mind, all knowledge is a response to a question. If there is no question, there is no scientific knowledge. Nothing is self-evident. Nothing is given. Everything is constructed. (1999: 14, our translation)

The argument developed in the section devoted to your problem and your theoretical framework should logically lead to the presentation of your research question within the methodology section. The purpose of this section is to present the **operationalization** of your theoretical problem – in other words, how you present hypothetical assertions. You have already touched upon the question in the introduction – you should develop it in the methodology as well as the hypothetical assertions that will guide your research: what are the provisional responses to your research question? This is not a matter of developing a research hypothesis to be falsified, as required by a hypothetico-deductive approach, but rather to develop pathways that will allow you to explore the research material.

In the methodology section, you will need to persuade your audience of the merits of using inductive qualitative methods to answer your question. To this point, we have mentioned several reasons to do so and they should be directly related to your goals. In this section, you are advocates of your own cause! You must justify all the choices you have made: Why is your methodological approach (Chapter 3) the one most relevant to your fieldwork? Why are you conducting interviews instead of observing? Based on which criteria will you select your sources of data? Why? Which tools will you use (Chapter 4)? How do you plan to analyse the data? Will you use software? How will you protect the anonymity and confidentiality of the people involved in your research (Chapter 5)? How will you ensure the validity of your project and your results (Chapter 6)?

These are the questions that your evaluation committee or your client – if the research is sponsored – will want answered before allowing you to start your fieldwork. And to this project, you must append all the documents that you will use: the guides, data gathering tools, consent forms, etc.

READING NOTES AND SCIENTIFIC LITERATURE REVIEW

A scientific literature review consists of producing a text that synthesizes and evaluates a number of documents on a specific subject or research problem. Documents that are used can come from a diversity of sources, such as books, scholarly articles, research reports, and so on. This tedious work often precedes the writing of the research design since it gives you the information you need to:

- identify what has been done in the past, what theoretical approaches were used and how you will justify your own theoretical choices;
- identify what has not been analysed yet or could be studied differently;
- identify your research goals and decide if the emphasis will be on theoretical or empirical goals;
- identify whether you should approach your research problem from a diachronic or synchronic angle;
- formulate your research question;
- identify the object that you will observe: a situation, a discourse, practices and representations or a narrative.

PRODUCING READING NOTES

One of the tools used to produce a good literature review is the 'reading notes template'. The template takes the form of a series of tasks that guides you in producing and organizing your reading notes. Such a template will help you assess the pertinence and the importance of the reviewed documents for your research design. It will allow you to preserve the complexity of the argumentation in the original texts. Here are a few tasks that should be part of completing your reading notes template:

1. Write down the complete reference of the document.
2. Summarize the text:
   a. Summarize each paragraph in one sentence.
   b. For each paragraph, identify the argument brought forward by the author. Note that an author can develop an argument over many paragraphs.
3. Identify the key concepts and theoretical approach used in the research as well as the authors that are referenced as theoretical inspirations.
4. If the document you are reading is on empirical research, identify the methods used to produce and analyse the data.
5. Identify keywords.

Table 2.2 illustrates what a reading notes template can look like.

Table 2.2   Reading notes template (from Lefrançois et al., 2009)

Summarize each paragraph in one sentence	Main argument
Para. 1 Democratic education programs for youth are conceived as the panacea to solve the crisis in democratic societies. In this context it is important to know whether the program taught in Quebec emancipates or reproduces a specific style of citizen	Democratic education programs are not emancipatory per se, but can liberate/ reproduce a specific style of citizen
Para. 2 The article is divided into two parts: (1) the presentation of the Québécois program; and (2) the presentation of the Westheimer and Kahne (2004) typology	
Para. 3 The school structure is heavily influenced by the socio-economic context. Democratic education program should go beyond and above the school walls	It is necessary to analyse the socio-economic context because structural elements impact on curriculum development
Para. 4 The objectives of the program are to sensitize students to issues of justice and reciprocity	
...	

Summarize each paragraph in one sentence	Main argument
Para. 9 The notion of 'common good' underlies the program	The notion of 'common good' that underlies the program encourages conformism rather than subversion
...	

Theory: Identify the main concepts used in the text
Concepts used: Citizenship
Theoretical approach: Citizenship typology of Westheimer and Kahne (2004).
Methods: Identify the source and the methodology used
Empirical material used: government documents; discourse analysis
Keywords: Identify keywords for further bibliographic research – Citizenship, justice, common good, school, students

This template simplifies the process of writing your literature review since you can just write the main arguments that you identified in your template and further explain in your own words the important concepts and results that were presented.

USING THE TEMPLATE TO DO THE LITERATURE REVIEW

After you have completed your reading notes template for all the documents you wished to review, you need to group the information that you found around themes. Creating another grid to group these various texts around these themes as well as the methodologies that were used and important concepts is a useful thing to do. The finished document presents an exhaustive review of available knowledge. This will help you identify what is left to learn or what you could aim to interpret in a different way. Do not forget that, when writing the conclusion of their literature review, authors often mention the questions that are left open or the ones they would like to shift their focus to. Such information will be of great value in defending the originality of your research when you define your research problem.

CHAPTER SUMMARY

In this chapter, you learned how to make fundamental choices that play a key role in formulating your research question. Your research question is at the heart of your design. Plenty of choices need to be made, but deciding whether you will put more emphasis on your empirical or your theoretical goals is a priority in order for you to sketch your plan. You were then asked to opt for a preferred object of empirical analysis, whether situations, discourses, narratives or representations and practices. The three graphs presented examples of research questions related to these different options. In this chapter, you also learned that the design process and the writing of your research project are two different types of intellectual tasks. You learned that articulating a clear research design means connecting your goals, theoretical framework, question, methodology and the imperative of validity for your project. Moreover, you learned that writing a project is a communicative act and that you need to convince an informed reader of the value and the validity of your project. You learned that your literature review plays an important role in showing the need for your research project. In the previous section on scientific literature review, you learned how to prepare a reading note.

Your project checklist

Now that you are more familiar with research design you can:

✓ Complete your library research and literature review to identify what studies have been conducted and what gaps remain in your topic.

✓ Identify the research objectives that you are aiming to fulfil at this stage with your project.

✓ Rewrite your research question, if needed (do not worry – it will keep being tweaked and improved upon until the end of your research).

✓ Choose your research design.

✓ Write a first, even partial, draft of your research proposal knowing that you still need to make a decision on your methodological approach later on (Chapter 3).

What you should read next

Green, Helen. 2014. 'Use of Theoretical and Conceptual Frameworks in Qualitative Research'. *Nurse Researcher* 21(6): 34-8.

• In this paper, the researcher debunks how authors use the terminology 'theoretical and conceptual framework' in qualitative research. She explains that there are few differences, it all depends on how authors define theory. Theory can simply be defined by the relation (causality, opposition, subordination, etc.) between several concepts.

Maxwell, Joseph. 2013. *Qualitative Research Design: An Interactive Approach*, 3rd edition. Applied Social Research Methods Series, Vol. 41. Thousand Oaks, CA: Sage.

• This book is one of the 'essentials' any qualitative researcher should have on his or her desk. Maxwell explains in a very comprehensive manner the mechanics of iterative research and the importance of research design. Each chapter finishes with examples and exercises, helping new and not so new researchers to adopt a reflexive stance toward each step of research design. This book is a good companion for understanding iterative design.

Website: http://uottawa.libguides.com/c.php?g=265260&p=2314609

- University of Ottawa Libraries offer information to define your research topic and to aid your library research in the social sciences. The website has a link to a strategy worksheet to begin your library research. It shows the importance of using a thesaurus to identify synonyms for your keywords. Each keyword should relate to the concepts of your research question.

Website: http://libguides.usc.edu/writingguide/researchproposal

- University of Southern California Libraries present a comprehensive website to help students prepare their research proposal and their research report. Some rubrics are intended for quantitative projects, but most of them apply to any type of proposal. They give relevant information on how to write an introduction, an executive summary or how to prepare a literature review and manage group projects.

Website: http://slideplayer.com/slide/4930414/

- This is a PowerPoint presentation by John Creswell and Viki Clark. Creswell has written several books on qualitative inquiries and he presents in a few slides the essentials of qualitative research design.

Want more support and inspiration? The online resources are here to help! Get to grips with key terms using **glossary flashcards**, see methods in action with a **library of SAGE cases and journal articles**, and follow analysis step-by-step with full transcripts of the sources discussed in the book.

3

CHOOSING AN APPROACH TO GUIDE METHODOLOGICAL DECISIONS

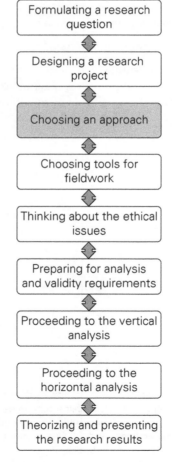

Figure 3.1   Where we are in the research process

IN THIS CHAPTER YOU WILL LEARN:

- To define five main traditions in qualitative research: phenomenology, grounded theory, discourse analysis, narrative analysis and ethnography.
- To recognize the underpinnings and premises of each tradition.
- To distinguish schools of thought that coexist under the same generic tradition.
- To describe the main steps taken to accomplish the analysis of the material in each tradition.

INTRODUCTION

In order for your research to be coherent, which is one of the most important quality criteria in science, there has to be a good fit between your research question, the epistemological grounding and design of your project, as well as the approach you choose or create to carry out the data production and analysis. This chapter will give you an overview of some traditional approaches in qualitative research (see Table 3.1). A methodological approach refers to the way empirical reality can be perceived and grasped. We understand an approach as a way of engaging with the research material. An approach has its sources in a philosophy or discipline, it is made of a series of concepts and axioms, and it also proposes concrete methods and techniques to analyse the material.

There are elective affinities between epistemological positions and methodological approaches. Choosing to conduct research using a certain epistemological position will likely lead you to consider some approaches, or schools within an approach, more than others. Note, however, that there is more than one good fit possible for a specific research project. Note also that every approach presented in the following pages has gone through many versions and led to the formation of different schools over time. Hence the importance of specifying which school(s) or which version(s) of an approach you use in your study and to explicitly question how it relates to your epistemological grounding. For example, the Glaser and Strauss (1967) version of grounded theory is closer to the post-positivist epistemology, whereas the Charmaz (2014) version is closer to the constructionist epistemology. It would be a detrimental shortcut to equate a generic approach with a definite and unique epistemological position.

For the purpose of this book, selecting the qualitative methodological approaches to cover is a necessary exercise – albeit a difficult one. This is so for two reasons. The first refers to the necessary partiality that a selection requires. There is not one selection that will agree with everyone's view of the field and be deemed complete. In this book, we decided to highlight five methodological approaches, necessarily leaving out others (see 'What you should read next' at the end of this chapter for other important approaches). Others have proposed their own selection (Creswell, 2012; Jacob, 1987; Marshall and Rossman, 2006; Silverman, 2005b).

Table 3.1   The five selected methodological approaches

	Approach				
	Phenomenology	Grounded theory	Discourse analysis	Narrative analysis	Ethnography
Field of origin or reference	Philosophy	Sociology	Applied linguistics	Literature	Anthropology
Main aim	Unearthing the lived experience of a phenomenon	Creating substantive theories of a social process	Documenting the ways language in use contributes to producing structures and practices	Showing the work and effect of stories in individual, social and political situations	Offering a rich description of a milieu or a situation through witnessing or participating in it

The second reason that makes a selection of qualitative methodological approaches difficult is that we end up with an artificial classification. Following Atkinson et al. (1988: 233), we want to emphasize the limits of the selection we propose below. First, there are controversies pertaining to the characteristics of a tradition and 'whose work is representative' of this tradition. Second, many approaches share common features. Third, the guidelines provided by some approaches are broad to the point where one has to build one's own methodological roadmap to conduct a project. Finally, many empirical studies happily combine, explicitly or not, a few approaches.

In Chapters 7–9, we will give you detailed examples of the way we use some of those approaches, namely one school of discourse analysis and a combination of grounded theory and narrative analysis, to tackle a speech and an interview with two activists, Parenti and Jodi. The speech and interview were gathered and produced for a research project on social participation. Before this, you need to become familiar with the approaches available to you. This is essential so that you can choose from them to conduct your research, or else select compatible elements that you can combine from those approaches to propose your own if you wish. The goal of this chapter is to give you some points of reference. This way, you will know what approach(es) you need to research further to properly guide your research project. For each of the five approaches covered here, we will give some brief elements of historical context; describe its underpinnings and premises; distinguish between different schools that have adapted the generic approach; and, finally, lay out the main steps suggested when analysing empirical material. Being introduced, even superficially, to the concrete ways in which analysis is conducted is a good way to grasp the specificities of each methodological approach. Following these important words of caution, let us try to define some points of reference in the broad territory covered by qualitative research.

PHENOMENOLOGY

Edmond Husserl (1859–1938) developed a method that aims at exploring subjective experience. It is phenomenology – the science of pure phenomena (Groenewald, 2004). The German philosopher was considered subversive because he rejected the view of his time, according to which **logical positivism** was deemed to be the basis of both natural and human sciences. Husserl acknowledged that the spatio-temporal world had been explored with great success using the hypothetico-deductive models and methods of physics and mathematics. However, he maintained that another portion of the natural world, the natural world as experienced subjectively by humans, as well as the social world, cannot be known in the same way (Fouche, 1993: 112–13).

According to Husserl, consciousness, the element that distinguishes human from natural phenomena, needs to be addressed by human sciences and requires a method that respects and considers its specificity. This characteristic marks phenomenology as one of the most important foundations of qualitative research because its *raison d'être* is to develop and use approaches and methods that are sensitive to the very subjective nature of human realities. That is certainly why some qualitative researchers advocate beginning the qualitative analysis phase of any study by a first 'layer' of phenomenological analysis (Paillé and Mucchielli, 2010: Chapter 5). Thus, we can say that almost all qualitative methods are rooted in Husserl's project. However, as we will see later in this section, phenomenology as a methodological approach, used to conduct an empirical study, is more specific than phenomenology as a broad philosophical tradition.

UNDERPINNINGS AND PREMISES

Phenomenology has its own elaborated vocabulary and system of thought. However, for introductory purposes, we will acquaint ourselves with only four of its concepts and premises:

- The focus on the lived experience.

- The imperative of bracketing one's own worldview.

- The analytical process of reduction.

- The goal of describing rather than explaining.

THE LIVED WORLD

For Husserl, the center of investigation is the lived world. We can know the 'outside world' only as we perceive it through our consciousness. This applies, a fortiori, to the world of emotions, relationships and experiences. Therefore, all that we know is mediated through our consciousness. The world 'as it is' is not a relevant (or possible) object of investigation – however, the lived world is. The lived world refers to the untheorized experience, some kind of unarticulated common sense. The object of phenomenology is to access the unprocessed experience, the deep layer of the 'felt' that is not distorted by conceptual frameworks. Phenomenologists long for the 'raw' experience of a phenomenon. It is only accessible through the people who experienced the phenomenon first-hand. Therefore, in the phenomenological tradition, the balance of expertise is explicitly challenged and participants are conceptualized as co-researchers.

BRACKETING

In order to access the lived experience, phenomenology, especially Husserl's phenomenology, requires that researchers bracket their own experiences, preconceptions and biases. Work is required to bring those into full view (through journaling, for example) so as to allow one to distance oneself and develop an untainted attitude toward the phenomenon under study. It is at the cost of bracketing their own experience and voice that researchers will be open enough to fully hear and see the co-researchers' lived experiences.

LOOKING FOR ESSENCE THROUGH REDUCTION

By accessing the lived world, as opposed to the theorized world, phenomenologists aim at identifying the essence of the phenomenon under study; that is, all the components and properties that distinguish a phenomenon from the next one: 'This method – the method of eidetic reduction – consists in arbitrarily adding to or subtracting qualities from the concept under investigation until one arrived at its invariant structure, that without which the colour red could not be red' (Fouche, 1993: 122–3). For example, what is the difference between a spiritual and a religious practice? One could make the case that they are very similar in substance and share the same components, except for the fact that religious practice entails participation in cyclical collective rituals. Hence, by comparing the experience that many co-researchers have of a phenomenon it is possible to boil it down, to reduce it, to its essential and necessary components. By doing so, phenomenologists get to identify the essence of a phenomenon and mark the border between one phenomenon (e.g. religious practice) and another similar but not identical phenomenon (e.g. spiritual practice).

DESCRIBING RATHER THAN EXPLAINING

Phenomenology aims at producing wisdom, not explanatory science. The analytical process of phenomenology attempts to generate texts that echo people's experience – descriptions that are such that they make the reader understand the studied phenomenon by identifying with the co-researchers and by bringing the readers' own experience of the phenomenon to the surface. This is the equivalent of the effect accomplished by good novels. Novels do not try to explain the world but, as readers, we can develop an understanding of it if we identify with the characters.

DIFFERENT SCHOOLS OF PHENOMENOLOGY

Husserl's vision of phenomenology, called transcendental phenomenology, has been described by some as a positivist attempt to reveal the lived world. Indeed, Husserl rejects relativism, the idea that there is no true or single description of the lived experience. He believed that, with proper distance and through bracketing, a researcher could describe the co-researchers' experience as it was lived. This position is noticeable when researchers adopt a point of view 'from nowhere' and erase their presence from their analytical work and their writing. Here is an example of what we mean by the point of view 'from nowhere': 'The experience of mourning entails four phases.' This is quite different from a qualified assertion such as: 'Our analysis of the co-researchers' narratives shows that mourning is experience through four phases.' In a way, Husserl's pursuit is similar to the objective perspective of positivists.

On the other hand, Merleau-Ponty (1945/2012), and his existentialist phenomenology, departs from Husserl's position in that he insists on situatedness. For him, consciousness is empirical and situated in a specific context. No matter how much bracketing one attempts, the point of view developed is never 'from nowhere'. Making explicit the researcher's position is therefore critical because one only speaks from somewhere, from a specific point in time, in life and in the world.

Also departing from Husserl's tendency toward positivism and his insistence on producing descriptions of phenomena is Heidegger and his hermeneutical phenomenology. Heidegger (1927/1962) sees the product of phenomenological research as an interpretation of the researcher. Here again, the researcher is problematized as an active agent in the making of knowledge.

Table 3.2 distinguishes those three schools of phenomenology according to the researcher's stance it supposes and the status given to the researcher's account.

Table 3.2   Different schools of phenomenology

	Transcendental phenomenology (Husserl)	Existentialist phenomenology (Merleau-Ponty)	Hermeneutical phenomenology (Heidegger)
Researcher's stance	The researcher adopts a point of view from nowhere	The researcher is situated, so is the participant, and this has to be taken into account	
Status of the researcher's account	The researcher's description matches the lived world		The researcher proposes an interpretation of the lived world

This first generation of philosopher phenomenologists paved the way for researchers who became phenomenology's icons in human and social sciences as well as education later in the twentieth century. We refer for example to Giorgi (1985) (psychology) and Schutz (1973) (sociology), as well as to Moustakas (1994) (psychology) and van Manen (1990) (education). Those writers are well worth reading if your research question pertains to the subjective experience of a specific phenomenon.

PHENOMENOLOGICAL METHOD

Since phenomenology cultivates an attitude of 'unknowing' to become aware and receptive to co-researchers' experience, it requires an important phase of introspection and work on the self (Munhall, 2007: 170). This attitude is as crucial to generating empirical material as it is to analysing it. This attitude contrasts with the post-positivist scientific project of producing knowledge and makes some researchers cautious about following rigid analytical steps. Indeed, some underline the importance of 'dwelling' upon and 'contemplating' one's material, sitting with it and letting it generate some insights (Munhall, 2007: 179–80). Others jump more quickly to a series of more formalized steps to unearth the essential meaning of a lived experience. Following Butler-Kisber (2010: 53), the analytical phase of the research can be schematized into five steps, each of which aims at boiling down the material to its essence. Having an overview of those steps will give you a better idea of what phenomenology can mean, concretely, for your project. To illustrate the steps, we will refer to the application we made of phenomenology to an allocution by Michael Parenti on his political involvement. You will find his allocution, titled 'How I became an activist', on the companion website of this book (https://study.sagepub.com/gaudetandrobert). It is also part of the material we use later on to illustrate different analytical strategies in action in Chapters 7–9. This allocution lasts 20 minutes and is 10 pages or 486 lines long when transcribed.

IMMERSION INTO THE MATERIAL

Researchers need an intimate knowledge of the materiel, its logic, its tone, its content. To ensure this, they must read the material over and over. Researchers have to be inhabited by their material. This step is especially important when researchers have not produced the material themselves, whether they work with documents or **verbatim** interviews conducted by others. That was the case when we used phenomenology to analyse Parenti's allocution since we were not present when it took place.

EXTRACTION OF SIGNIFICANT STATEMENTS

Every significant statement regarding the experience under study is then extracted from the material. Statements on a different topic or redundancies are eliminated. The end product of this step is a numbered list of significant statements. From his talk, we identified 69 such significant statements pertaining to the process by which Parenti became an activist. For example: Significant statement 8: 'My home was politically relatively impoverished. It was blue-collar, Italian-American, working-class, low income. We were really poor.'

FORMULATION OF MEANINGS

The significant statements are read over a few times to identify the main aspects expressed in the material. The researcher writes a sentence or two that expresses the explicit and implicit meanings of a series of significant statements relating to an aspect of the experience. The end product of this step is a numbered list of formulated meanings, each followed by the number of the various significant statements they refer to. From the 69 significant statements identified in the previous step, we ended up with 17 formulations of meanings that encompass them all. For example: formulation of meaning 4: 'I grew up in an environment deprived financially and politically' (significant statements 8 and 19).

IDENTIFICATION OF THEMES

The formulated meanings are clustered into broader themes that pinpoint the common key elements that compose the experience. For example, we identified the theme 'Hardship as the (fertile) ground to become an activist.' This theme encompasses two formulations of meanings, including the formulation of meaning number 4 identified above.

WRITING THE PHENOMENOLOGICAL NARRATIVE

On the basis of the themes identified and all the previous steps performed, researchers write a narrative that expresses the essential components and meanings of the phenomena under study. 'The text must convey the intimate experience of the participant from his or her point of view' (Paillé and Mucchielli, 2010: 92, our translation). From Parenti's allocution, the phenomenological narrative we arrived at from writing up the themes is a short text (half a page) written in the first person.

After the individual analysis of each source is performed, the researchers are faced with a series of phenomenological narratives. It is now possible to identify the recurring patterns and differences in all the narratives and either to write a narrative that reflects the general structures found in the singular phenomenological narratives (Paillé and Mucchielli, 2010: 94), or to elaborate a typology that shows the diversity of the lived experience for the phenomena under study.

GROUNDED THEORY

In the United States of the late 1960s, the post-positivist paradigm, with its emphasis on objectivism, replication, explanation, **generalization** and instrumental rigor, was still predominant. But ethnomethodology and social constructionism were emerging. So was grounded theory, with the publication of Barney Glaser and Anselm Strauss's book, in 1967, *The Discovery of Grounded Theory*. Around the same time, they also published grounded theory works on the trajectory of dying patients (Glaser and Strauss, 1965/1970; 1968; 1971). Glaser was trained in the quantitative and functionalist traditions while Strauss was a product of the Chicago school and a proponent of symbolic interactionism. Founded on the works of Mead (1934/1963), Blumer (1969), Goffman (1961) and Becker (1963), symbolic interactionism had a strong influence on grounded theory with its conceptualization of social experiences in terms of process, learned and negotiated meanings, interaction, trajectory and identity. Glaser and Strauss are explicit as to the usefulness of both quantitative and qualitative material, even if their influential books emphasize the latter. At a time when qualitative research was mostly conceived of as an auxiliary method, dedicated to the preliminary phase of a grand-scale quantitative research project, grounded theory both systematized and legitimized qualitative research (Bryant and Charmaz, 2007).

UNDERPINNINGS AND PREMISES

Grounded theory is likely one of the most popular traditions in qualitative research. Many books have been written on it and we are tempted to say that a majority of qualitative researchers acknowledge their connection to this important tradition. To navigate the rich waters of grounded theory, we will focus on four of its concepts and premises:

- The goal is to produce theories.
- Those theories are anchored in the empirical material under study.
- The analytical process of constant comparison is key to the method.
- **Theoretical sampling** is at the basis of both data gathering and theorization.

PRODUCING THEORIES

In its original form, the objective of grounded theory is to produce theories. Here, theories are conceived of as an evolving process rather than a final product. The obsession of social sciences to replicate already known hypotheses is deemed insufficient by Glaser and Strauss. While the grand theories are fruitful, the two founders thought sociology needed more mid-level theories. Therefore, the project of sociology should not be restricted to verifying hypotheses drawn from the grand theories but to generate new theories (Glaser and Strauss, 1967: vii–viii; 2). Grounded theory calls for conceptualizing social experience. Note, however, that studies often borrow the tools of grounded theory (coding, categorization, etc.) without the ambition of producing theories.

THEORIES MUST BE EMPIRICALLY FOUNDED

The inductive theories created by grounded theory are the product of empirical analysis. According to the founders, it is because they are empirically anchored that produced theories can 'enable prediction and explanation of behaviour ... [and] be usable in practical applications' (Glaser and Strauss, 1967: 3). Theories are not to be found, ready to be collected, in the material. Theories are generated from the researcher's analysis. To achieve such a goal, inductive work is key, especially at the early stages when the theory is given shape. Indeed, grounded theory is often portrayed as requiring researchers to proceed directly to the fieldwork before even getting acquainted with the literature on the investigated topic (Glaser and Strauss, 1967: 37). Proponents of this approach suggest that researchers conduct fieldwork and analyse their material using their general knowledge and their sensitizing concepts. They owe the latter term to Blumer:

> Whereas definitive concepts provide prescriptions of what to see, sensitizing concepts merely suggest directions along which to look. (1954: 7)

Through their sensitizing concepts, researchers can therefore study their material and identify the specificities of the phenomenon under study. When the categories to describe the phenomenon have been solidified, the researchers can use them to enter into a systematic dialogue with previous literature on the topic.

CONSTANT COMPARISON

The inductive process of generating an interrelated set of conceptual categories to explain a phenomenon, a theory, is made possible by the use of an essential tool: constant comparison. Proponents of grounded theory use it to build their way to higher levels of abstraction. For example, one starts from empirical observations (empirical observation in hospital wards about dying patients), to generate conceptual categories (loss, value of a dying person), to construct substantive theories (theories about a specific phenomenon such as dying), and finally proposes formal theories (the theory of status passage, an abstract theory that explains dying and other transformations occurring throughout one's lifetime). Grounded theorists compare empirical observations to one another to generate conceptual categories; they compare empirical observations to conceptual categories to identify or refine the dimensions and properties of the conceptual categories; they compare conceptual categories to one another to pinpoint their specificities and build substantive theories; they compare empirical observations and conceptual categories to substantive theories to improve upon them; and, finally, they compare substantive theories to one another to generate a formal theory that has even more explanatory power.

THEORETICAL SAMPLING

The progressive process of generating a theory solidly anchored in the empirical material rests on a continuous loop among the generation of material, its analysis and the **sampling** of further material, cases or participants. Indeed, writing up the research report starts as soon as the analysis begins and, in the ideal grounded theory world, the analysis starts right after the first interview is conducted, the first observation session is completed or the first document is gathered. On the basis of the analysis of this source, purposeful selection criteria are identified to choose the next participant, observation site or document. Sampling decisions are therefore always the product of lessons learned from the analysis, conceptual insights and nascent ideas that need to be tested. Theoretical sampling also means that the sampling decisions are always made with the aim of finding, improving, refining all the categories (e.g. prestige), and the properties of each category (e.g. the level, source and effect of the category prestige), that compose the developing theory (e.g. a theory on political influence) (Charmaz, 2014: 96).

DIFFERENT SCHOOLS OF GROUNDED THEORY

Following the publication of their 1967 book, the two founders continued refining the method over time, either together, or separately. Indeed, at one point their views on the appropriate level of induction in grounded theory diverged. Glaser pleaded for strong induction; that is hitting fieldwork first, while Strauss saw the usefulness of starting a project with a literature review before fieldwork (Corbin and Strauss, 1990; Glaser, 1978; Strauss and Corbin, 1990). Their students and other grounded theorists also continued to adapt the approach (Charmaz, 2014; Clarke, 2005). In a very schematic way, based on their epistemological underpinnings, Table 3.3 distinguishes four versions of grounded theory.

This typology is partial and does not account for the multiplicity of adaptations of the approach initially proposed by Glaser and Strauss. Indeed, many researchers refer to grounded theory as their method but rarely use it in its entirety, as an approach to the phenomenon under study that embodies the strongly inductive process, the constant comparison and the theoretical sampling principles that aim at producing theories. Rather, many researchers are inspired by grounded theory but simply use some of the analytical tools popularized by this approach – specifically, coding and categorization.

Table 3.3   Different schools of grounded theory (GT)

Classic GT		Constructionist GT	Critical realist GT	Postmodern GT
Post-positivist: insistence on verification and explanation (causal mechanism)		Constructivist: acknowledgment of situated knowledge and the role of the researcher as a selection agent	Critical realist: insistence on abduction rather than induction	Postmodern: emphasis on situatedness, partialities and contradictions
Pure induction	'Informed' induction	Charmaz (2014)	Oliver (2011)	Clarke (2005) Kools (2008)
Glaser (1978)	Glaser and Strauss (1967)			
	Corbin and Strauss (1990)			

GROUNDED THEORY'S METHOD

While grounded theory, like phenomenology, is a broad research approach to social experience and a scientific project on its own, it is also of interest for the tools it provides us with for analysing data. Hence, Paillé (1994), based on the works of Glaser and Strauss (1967), details an iterative analytical process in six steps that can be used with any kind of material, whether verbatim interviews, observation notes, media clips, etc. For the remainder of this section, we will rely on his excellent descriptions of these steps. Again, we believe that having an overview of them will give you a better idea of what grounded theory can mean, concretely, for your project.

INITIAL CODING

This step requires a close reading of the material with a question in mind: 'What is this about?' (Paillé, 1994: 154). Coding means reading the material, line by line, in order to identify concisely the best keywords to synthesize the substance of the material and annotate the material accordingly. Those keywords, called codes in grounded theory, can come from the researcher (**etic**) or the participants (**emic**). At this stage, the job is still closer to description than to interpretation. While coding is a central step at the beginning of grounded theory research, it will be progressively abandoned as the material is generated and analysed. Indeed, the goal of the initial coding step is, for the researcher, to immerse him- or herself in the material and slowly proceed to a more abstract reading of it which is embodied in rich conceptual categories.

CATEGORIZING

In an odd way, the second step of the process resembles the first. One reads the material again and asks the following question: 'What phenomenon am I facing?'

(Paillé, 1994: 159) The difference between this step and the previous one, the coding phase, is that categories elevate the analytical process to the comprehensive rather than the descriptive level (codes). The theoretical sensitivity of the researcher comes into full play here because the categorization step is about seeing meaning in the data, not just identifying substance. It is therefore to be expected that there would be fewer categories than codes for the same excerpt of material. Generating categories is a complex trial and error process. That is why writing memos to oneself is an intrinsic part of this step. A memo is an entry in an analysis journal that details the mental processes occurring as the categories are produced. Table 3.4 shows a memo on a category: politicization. Early in our categorization process of Parenti's talk, we labeled three excerpts as 'politicization'. We need to define this category from the ground up; that is, in a way that is congruent with the three excerpts tagged under this category. This initial definition and characterization of a category will evolve as more excerpts are labeled under this category and compared to it.

Table 3.4   Example of a memo on the category 'politicization'

How do I define this category (1994: 164)?	'Politicization is the process of becoming conscious of the inequalities at the basis of and resulting from institutional, collective or individual actions.'
What are the characteristics of this category (1994: 165)?	'Politicization' is a process that is made of steps such as being exposed to early influences, experiencing turning points, becoming actively engaged with a cause, living through changes of heart, learning to cope with the social costs of one's political actions, etc.
What are the social conditions necessary to the category (1994: 165)?	For 'politicization' to take place, a vocabulary to recognize and talk about power issues has to be developed, one's disagreement with conventions or official order has to be publicly voiced and it has to be acted upon.
What forms or dimensions does a category take (1994: 166)?	'Politicization' is a process that can be progressive (developing through one's childhood) or sudden (after having met politically aware and engaged college friends); it can be situated on a spectrum of consciousness ranging from awareness and choice (attending non-violence workshops) to being subtle and involuntary (a continuous feeling of not fitting into the middle-class Jewish neighborhood); it can be acted upon in different ways (participating in demonstrations, organizing political events, writing letters to elected representatives).

ESTABLISHING RELATIONS AMONG CATEGORIES

The third step of grounded theory suggested by Paillé (1994) is to identify the links that emerge among categories. What orders, logics and patterns connect them? The links among categories might be of different natures: hierarchy, dependence, functional relationships, causal links, etc. Which categories are central, which are marginal? At this stage, the researcher might want to draw a figure (or multiple figures) and write memos that describe the arrows or lines that connect categories together in the figure.

INTEGRATING

Each step of the grounded theory method requires bringing the data to a greater level of abstraction. The researcher has traveled progressively from the initial research question to a more general inquiry. Hence, at the integration stage, the research object needs to be more explicitly delineated. In the end: 'What does my research pertain to?' (Paillé, 1994: 172). What is the theme that unifies the categories and figures generated earlier? For example, the analysis of Parenti's talk on how he became an activist coupled with that of talks and interviews with other participants on the topic could lead to a narrative thread that pertains to finding one's vocation; that is, not just practicing a political activity but finding and developing in oneself an intense passion (in Parenti's case, it was his love of justice) that shapes and consumes most areas of one's life and justifies going through hardship. Moreover, the vocational angle transforms hardship into a proof of one's commitment and higher moral purpose.

MODELING

The objective here is to progressively formalize the research object constructed so far into a model with clear characteristics, explicit processes and predictable consequences. In order to do so, the researchers have to ask themselves: 'What are the components or dimensions of the phenomenon?'; 'What are the necessary conditions for the phenomenon to emerge?'; 'What are the consequences of the phenomenon?'; 'How is it related to other phenomena?'; 'What rhythm or dynamic does it obey?' (Paillé, 1994: 173–7). Answering those questions helps us develop a model that, in our example, does not just portray how people become activists but, more broadly, the process of finding one's vocation.

THEORIZING

Once the model has crystalized, it is tested. Theorization is a process that aims at reinforcing or revising the theory that emerged from the previous steps. Following Glaser and Strauss, one way of doing that is to continue applying the theoretical sampling principle but, this time, at the scale of the phenomenon and its components. To continue with our example, let us say that the grounded theory analysis of Parenti's talk and other similar material on becoming an activist led us to develop a model that pertains to finding one's vocation. That model could be made of different components, such as being open to a 'calling', framing one's problems as 'tests', etc. Theoretically sampling each component of the model would require going back to the original material and/or generating other material and finding multiple examples of being open to a 'calling' or framing one's problem as 'tests'. These examples would help to refine the model and ensure that all its properties are explicitly laid out – to the extent that there are no other properties to discover.

Theorizing could be accomplished by analytic induction where the researcher continues gathering new data and searching for a 'negative case': a participant or an experience that contradicts some component of the model. Then the researcher can revise and tweak the model to make it general enough so that it can apply to the negative case as well.

It should be understood that, to be true to the spirit of the founders, grounded theory must be more than a series of steps to conduct qualitative research – it must be an ambitious research program (producing mid-level theories) and a commitment to inductive analysis. Of course, many researchers trained in that tradition critiqued it and modified it to create different versions of grounded theory. Moreover, as we mentioned above, many researchers are content to simply use the first tools in the original grounded theory toolbox (coding and categorization). In those cases, while it may be inspired by grounded theory, in our view the analysis is closer to qualitative content analysis or thematic analysis.

DISCOURSE ANALYSIS

The meaning of discourse analysis is not always clear in the methodological literature. For our sake, we trace the line to the 'linguistic turn' in social sciences. Discourse analysts took the linguistic turn and decided to 'take language seriously' (Alvesson, 2002: 63). By that, they mean that they focus their analysis on language in use. To better understand what this turn involves, we need to first lay out the default position often adopted by qualitative researchers: the correspondence theory of language (Alvesson, 2002) or the factist perspective on language and data (Alasuutari, 1995c).

Many qualitative researchers implicitly accept the idea that language mirrors more or less directly the beliefs held by people and the practices those people have. For them, there is a preoccupation with making the language and data as 'transparent' as possible onto the 'real' beliefs or representations and the 'real' actions or practices. They want to make language correspond to 'facts'. Finding a way to neutralize language is a necessary condition to study reality. For example, you might want to conduct interviews to document the use of solitary confinement by prison officers. Your interest is the practices that prison officers develop and put in place regarding the use of solitary confinement. For this reason, you want to make sure that what they tell you reflects as closely as possible what they actually do. Hence, there is a strong concern regarding 'biases' introduced by the participants and the researcher in the material production or gathering phase of the project, as well as a strong concern for **triangulation** of the information to ensure that the participants are giving a true picture of their thoughts and actions. Concerns like the following take center stage: Is the participant leaving out information or embellishing the story to hide unsavoury concerns or actions? Is the interviewer unknowingly leading the participants with prompts and questions toward a 'desirable' answer? In order to reduce, if not eliminate, those biases, many will want to establish a close connection with the participants so they will share their true stories with ample details and with complete trust (Alasuutari, 1995c). The thinking is: the better the connection between researcher and participants, the truer and more complete the research material will be. With trust, the participant will not use words in a way that distorts reality. Or, researchers might go a different route and choose to conceal their research questions or objectives from their participants so as to avoid influencing them into describing their experiences in such a way that could please the researchers. In this case, the thinking is: not knowing the research objectives, hypothesis and the researcher's stand on the issue will make it difficult, if not impossible, for a participant to 'fool' the researcher (Alasuutari, 1995c). The correspondence theory of language, or the factist perspective, sees language as an obligatory passage toward reality as it is thought and lived. It is assumed that language has the capacity to portray thoughts and actions perfectly, if certain conditions are met: complete trust or ignorance from the participants. It is up to the researcher to use techniques and skills that will increase the reliability of the empirical material. Discourse analysts reject this correspondence theory of language or the factist perspective. They see language as we use it in our interactions as a level of reality worth analysing in itself.

UNDERPINNINGS AND PREMISES

Maybe even more than phenomenology and grounded theory, discourse analysis is a varied tradition. We emphasized the rejection of the correspondence theory of language or factist perspective as a commonality among the schools of discourse analysis. More positively, though, we suggest that they share the following three concepts and premises:

- As a specimen of our culture, the way people mobilize language deserves its own analysis (Alasuutari, 1995b).

- Language is performative; it constructs a version of the world.

- The analytical process is focused on situatedness, otherwise called language in use.

LANGUAGE/DATA AS A SPECIMEN

Discourse analysts take the linguistic turn and make language the main focus of their study. In this context, you would still want to conduct interviews to learn about the use of solitary confinement by prison officers. But those interviews would be occasions to gather information on the way prison officers talk about their use of segregation. What they say about solitary confinement would be the focus of the study. You would not assume that it reflects what they really think or do. Language is not, or not simply, a medium to convey something else, such as beliefs or behaviors as it is conceived of in the correspondence theory (Alvesson, 2002). Chosen vocabulary, oppositions and associations made, level of language, figures of speech, repetitions should all be attended to in the analysis. Words are specimens, an intrinsic part of a culture (Alasuutari, 1995b). The same way an archeological dig leads to finding artefacts that belonged to a society, language is part and parcel of a society, a segment of a population or a group. It is not, or not just, the reflection of another level of reality such as thought or actions. Like each specimen discovered, it deserves an analysis in its own right.

PERFORMATIVITY

Language does things to people and people do things with language. Language creates paths for action. It makes some actions and thoughts more likely, others less so. For example, when faced with a problem and a potential solution on which to vote, participants are inclined to ponder the solution offered and vote for or against it. Presenting the same problem and solution but asking the participants to comment, rather than asking them to vote, on the solution will likely allow additional solutions to be generated. This is not to say that people simply do what they are told and think what they are taught. It is always possible for someone to choose to revisit the definition of the problem in the first place. But language traces certain parameters for action. It is not the same to be asked to vote or comment. Moreover, people accomplish things with language: boast, plea, reprimand, flatter, convince, appear authoritative, etc. The terms prostitute or sex worker summon different registers, connotations and social imaginaries. The former is more likely to suggest marginality, the latter, labour. Hence, reality is performed through language.

SITUATEDNESS OR LANGUAGE IN USE

There is hardly a neutral use of language. This is the reason why many schools of discourse analysis favor studying language in use – so as to grasp the context of utterance. This context is essential to understand the meaning that is conveyed with the choice of certain words. Alvesson (2002: 63) gives a good example of this. The sentence 'It is 9 o'clock' can mean 'It is 9 o'clock, let's congregate and start the meeting', or 'It is 9 o'clock, the meeting has already started and you are late', or else 'It is 9 o'clock, and therefore too late to start the meeting.' Language is a situated practice that has to be studied in its context of use.

DIFFERENT SCHOOLS OF DISCOURSE ANALYSIS

Every school of discourse analysis defines discourse in its own way and has its own strategies to analyse it. To give an idea of the range of schools, we borrow a useful typology (Figure 3.2) developed by Phillips and Hardy (2002: 20).

Discourse analysis schools can be positioned along the constructivist–critical axis. At one end of the spectrum, a researcher might want to focus on a process of social construction. For instance: how was the label 'school

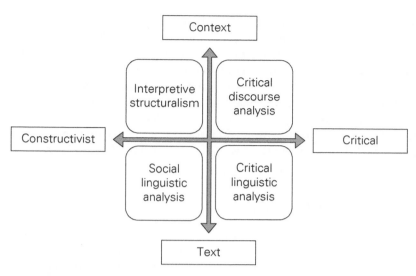

Figure 3.2 Different schools of discourse analysis (from Phillips and Hardy, 2002: 20)

bullying' popularized to designate hurtful schoolyard interactions among youth and how did it become a social problem? At the other end of the spectrum, a researcher might want to investigate the power dynamics at play in this phenomenon. For example: how is public health imposing its definition of school bullying (thus marginalizing pedagogical, psychological, legal definitions) and contributing to the medicalization of social policies? Of course, it is difficult to focus on processes of social construction without considering power and vice versa; that is why, following Phillips and Hardy (2002), we chose to represent this choice not as a dichotomy (either/or) but as a continuum.

Moreover, discourse analysis can be positioned along the text–context axis. Here again, this choice is a matter of degree. In the vast majority of studies using discourse analysis, special focus will be directed on the text itself or what some call the proximate context: the document's genre, its position in relation to other texts, its structure, and the direct conditions of its production. In other studies, the distal context will be of paramount importance: the socio-political climate at the time the text was produced, the cultural norms that prevailed, and the institutional rules under which the text was created.

At the intersection of those two axes, we find four broad schools. Social linguistic analysis focuses on construction processes and text. Under this category, we find a study aimed at identifying the rhetorical features of 'green evangelicalism' (Prelli and Winters, 2009) or one documenting the position attributed to every member of a board by doing a conversation analysis of their meetings. Critical linguistic analysis is similar but centered on power issues. Here, a study would analyse closely the transcripts of family verbal interactions to reconstitute discursive strategies that ensure the dominance of adults over children. Another could analyse the prevalence of bio-governance by focusing on the metaphors used in the press about the necessity to collect a DNA sample from children for prevention purposes. The interpretive structuralism school aims at showing processes of construction while locating them in a distal context. For example, studying the discursive evolution of company takeovers to show a change in business culture over time (Hirsch, 1986) exemplifies this approach. Finally, critical discourse analysis is interested in mapping power dynamics and pays close attention to distal context. Peled-Elhanan's (2010) study on the legitimation of massacres in history manuals in Israel or Carabine's (2001) genealogical analysis of unmarried motherhood over a century in Britain fall under this approach.

DISCOURSE ANALYSIS METHOD

The previous section suggests that there is no common analytical strategy in discourse analysis. To illustrate one possibility, and give you an idea of what it means concretely to do discourse analysis, we will rely on a strategy systematized by Fairclough (2001), one of the main theorists, with van Dijk (1985) and Wodak (2002), of critical discourse analysis.

Fairclough (1995) is influenced by Foucault, the Frankfurt school and Roy Bhaskar's (1975/1997) work. Fairclough is interested in showing how semiosis (all meaning-making activities, including talk and texts) contributes to the ideological reproduction of relationships of domination. He focuses mainly on discourses of globalization and exclusion and wishes to contribute to social change by unveiling the power relations at play in those processes. In order to achieve this, Fairclough's discourse analysis strategy (2001: 236) is embedded within a whole framework consisting of five steps. For the sake of the presentation here, attention will be restricted to the second step of analysis where a close reading of the text occurs. At this moment of analysis, the question is: what is the discourse itself on this problem? Close attention to the language thus takes place using four layers of query, as follows.

STRUCTURAL ANALYSIS AND THE ORDER OF DISCOURSE

How and where does a text occur in the chain of texts that precede and follow it? Said otherwise, where does the text under study fit in the landscape of meaning? It is important to understand that a text is not necessarily meant as a document but can be a billboard on a highway, an interview transcript or a video game. Each text is an answer to another. Therefore, it is important to conceive of a text as a point in time in a broader interactional process, whether a personal or social conversation (Fairclough, 2001: 239–40).

INTERACTIONAL ANALYSIS

Each text is productive and must be analysed to uncover four types of productions (Fairclough, 2001: 241):

1. Representations: How are the facts and stakes represented in the text?

2. Identities: What identities does the text create?

3. Values: What is presented as desirable, positive, good versus undesirable, negative, bad?

4. Relations: What social spheres (personal, public, government, politics, etc.) are related or connected in and by the text?

INTERDISCURSIVE ANALYSIS

A text is rarely homogeneous. It is often made up of different genres. Therefore, the question at this stage is: what genres does the text borrow from? Comedy, interview, commercial, address, etc. (Fairclough, 2001: 241)?

LINGUISTIC AND SEMIOTIC ANALYSIS

Finally, the text is read to uncover the very fabric of meaning in terms of choice of sentences and words:

1. How is the text organized? Is it narrative, argumentative, declarative (Fairclough, 2001: 241)?

2. How are the clauses combined? Is the text using complex or compound sentences or simple ones (2001: 241)?

3. What type of clauses does the text contain? Grammar and semantics of clauses, transitive or intransitive verbs, action verbs, choice of pronoun, modality, etc. (2001: 242)?

4. What words are used? Vocabulary, connotative and denotative meanings, metaphors, etc. (2001: 242)?

Looking at pronouns used, action verbs, choices of vocabulary, clause combinations and all the other linguistic aspects are all ways of seeing how reality is constructed and how power, such as racial, gendered, heteronormative or ableist structures, is produced and reproduced. When the critical angle is added to this, a discourse analyst can then interpret these choices as mechanisms by which ideological reproduction, or resistance to it, operates.

NARRATIVE ANALYSIS

Narrative analysis is an umbrella term that refers to a variety of methodological positions and tools, all of which concern themselves with stories that humans produce and the storied nature of their lives. Like the other approaches described in this chapter, narrative analysis is a qualitative research tradition as a whole with its history, debates and specific types of research questions or problems. However, and again like the other traditions presented in this chapter, researchers sometimes choose to borrow specific analytical tools from narrative analysis (e.g. a study of the characters portrayed in a source) without necessarily conducting their whole project within this specific tradition. Some classify narrative analysis as a branch of discourse analysis. Both traditions certainly share important commonalities, such as making language in use the focus of analysis. For clarity, though, we prefer to introduce narrative analysis as a tradition on its own. For the purpose of our discussion, we will suggest a definition that borrows some key elements from Prince (in Alasuutari, 1995a): a story is more or less a sequential telling of past events containing a plot; that is, changes to a state of being. Alasuutari gives the following example of a story: 'John was happy until he met Mary and then he became unhappy' (1995a: 71). Hence, a narrative is different from a simple description, a list or an argument. There are individual narratives that can be analysed with a focus on personal identity issues – for example, Elizer's narrative of his youth (Spector-Mersel, 2010). There are also collective narratives – for example, the 'diaspora narrative' as applied to Indians, Jews or Palestinians around the world (Said, 2000) or the 'green narrative' (Starkey and Crane, 2003).

The origins of narrative analysis can be traced in literary studies as far back as Aristotle (384–322 BCE) with his dissection of Greek tragedy, then the Russian formalist school (1910s–1930s) with Propp (1968) and his work on folk tales or linguistic structuralism and its rediscovery and popularization by Lévi-Strauss's (1963/1999) study of myths (1950s–1960s) (Kohler Riessman, 2008). For the sake of this overview, though, we will focus on what has been called the 'narrative turn': that is, the application of literary conceptual and methodological tools, such as sequences, plot, character and story line, to non-literary material such as archives, political texts, verbatim interviews, observation notes. This wave of interest started in the 1960s but bloomed in the middle of the 1980s (Kohler Riessman, 2008: 14) in a number of disciplines in social and health sciences. According to Pinnegar and Daynes (2007), the 'narrative turn' is born out of a reaction to the conventional or positivist way of doing science, the reification of research participants, the fetishism of numbers and the focus on generalizable truths.

UNDERPINNINGS AND PREMISES

Because of the multiplicity of definitions of the term 'narrative' and understandings of 'narrative analysis', pinpointing the fundamental commonalities among narrative studies runs the risk of misrepresenting some traditions (Robert and Shenhav, 2014) but we suggest three commonalities in the field of narrative analysis:

• Narratives are conceived as fundamental ways of knowing and portraying the world.

- The interest of narrative analysts is not the truth so much as the **verisimilitude** of the narratives.

- The analysis focuses on the study of connectedness, for each agent or character in a story needs to be understood relationally.

A FUNDAMENTAL WAY OF KNOWING

Bruner (1987) identifies two ways of knowing. The first is the rationalist and empiricist way that is characteristic of science. For a long time, this way of knowing has been promoted as the ideal way our minds work or should work. The rationalist–empiricist way is preoccupied with using facts to produce a formal and systematic description and explanation that reach the standard of universal truth (Bruner, 1991). The second is the narrative way of knowing that pervades all aspects of human experience. It is preoccupied with the way humans construct particular stories to represent and constitute experience. The 'narrative turn' is premised on attending to those stories that are constantly produced by humans and identifying the way they are shaped and shared, as well as the content of the stories, the characters that are involved, the sequence of actions, the plot and their effects on the audience.

VERISIMILITUDE RATHER THAN TRUTH

> Unlike the constructions generated by logical and scientific procedures that can be weeded out by falsification, narrative constructions can only achieve 'verisimilitude' or plausibility and realism. Narratives, then, are a version of reality whose acceptability is governed by convention and 'narrative necessity' rather than by empirical verification and logical requiredness. (Bruner, 1991: 4)

Stories are not true or false; they are more or less believable, they more or less achieve their aims of convincing, teaching a lesson, entertaining an audience and conveying a feeling. One event can lead to multiple accounts, each of them being partial and the bearer of one point of view (Bruner, 2002). Indeed, there are many ways to tell the story of how one came to decide to undertake and complete a university degree. For example:

> I was always fascinated by the crime shows that I saw on TV. When came the time to decide what I would study after high school, I was excited to see that I could become a criminologist by applying to a criminology program at the university in my city. I did, was accepted, and after my first semester soon understood that being a criminologist had little to do with what I saw on my favorite TV shows. Still, the courses interested me and I decided to complete the degree I had begun.

The same person could tell a different story:

> My brother and sister had both gone to university and there was little question that I would too. In fact, it was never even brought up at home and I never considered the possibility of going to professional college. I always liked school and going to university was just natural. I think my parents would have been shocked if I had told them that I did not want to go. When I started, it was a bit harder than I had anticipated but I made friends in my program and we struggled together. We organized study groups, where we did quite a bit of chatting rather than studying, but after the first year, I adapted. Despite being a little disillusioned as to what a criminologist does, there was never a doubt that I would finish my degree. These days, having an undergrad. degree is a necessity.

While the first emphasizes the emotional connection to a topic, the second lays out the implicit expectations that influenced the educational trajectory of the story teller. Those narratives are equally true and equally partial, equally factual and equally interpretative.

CONNECTEDNESS

In the same way that one needs to consider the Evil Queen's motives to wholly understand Snow White's actions, every sequence of a story and each of its characters need to be considered in relation to one another. In narrative analysis, meaning is relational; it is not a property of an event or a character. Therefore, the material under study needs to be considered wholly. The part is only meaningful in relation to the other parts of the story. Fragmenting the material, through detailed coding for example, hinders narrative analysis. The focus of analysis is on the relations that unite events and characters, not only the events and characters themselves.

DIFFERENT SCHOOLS OF NARRATIVE ANALYSIS

For the sake of clarity, we can divide the scholarship on narrative analysis into two broad schools: the classical and the post-classical (Robert and Shenhav, 2014). Figure 3.3 captures these distinctions visually.

What we will call here the classical school in narrative analysis encompasses different models. The Russian formalists (Propp, 1968) and their successors, such as Labov and Waletzky (1967), adopt a syntagmatic perspective focused on identifying the chronological sequences of events in a narrative. In these approaches, the analysis is inspired by the study of sentences. The researcher aims to uncover the 'syntax' of the narrative – the way its components are put together. How does the narrative open? What events complicate the progression of the action? How does the protagonist fare in adversity?

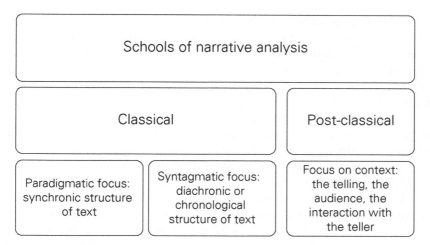

Figure 3.3   Different schools of narrative analysis.

With this interest for narrative progression in mind, Frank (1995) conducted an extensive interview study on the experience of chronic illnesses. He showed that there are basically three types of chronic illness narratives:

1. 'A narrative of restitution: I was healthy, now I am sick but tomorrow I will be better' (Frank, 1995: 77).

2. 'A quest narrative: illness is an opportunity to reinvent oneself' (1995: 166).

3. 'A chaos narrative: my life is in shambles and will stay as is; nobody is in control' (1995: 101).

This shows that the experience of chronic illness is varied, there is not one model and these different experiences might call for different types of support by the medical professionals and family members.

Another classical perspective on narrative analysis adopts a paradigmatic point of view, inspired by Lévi-Strauss (1963/1999) and Greimas (1966/1983). Rather than a syntagmatic one focused on a chronological structure, this approach aims at discovering the structure of meaning, also called the semiotic structure, of a narrative based on identifying fundamental oppositions. Wang and Roberts (2005) use this approach to explore the narrative construction of identity in the case of a peasant's daughter who becomes a school teacher and works with the children of peasants in communist China in the 1970s. That type of study highlights the relational reconfiguration needed for a peasant's daughter to assume authority in a classroom as a teacher.

In the post-classical school of narrative research, the focus is more on the context of production and transmission of the narrative than on its structure per se. In other words, it shifts the focus to storytelling as a performance (Peterson and Langellier, 2006). Therefore, a narrative is not a structure to be found in the empirical material but an open and dynamic process to be studied (Herman and Vervaeck, 2005). Since the interest is focused on the production rather than the product, the role of the reader or the interlocutor (or the researcher) is examined as a factor that contributes to the co-construction of the narrative: 'A particular self is constituted through ... narratives, occasioned by the presence of a listener, her questions and comments' (Kohler Riessman, 1990: 1195). In her analysis of interactions in support groups for chronic fatigue syndrome patients, Bülow (2004) explicitly analyses the way narratives are jointly produced by the facilitator and the participants. From this perspective, the facilitator orchestrates a chain of stories from the participants and co-narrates collective stories.

In addition, the post-classical approach insists on the fact that the attributes of a presupposed audience are likely to interact with the writing of the text. This interactional view opens up whole areas of research for narrative analysts: 'such as telling roles and telling rights, audience reactions, etc.' (De Fina and Georgakopoulou, 2008: 381). In these interactions, notions of identity, power, gender, seniority and culture are central.

NARRATIVE ANALYSIS METHOD

Narrative analysis encompasses many schools and, among them, many methodological strategies. We will use only one example to make narrative analysis more concrete and help you decide if it could be an option for your project. Wondering how transformations in Western movies since the 1930s are related to social changes in the United States, Wright (1975) produced an interesting structural narrative study. Using both syntagmatic and paradigmatic tools, he conceives of Western movies as modern myths and relates them to the stages of capitalism. Wright's method has been described in four steps by Harvey (2011).

IDENTIFY THE BINARY OPPOSITIONS

Determine which characters of which groups are in opposition to one another (cowboys and Indians, sedentary farmers and nomad tribes). Only by identifying what it is opposed to can we reveal the meaning of a character. For example, if black is opposed to white, then black likely refers to an absence of light; if black is opposed to pink, then black likely refers to a negative mood or outlook.

PROVIDE A SYMBOLIC CODING FOR THE CHARACTERS

For structuralism, oppositions found in the myth (in a Western in this case) always represent conceptual oppositions at the cultural and conceptual levels. Therefore, at this stage, one has to identify what concepts each opposition of characters represents in the cultural or social conscience. Figure 3.4 shows what Harvey (2011: 2) suggests in this case.

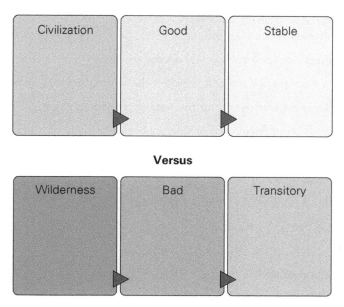

Figure 3.4 Example of symbolic coding for the characters

IDENTIFY THE FUNCTIONS OF THE PLOT

The goal at this stage is to reduce the narrative to its functions. To do so, one has to make a list of one-sentence statements 'that describe a single attribute or action of a character. For example, "the hero fights the villains"' (Harvey, 2011: 3). Those narrative functions are indicative of social or institutional actions and not just of society's conscience, contrary to the oppositions identified earlier.

DETERMINE THE NARRATIVE SEQUENCES

> The sequence ensures that the narrative 'makes sense', that is, tells a story rather than giving a listing of events. More specifically, the sequence provides rules by which characters are created and conflicts resolved. (Harvey, 2011: 3)

Narratives prescribe roles and conflict solutions that are coherent with the institution or society's needs. As institutions and societies change, so do the narrative structures of their myths. Here is an example of the classical plot Wright (1975: 48–9) uncovered in Westerns produced in the first period of his study:

1 'The hero enters a social group.'

2 'The hero is unknown to the society.'

3 'The hero is revealed to have an exceptional ability.'

4 'The society recognizes a difference between themselves and the hero; the hero is given a special status.'

5 'The society does not completely accept the hero.'

6 'There is a conflict of interest between the villains and the society.'

7 'The villains are stronger than the society; the society is weak.'

8 'There is a strong friendship or respect between the hero and the villains.'

9 'The villains threaten the society.'

10 'The hero avoids involvement in the conflict.'

11 'The villains endanger a friend of the hero.'

12 'The hero fights the villains.'

13 'The hero defeats the villains.'

14 'The society is safe.'

15 'The society accepts the hero.'

16 'The hero loses or gives up his special status.'

Among the Western movies from the 1930s to the 1970s Wright identified four narratives, chronologically ordered. After the classical plot depicted above, he finds the vengeful plot, the transitional plot and the professional plot.

LOCATE THE MYTH IN THE SOCIO-ECONOMIC CONTEXT

The strong hypothesis of Wright's research is that institutions and society structure individual interactions. Therefore, change in society should provoke change in its foundational myths. If that is the case, after each major social transformation we should observe a change in the narrative structure of the Western. The final step in Wright's method involves showing how the meaning of the narrative structure represents dominant ideological forms grounded in existing social structures. He convincingly shows how the progression from the classical to the professional plot reflects the transformation toward a corporate economy.

Again, narrative analysis is diverse. Like Wright, who crafted an approach that focuses on meaning structure (oppositions) and chronological structure (sequences), many researchers using narrative analysis borrow tools and principles from many schools both inside and outside narrative analysis.

ETHNOGRAPHY

While for some researchers any period of fieldwork dedicated to gathering documents, conducting interviews or observing settings can be qualified as 'ethnographic', O'Reilly suggests a 'critical minimum definition' of the term that is useful for our purposes. In her words, ethnography is:

> an interactive-inductive research (that evolves in design through the study), drawing on a family of methods, involving direct and sustained contact with human agents, within the context of their daily lives (and cultures), watching what happens, listening to what is said, asking questions, and producing a richly written account that respects the irreducibility of human experience, that acknowledges the role of theory, as well as the researcher's own role, and that views humans as part object/part subject. (2005: 3)

It is said that necessity is the mother of invention. Ethnography, as a systematic way of documenting cultures, is owed to anthropologists, namely Malinowski (1922/1966), who developed the methods of participant observation while studying the inhabitants of the Trobriand Islands in Melanesia at the beginning of the twentieth century. Anthropologists needed to find a way to gather information about the societies that interested them. Since no written records were available apart from travel journals written by explorers, colonizers and missionaries, the only other way to learn about undocumented cultures would be to actually go and integrate with this society. By being present and involved, an accurate account of a group could be written.

Another pillar of ethnography was the Chicago school of sociology (Atkinson et al., 2001). The Chicago school was dominant in the United States from the mid-1910s to the early 1940s in an era where immigration, urbanization and related realities, like homelessness, were on the rise. Following the invitation of Robert Park (1864–1944) and Ernest Burgess (1886–1966), sociology students used the transforming city as their laboratory. They learned to study people and activities (immigrants' ghettos, youth groups, etc.) *in vivo*. After the Second World War, the second school of Chicago, a school which went hand in hand with symbolic interactionism, continued the tradition of ethnographic fieldwork and applied it to institutions such as hospitals and psychiatric wards as well as marginalized populations.

UNDERPINNINGS AND PREMISES

While ethnography is the method of choice in anthropology, nowadays it is an approach used in many disciplines: nursing, education, sociology of health, organization studies, social psychology, to name a few. No matter what discipline a researcher identifies with, when undertaking ethnographic research, three main issues arise:

- Spending time.

- Distributing the focus on observation and/or participation.

- Choosing one's point of view.

TIME

One of the main characteristics of ethnography is the extended period spent by a researcher immersed in the studied milieu – often many months, if not years. It takes time to integrate into a milieu to a point where it becomes intelligible: having a sense of the ways a group structures time, divides tasks, allocates ranks and positions, cherishes symbols, values attitudes, disciplines, disobediences, etc. The time spent documenting all aspects of a milieu is not just important in the case where a researcher wants to write a comprehensive monograph on a group. The researcher can choose a more specific topic, such as the rapport with the body developed by tattoo artists, yet still the time spent documenting the wider context in which the artists' work will deepen the outlook of the researcher on tattoo artists' conceptions of the body.

OBSERVATION/PARTICIPATION

Ethnography often means being eclectic and gathering material through informal conversations, formal interviews, archival work and documentary analysis, but mostly it requires time spent observing, being there, 'hanging around' (Shaffir, 1999). Observing and participating (to one degree or another) is a condition for breaking the 'word barrier'. Some claim that observing more closely better guarantees an accurate rendition of an experience. Some would rather emphasize the texture of reality that observation can convey. For example, we are not always capable of expressing in words what goes on in our daily lives and we are not always aware of what we do in a day. Relying on Joe's account of his day as a portrait of what he did is one thing. Being there and observing him in action will likely yield another account – not because, as an interview participant, Joe lied about what he did, but because he is unaware of how many phone conversations he had in a morning, or the number of times he gazed at the sky daydreaming, or the tone he used when explaining an assignment to a co-worker, etc. Gathering such details is what give richness to an account, what allows a researcher to convey to a reader the feeling of 'being there'. By participating, that is assuming a role in a milieu, a researcher goes even further and can feel for him- or herself what an experience entails. For example, by being involved, a researcher can experience the feeling of dependence of an apprentice carpenter on a master or being in a position of authority when endorsing the role of a teaching assistant and marking undergraduate students' essays.

On the importance of observing in a milieu, watch Sarah Delamont's interview on ethnography on the website **https://study.sagepub. com/gaudetandrobert**.

POINT OF VIEW: EMIC/ETIC/AUTO

The monographs traditionally written by ethnographers to describe the practices of the groups they researched were often written 'from nowhere', using the impersonal form. In a study about skateboarding, this style of telling could sound like this: 'What stimulates the urban skateboarders is the search for risk/pleasure. They crave strong sensations, sometimes to the point of under-evaluating the dangers they take and represent to others.' The narrator of a monograph written in such a style is absent, giving an impression of describing life as it unfolded in a detached, objective manner. This is what is referred to as 'naturalism' in ethnography (Spencer, 2001: 448–9). This outsider's or etic point of view, while being a key tool of scientific rhetoric, was later questioned in human and social sciences.

Many ethnographers chose to leave this convention behind and made sure to give voices to the members of the group they worked with and tried to give predominance to the emic point of view: that is, the insiders' point of view. Quotes from the participants were included in monographs, accounts of events or experiences were accurately attributed to participants, the monographs aimed at making the underprivileged point of view heard. In a monograph on skateboarding that adopts the emic point of view, we would rather be faced with statements like the following:

> Andy, who qualifies himself as an intermediate skateboarder, explains: 'I want to push my limit and use the urban fixtures as my playground. I want to increase my skills and speed. Skateboarding is about saying no to conventions and the so called proper ways of going from one place to the other.'

This desire to give a voice to participants came under scrutiny and was debated. After all, was it not always the researcher who was in charge, selecting which participants to quote, whose point of view to adopt? Were we fooling ourselves in pretending that our monographs reflected the point of view of the participants?

For some, the answer to this debate is to confess to the authorship of their monograph, rejecting both the attempt to describe a group from nowhere and the attempt to render the point of view of the research participants. Monographs began to be written using the first-person narrative style and the positionality of the author was explicitly reflected upon. In autoethnographic research on skateboarding, we would probably read assertions like the following:

> I [the researcher] was scared the first time I set foot in a skateboard park and tried my moves. The guys and girls there were clearly more skilful than me. They were going past me at such speed. As a twenty five year old beginning skateboarder, I felt out of my league. That is when I met Andy.

The authors who adopt such an autoethnographic style reflexively discuss their gender, race, nationality, socio-economic background and their relation to the 'Other' as they write the account of the time spent with their participants (Madison, 2005).

DIFFERENT SCHOOLS OF ETHNOGRAPHY

Categorizing ethnographic works is a task that even the best ethnographers find difficult (Loseke and Cahill, 1999). It is nevertheless useful to try and, to do so, we will rely heavily upon the classification proposed by Roy and Banerjee (2012) as shown in Figure 3.5, despite the fact that they tend to equate ethnography as a methodological approach with anthropology as a discipline. We have modified their typology slightly and will not go into much detail here, but this might be enough to shed some light on the basic distinctions that exist among ethnographic studies.

The holistic school of ethnography has its source in the American anthropological work of Franz Boas. It favors an inductive and historical approach to studying culture formation. The holistic school perceives culture as a 'whole' and tends to study all the life dimensions of a group: family, community, politics, economy, beliefs and rituals, etc. According to the proponents of this school, patterns of behavior emerge; they slowly crystallize and become the norms of conduct of a group. Some ethnographers compare the development of those cultural personalities, searching for the commonalities among them, the features shared by many if not all cultures; this is the universalist branch of the holistic school headed by Ruth Benedict. Others, at the opposite end of the spectrum, are interested in the peculiarities and idiosyncrasies that

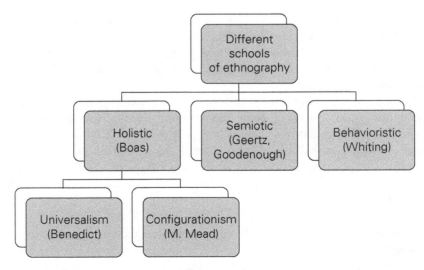

Figure 3.5 Different schools of ethnography (adapted from Roy and Banerjee, 2012)

each culture develops; this is the configurationist branch of the holistic school of which Margaret Mead (1901–1978) is an icon.

The semiotic school of ethnography is associated with the documentation of meaning. According to this school, culture is a system of signs that needs to be interpreted both by the natives of a culture and by the ethnographer. Therefore, the focus of the ethnography is not only on observed behaviors, but on the points of view people hold about these behaviors. To convey those points of view to a reader, a 'thick description', that is a detailed account of the context and the lived experience, is important. Such a detailed and vivid account is key to creating the verisimilitude effect (the impression for the readers that they know the participants) which is an important quality criterion of good ethnography.

The behavioristic school of ethnography is associated with John Whiting (1908–1999) and Beatrice Whiting (1914–2003) and is a form of post-positivist cultural psychology research. It posits that there is a relation between the culture of a group and the personality of its members. This school of ethnography has led to studies on children's personality development or children's aggressive behaviors across different and contrasted cultures. On the bases of the biology of a people, the ecology in which they live, the social interactions and culture they have, a series of hypotheses are drafted about the personality that the members of a society are expected to have. Those hypotheses are then tested following carefully sampled data and often quantitative analysis.

ETHNOGRAPHY'S METHOD

In this section, as well as presenting a specific analytic method used in ethnography, we want to draw attention to two interrelated methodological developments within this approach: multi-sited ethnography and digital ethnography.

MULTI-SITED ETHNOGRAPHY

Ethnography often evokes bounded territories, the idea that an ethnographic research object is materialized into a delimited location. As with the research by Malinowski we referred to earlier, studying the Trobriands' culture at the beginning of the twentieth century meant spending time with them on the islands they inhabited. The emergence of multi-sited ethnography has questioned the contrived association between ethnographic object and physical location. Moreover, multi-sited ethnography highlights the fact that a research object is never given, whether by a territory, era or group, but always the result of a series of selection decisions (What is part of a culture? What aspect to emphasize? What aspect to downplay?) (Marcus, 1995). Moreover, 'contemporary society is increasingly characterized by mobility, connection and communication' (Hine, 2007: 655). Therefore, multi-sited ethnography emphasizes the connections and relations that a research object is made of.

An ethnographic study must therefore cover a diversity of interconnected sites that are dictated by the research object itself. For example, when conducting an ethnography of a pharmaceutical agent it might mean conducting a long period of observation in a microbiology laboratory, followed by or interspersed with reading and analysing the research articles produced from that laboratory, then another period of observation in a 'rival' laboratory, followed by attendance at conferences where those scientists socialize and debate their latest scientific statements. The study might continue with a period of observation in a pharmaceutical laboratory where a molecule is created on the basis of the microbiology statements and clinical trials are conducted with patients all the way through to commercialization of the new medicine, etc. In a multisited ethnography, the researcher follows the connections that create and are part of the research object (for more, see the following: Latour, 2005; Latour and Woolgar, 1979/1996; Mol, 2002).

DIGITAL ETHNOGRAPHY

The virtual world plays an important role in the fluidity and connectedness that characterize contemporary life. In human and social sciences in general and in the ethnographic tradition in particular, the virtual world is a subject of study. Researchers are interested in documenting how people relate to the virtual (Ochoa et al., 2011). It can also offer tools for conducting research, such as online questionnaires and interviews, digital videos and research blogs (Hsu, 2014; Murthy, 2008). Finally, the virtual world offers an important source of ethnography sites and communities such as those from the gaming world, social media, virtual communities, organizations' websites, among others (Burke and Goodman, 2012; Cooper et al., 2012; Moore et al., 2009). In order to conduct observation in the virtual world, Marcus et al. (2012) emphasize the importance of preparation. Conducting ethnographic research of the virtual world requires you to set up your workspace so as to be comfortable spending long hours online, be well equipped in terms of hardware (microphone, headphones, joystick, etc.) and with Internet access so as to minimize the technical bugs that could hinder your fieldwork. You must learn the language and the mores of the community you want to integrate, as well as build technical proficiency (commands, options, speed, dexterity, etc.). You must create an avatar that will embody your online self for your participants (a gnome or a sexualized demon?), selecting the kind of presence you want in the online world (observation only; part of this or that group or forum; building a station/dwelling or not?). As part of participant observation, the online world also allows for individual or group interviews and documentary research through capturing chatlogs, screenshots, video and audio material, and visual artefacts. Lives are lived in the physical and online world, and following the connections that create and are part of our research object means being capable and willing to navigate both.

On the richness of netnography, watch the interview with Robert V. Kozinets on the website **https://study.sagepub.com/gaudetand-robert**.

ETHNOGRAPHIC ANALYSIS

Whether the fieldwork is conducted online, offline or both, ethnographers, especially if they have affinities with the semiotic school of ethnography (see above), are often interested in deciphering the meanings that things have for members of a culture or group. The focus is on the way a culture is organized, the classifications and categories that members share. Spradley (1979: 93), in a classic ethnography method, expresses it in these terms: '*Ethnographic analysis* is the search for the parts of a culture and their relationships *as conceptualized by informants*' (emphasis in the original). Could that type of analysis work for your project? To help you reflect on this, let us see what it means concretely. In order to uncover the system of cultural meaning people use, Spradley proposes four analytical tools:

1. Domain analysis: identifying the large categories that embrace items sharing common properties.

2. Taxonomic analysis: uncovering the internal structure of the domain.

3. Componential analysis: finding the attributes that distinguish items that are part of a domain.

4. Theme analysis: identifying the relationships that exist among domains.

We will limit ourselves to illustrating domain analysis here. To do so, we adapt an example provided by Spradley (1979: 100–5) based on his study of women working in a male-dominated environment, Brady's Bar.

Step 1: Selecting a sample of verbatim interview or observation notes.

Spradley selects the following short excerpt from a verbatim interview with a cocktail waitress:

> A table of about seven guys deliberately gave me a lot of grief, each ordering separately instead of in a round like most guys do. They all wanted to pay with large bills, too. I ordered four Buds with and passed the glasses out and they decided they didn't want glasses after all. I was mad but I kept smiling and saying, I'm sorry. (Spradley, 1979: 101)

Step 2: Looking for folk categories, names of things or actions as termed by the participant (the items part of a potential domain). Here are the actions of the clients as phrased by the waitress in the excerpt:

a.   ordering separately;

b.   paying with large bills;

c.   decided they didn't want glasses after all.

Step 3: Identifying a possible domain name; that is, a cover term for the folk categories.

Those three actions can be encompassed under the umbrella term 'give waitress grief'.

Step 4: Identifying the **semantic** relationship between the domain and the folk categories:

The three actions accomplished by the clients are means or ways to 'give waitress grief' (see Figure 3.6). In other words, [X: folk term] <u>is a way of</u> [Y: domain].

Is a way of:
Y: Give waitress grief

Figure 3.6   Identifying the semantic relationship (adapted from Spradley, 1979: 102)

Step 5: Searching through additional interview or observation notes for other folk terms that are part of the identified domain.

The main difficulty in identifying domains in our material is in imposing upon the material analytical categories that we, as researchers, are familiar with. Empirical accuracy is of utmost importance in such ethnographic analysis. In order to produce the cultural map shared by the research participants, the analysis has to be anchored in the participants' vocabulary; that is, the emic categories. As was said earlier, domain analysis is just one aspect of the ethnographic analysis proposed here. It is worth looking at Spradley's book to discover the richness of ethnographic analysis.

CHAPTER SUMMARY

This chapter introduced you to five traditional approaches in qualitative research: phenomenology, grounded theory, discourse analysis, narrative analysis and ethnography. We discussed their central premises and philosophical underpinnings. We showed the diversity among all the approaches as they have evolved and been adapted. And we also looked at an example of the very practical type of analytical steps the tradition suggests to analyse empirical material. You have therefore some options to choose from or elements to mix and match to create your own approach.

Your project checklist

Now that you are more familiar with some of the main approaches in qualitative research, you can:

✓ Go back to the empirical studies you have already read on your topic and identify the approaches they used, implicitly or explicitly, to appreciate the difference they make in the design, analysis and results of specific studies.

✓ Decide on the two or three approaches that are best suited for the project you are designing.

✓ Read additional texts on the selected approaches to broaden your understanding of them and narrow your selection further. See the annotated list below as a start.

✓ Justify your final choice of approach(es) laying out the specificities and analysing the way it fits with your research question, your epistemological grounding and the design of your project.

✓ Revisit your research question, your epistemological grounding and the design of your project to tweak them if needed and ensure the best fit possible with your chosen approach.

What you should read next

Creswell, John W. 2012. *Qualitative Inquiry and Research Design: Choosing among Five Approaches*. Thousand Oaks, CA: Sage.

• This book compares and delves in depth into narrative research, phenomenology, grounded theory, ethnography and case study. It also offers and comments on complete empirical studies to illustrate each of the covered traditions.

Jacob, Evelyn. 1987. 'Qualitative Research Traditions: A Review'. *Review of Educational Research* 57(1): 1–50.

- This journal article is, to our knowledge, quite unique in that it compares and condenses qualitative research traditions and theories in education that we have not covered in this chapter, but that might be of interest to you even if you are not from that discipline: ecological psychology, holistic ethnography, cognitive anthropology, ethnography of communication, and symbolic interactionism. It is a good complement to this book and the Creswell book suggested above.

Kindon, Sara et al. 2007. *Participatory Action Research Approaches and Methods: Connecting People, Participation and Place*. London: Routledge.

- A book dedicated to an important approach we have not covered here that might be of interest to you if you want to undertake collaborative research that aims at producing concrete social changes.

Wertz, Frederic J. et al. 2011. *Five Ways of Doing Qualitative Analysis: Phenomenological Psychology, Grounded Theory, Discourse Analysis, Narrative Research, and Intuitive Inquiry*. New York: Guilford Press.

- A whole book dedicated to the applied comparison of five different traditions in qualitative research. Each tradition is presented and applied by a researcher specialized in the tradition. This book is useful to gain more in-depth knowledge of the covered traditions, and help you decide which one(s) best suit your project.

Werunga, Jane et al. 2016. 'A Decolonizing Methodology for Health Research on Female Genital Cutting'. *Advances in Nursing Science* 39(2): 150–64.

- Centered on the topic of female genitalia cutting, this article examines the decolonizing methodological potential of postcolonial feminism, African feminism and intersectionality. While it is not a 'how to' article, it might tell you whether feminist and postcolonial methodologies are approaches you need to learn more about for your own project.

Want more support and inspiration? The online resources are here to help! Get to grips with key terms using **glossary flashcards**, see methods in action with a **library of SAGE cases and journal articles**, and follow analysis step-by-step with full transcripts of the sources discussed in the book.

4

CHOOSING TOOLS FOR YOUR FIELDWORK

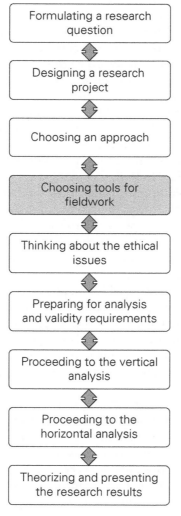

Figure 4.1 Where we are in the research process

IN THIS CHAPTER, YOU WILL LEARN:

- To identify the specificities of three main tools to conduct fieldwork: observation, interview and document.
- To distinguish the approaches used in working with these tools.
- To compare the types and forms that each tool can take.
- To describe the steps taken to conduct observations, interviews, and select documents for your own fieldwork.

INTRODUCTION

Empirical qualitative research, the focus of this book, requires a concrete base to work with: your material or sources. Collecting or producing your material or sources is often called the fieldwork phase. This work in the 'field' can be accomplished through the use of observations, interviews or documents – whether in the 'real' or virtual world, or some combination of those. In order to prepare for this task, you need to decide on the best way(s) to collect or produce your empirical material according to your research goals, your chosen methodological approach and your epistemological foundations. On that very issue, will you be collecting or co-constructing your empirical material?

The terms 'data collection' or 'data gathering phases and tools' are common in qualitative research. Those metaphors suggest a post-positivist or realist point of view from which the research material is waiting to be collected or gathered by the researcher. From a constructivist point of view, those metaphors are misleading. Indeed, they do not grasp the very active role the researcher plays in generating the material; hence, constructivists often prefer the expression 'co-construction' or 'production'. We will follow their lead. This chapter describes some potential tools, and some of their variations, available to produce your research material. As Figure 4.2 shows, your choices of data production tools are guided by two imbricate principles: coherence and flexibility.

In brief, the quality of the fieldwork phase requires an awareness to the connection and necessary coherence among the philosophical, theoretical and very practical choices made to gather or produce the empirical material. But the quality of the fieldwork phase also requires that researchers be open and responsive to the field's dynamics so that they may revisit their choices if necessary as the fieldwork progresses and as the interpretations develop.

Here, we will look at three ways researchers often use to generate empirical material: observation, interviews and documents. We consider these to be the three basic tools in qualitative research. But they have variations and the border between them is not as tight as one might think at the outset. Art-based research illustrates this porosity very well. For example, as part of your interview you might ask your participant to cut images from magazines to produce a collage expressing the reality you want to explore (e.g. raising a

Coherence	• All research tools (observations, interviews, documents) carry within them many philosophical assumptions. The initial choices regarding the type of tools used for fieldwork have to be coherent with the epistemological and theoretical choices made as well as with the research aims and approaches chosen
Flexibility	• But initial choices of empirical tools might change as the fieldwork evolves. When spending more time in the field, opportunities or obstacles might surface and so might change the research questions, and this might require altering or adding tools
... and some more flexibility	• Moreover, each tool has different models, types and styles. Those can also change according to the progress of the fieldwork. For example, on the basis of epistemological and methodological approaches, one might choose to conduct open observations but, after weeks or months in the field, one might need to verify an emerging interpretation and opt for a phase of more structured observation

Figure 4.2 List of 'warnings' on coherence and flexibility when choosing data production tools

child with autism). This collage then becomes a support to fuel the interview with your participant. In this case, the data production tool you are using crosses the borders of interview, observation and document. It becomes a bit of them all. We want to give you as much information about the basic form of observation, interview and document so that you can feel comfortable to adapt them and mix them up if you need to and also investigate the hybrid tools that have developed over time in qualitative research (see 'What you should read next' at the end of the chapter for a start).

In this chapter, one section is devoted to each of the three basic tools. Each section is loosely organized around a definition, a discussion of the different types and approaches regarding the tool under study, and a step-by-step guide to put it into practice.

OBSERVATION

At 2½ weeks old, Myriam is already captivated by the face of her grandfather. She studies his nose, his eyes and his mouth intently as he holds and speaks to her. Observing is something that we seem to do naturally. For researchers, though, observation assumes the status of a full-fledged research strategy.

Observation is the key tool in ethnography, one of the approaches covered in the previous chapter, but it can be used in many other approaches. As you read in Chapter 3, it was legitimized and academic applications were regularly found in the nineteenth century when fieldwork gained precedence over 'armchair' social science based on explorers' chronicles and missionaries' diaries.

DEFINITION OF OBSERVATION

Observation is the activity of researchers who interact in an environment, spend a significant amount of time in a milieu and document their experiences closely (inspired by Peretz, 1998: 48). Involving more than the eyes, observation is an all-encompassing research strategy in that it requires informal conversations and often includes interviews and the analysis of the documents that are produced or used by the researched milieu (Silverman, 2013). The idea behind observation is to get as close as possible to, if not actually into, the reality you are studying. While it requires time and involvement, as well as a welcoming observation site, observation has been associated with the in-depth study of milieus and groups such as a psychiatric hospital (Goffman, 1961), scientific researchers in a biomedical laboratory (Latour and Woolgar, 1979/1996), women in a roller derby league (Finley, 2010), or so-called 'subcultures' such as that of Italian immigrants in the United States (Whyte, 1956). The organizations, groups and 'subcultures' we refer to here also encompass online communities. While some underline the difficulties of maintaining an ethnographer's attitude online and staying attuned to the mundane (Silverman, 2013), others see digital ethnography as very fruitful (Murthy, 2008).

Whether it is offline or online, the variations on the theme of observational work can be classified under different models, approaches and types.

Observation is an umbrella term for observation *in situ*, direct observation, ethnography, field research, participant observation, digital or online ethnography, or else netnography.

APPROACHES TO OBSERVATION

Let us assume that you have decided it is important for you to document mostly observable actions and behaviors as well as the meanings that social actors ascribe to those actions and behaviors. The question then becomes: how will you approach your observation milieu? Will you present yourself as a researcher or will you decide to go 'undercover' and adopt another role (Peretz, 1998: 53)? This decision is directly in line with the epistemological position one adopts: is reality something waiting for the researcher to gather it as such or is it rather co-constructed by social actors including the researcher? In the first case, the researcher wants to 'gather' the 'facts' without impacting them. In the second, the researcher accepts that interaction in a milieu is necessarily going to transform it. Depending on your epistemological position, you will favor a certain position with regards to ethics and reactivity. Reactivity is the reaction likely to occur because of your presence as an 'outsider' in the research milieu. Again, while we present this choice as a dichotomy, the options are situated along a continuum with differences being a matter of degree as shown in Figure 4.3.

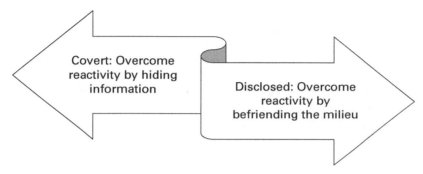

Figure 4.3   Approaches to observation depending on reactivity management choices

COVERT OBSERVATION

Covert observation refers to situations in which researchers divulge the least information possible about their identity and goals as researchers. In the most extreme case, they go 'undercover'. This seems to be a frequent practice when conducting online or digital ethnography since the information is often considered, a bit quickly, to be in the public sphere (Murthy, 2008). While it appeals to one's sense of adventure, covert observation presents many ethical considerations, affective issues, structural constraints and challenges for information recoding (see Chapter 5 on these issues). It is to be considered only in cases where the research could not be otherwise conducted.

Marquart (2003) tells his story of being a PhD student trying to document how correctional officers granted favors to some prisoners in exchange for their bullying services. They were asked to intimidate other prisoners labeled as disruptive and troublemakers by the correctional officers. It was reasonable to think that correctional officers would not want to be observed or would refrain from such arrangements with prisoners if they knew they were in the presence of a researcher. Bringing such activities to light would not only have made some correctional officers look bad, but also have produced the fear of being sanctioned for violating the rules of the institution that did not formally allow such practices. To overcome these difficulties,

Marquart chose to undergo the selection process and get hired as a correctional officer himself. While he accomplished the work that he was supposed to do as a correctional officer, his main purpose was to secretly observe and record information about the interactions and the 'deals' between the officers and prisoners. By hiding information that might have provoked reactivity (changes in behavior) on the part of the participants, he succeeded in documenting a phenomenon that was known unofficially but on which research was still silent.

One does not need to go completely 'undercover' to do covert observation. Researchers might choose to introduce themselves as researchers but present their research goals in such vague terms as to not reveal their real objectives. By keeping the participants partially in the dark, some researchers hope to ensure that the participants would act and react more 'naturally'. Again, before you consider that path, consider carefully the pitfalls of such an approach to observation. You will need a strong scientific rationale and a strong ethical justification before the ethics board of your institution allows you to conduct such a study. For example, you would need to show that the research cannot be otherwise conducted and that doing so will just minimally compromise the basic rights of participants since they are anonymous passers-by in a public place.

DISCLOSED OBSERVATION

At the other end of the spectrum, when entering a milieu one might choose to clearly reveal one's identity and purpose as a researcher and deal with participants' reactivity upfront. In this case, the researcher tries to develop trust and stay in the milieu long enough to 'blend in'. The possibility and desirability of becoming a 'fly on the wall' is debatable. To be part of a milieu and expect people to act and react as if there was no researcher present is somewhat naive. Nevertheless, choosing such an approach can help overcome some important ethical and relational concerns that will be discussed in the next chapter on ethics.

TYPES OF OBSERVATION

After choosing the model and approach that best matches your study, you have to decide on the type of observation you will conduct. Of course, because fieldwork is dynamic, the type of observation you choose might change as the empirical phase of your research progresses.

The distinctions among types of observations will show up in the characteristics of the observation grid developed by the researcher (Deslauriers and Mayer, 2000: 137–8). Indeed, before going into the field, one has to know and make clear to oneself what needs to be observed. An observation grid is basically a list of reminders to the researcher as to what elements of information are needed in order to answer the research question (see Figure 4.5 below).

STRUCTURED OBSERVATION

Structured observation is characterized by the elaboration of a detailed observation grid produced before the start of fieldwork. It is often found in hypothetico-deductive research where one has clear assumptions to falsify. In this case, the grid is made up of the indicators resulting from operationalization of the main concepts of the research question. For example, if you want to record consumption habits at a grocery store, you might have an observation grid that details the navigational patterns of consumers (outside perimeter only, or perimeter and aisles), the type of products they buy, even the brand of certain products they choose, etc. A potential shortcoming of this type of observation is that such a grid pre-structures the interest of researchers and makes them blind to the unexpected elements arising from the fieldwork, elements that could be pertinent for their project.

OPEN OBSERVATION

At the other end of the spectrum, open observation is characterized by a less detailed observation grid that is conceived of as work in progress. The researcher wants to identify what matters on the ground, in the observed situation or milieu. In the inductive tradition, those decisions cannot entirely be taken before the fieldwork begins. The observation grid develops along the time spent in the field. The assumption behind this type of observation is that the milieu will teach us what is pertinent and that we have to be sensitive to its inherent logic, unspoken rules and unexpected dynamics.

CONDUCTING OBSERVATIONS STEP BY STEP

The following seven steps, inspired closely by Peretz (1998: 49), are meant to give you an idea of the sequence of activities that you will accomplish as your observation fieldwork progresses. Keep in mind that those steps are not mutually exclusive or linear.

CHOOSING AN OBSERVATION SITE: THE NEED TO SAMPLE

Producing knowledge requires abstraction and generalization. Comparison, within or between observation sites and among diverse situations, can be used as a key tool to achieve this ambition. This is where the choice and sample of your observation site(s) come into play. Note that in qualitative research, what matters is theoretical and not statistical generalization. Therefore, your sample is not guided by the need to consider a certain number of observation sites that you would hope to be representative of all others. You aim to find a rich one or a few rich ones that will offer a diversity of situations to be analysed and that will make it possible for you to contribute to or open a specific theoretical discussion.

An observation site is a context made of a physical space where events (actions, activities) occur and where people or groups interact (Peretz, 1998). The selection of the observation site or sites depends closely on two aspects of your research question: the topic and the conceptualization of your research object. First, where are you likely to observe what is required for you to answer your research question? If you are interested in the relevance of workers' unions in the digital economy workplace, it would make sense to choose a unionized high-tech firm to conduct your observation. But there is also a second consideration. How did you conceptualize your research object? Is your focus of interest the group itself, the 'culture' or, said otherwise, the organization? If so, you might want to have a single case sample, elect one observation site only and devote yourself to it for the whole of your fieldwork. Many great works in social sciences are the product of a case study of one milieu: Goffman's (1961) famous study on a psychiatric institution or Festinger et al.'s (1956) research on a sect. If you choose to concentrate on a single case sample, make sure that the observation site is rich in terms of relevant interactions and situations to answer your question.

On the other hand, if you conceptualize your research object not so much as a specific group, culture or organization, but rather as a relationship like the one between teachers and pupils, a multiple case sample can be useful. In this case, you might not want to dedicate all your fieldwork to a specific classroom but rather observe teachers with different characteristics as they work with equally diverse pupils in many contexts. The issue of diversity is equally important if your question pertains to a situation (e.g. coping with an injury) or an event (e.g. students' demonstrations). In order to grasp the processes at the core of these situations and events, you might want to compare sites to achieve the desired level of abstraction that will allow you to generalize your specific research results to similar situations.

Deciding on the nature and on the number of observation sites in your sample is not the last of your sampling decisions. You will have to further refine your sample because an observation site is composed of sectors, moments and people (Spradley, 1979). Indeed, as small as it can be, an observation site is a collection of sectors (for example: public/private, employees/management, frontline/coordination). You have to choose among the different sectors you will observe. For instance, if you are interested in understanding the experience of clients in a casino, you will have to sample according to the different games played (slot machine, baccarat, keno), but also the play and non-play sectors such as the bars and restaurants in the casino. In the same vein, in an observation site, the action might vary depending on the time of year (high or low season), the month (beginning or end), the week (weekdays or weekend) and the hour (morning or evening). It is a good idea to get acquainted with rhythms of the observation sites so as to sample a diversity of moments to conduct your observation. Finally, an observation site is also a collection of people who pass through or remain (frequent players, occasional players, one timers, security employees, croupiers, catering services employees, cleaning services employees). Again, trying to identify and describe the variety of site users is an important first step before choosing to allocate your observation time according to the diversity or comparison imperative as well as the needs of your research question.

Moreover, choosing your observation site(s) is also dependent upon the following three practical considerations which help define the approach to and types of observation you will adopt (Laperrière, 2003; Peretz, 1998):

1. Accessibility and permission. It has to be possible to access the observation site; it does not have to be easy – just possible.

2. Non-intrusiveness. Although researchers observing in a milieu often impact the interactions taking place in a milieu they must nevertheless cause the least nuisance possible.

3. Possibility to participate, interact. While researchers want to limit the disturbances they might cause, they still want to interact with participants.

When the observation site is chosen, it is important to spend the necessary time writing down the assumptions you have regarding the chosen site: What do you expect it to be like? What is your impression of this site? What are your fears regarding this milieu? Moreover, how will you come across in such a milieu? How might your own characteristics influence the relationships you develop: your gender, your age, your cultural and ethnic background, your social class, your personality? How can all these aspects be perceived by the participants? This could be your first entry in your fieldwork journal, the valuable notebook in which you will be able to collect all the thoughts from your fieldwork experience.

NEGOTIATING YOUR ENTRY

When the observation site is chosen, the researcher must find a point of entry (covert observation) or negotiate access (**disclosed observation**) with the gatekeepers to the milieu (Laperrière, 2003; Peretz, 1998). The researcher has to ponder the three following items: (1) Who to negotiate with and get consent (the issue of consent will be covered in depth in Chapter 5). Should you start by asking people on the ground or those higher up in the hierarchy? Whose sensitivity to protect? What are the relative advantages of approaching from the bottom or top of the hierarchy? (2) What to ask for. How much time will you need in the field? What sectors of the observation site do you want to access? Do you want to be paired with a specific person (shadowing)? How should you negotiate permission to publish the research findings? (3) What to promise. What will you give back in return? Will you share your results with the people you observed? Will you ask them to react or even validate the research findings?

If researchers are not already familiar with the observation site they choose, the negotiation phase represents a key moment to learn the hierarchy in the observation site (formal and informal power, potential allies, potential resistance) and the different networks that populate it. It is a phase where we have to be aware of the initial alliances we forge because 'outsiders' such as researchers can often attract people in the observation milieu who identify themselves or are identified as also being marginal.

DECIDING ON YOUR INITIAL ROLE AND DEVELOPING RELATIONS

Now that you have access to the observation site, you will get a better sense of the characteristics and rhythms of the milieu and the extent to which you can participate in it. Four aspects are at the forefront of this observation phase (Laperrière, 2003; Peretz, 1998):

1. Balance between observing and participating. Should you start slowly by observing mostly while you get acquainted with the place and the people? On the contrary, would it be more difficult that way (e.g. in a kindergarten) or too informatively poor (e.g. in a warehouse)? Would it be better, then, to adopt an active role from the start, even one on the fringe, to become steeped in the milieu (e.g. as a cleaner)? This initial role will have to be revised as the observation progresses.

2. The role attributed to you. How do the participants see you? What ideas do they entertain about you? It is important to pay attention to signs about the participants' perceptions of the researcher and rectify erroneous beliefs that can act as a barrier to accessing information.

3. Presentation and language. This initial phase of the fieldwork is also the moment where the researcher pays attention to the particular verbal and physical language of the participants. Not only is this precious material in itself, it is also important to make sure that the researcher adapts, and if not blend in, is at least aware of it and does not irritate the participants with his own language and presentation of self.

4. Note taking and observation planning. Getting acquainted with the observation site is also when the researcher discovers the possibilities for recording information (Will it realistically be possible to take notes without distracting the participants? When? Where?) and to develop a more precise fieldwork calendar (which weeks, days, hours?) and estimate more clearly the time the observation is ultimately likely to last, in the ideal situation.

In the initial observation stage, it is essential to avoid exclusive relationships with any of the participants. The idea is to multiply the points of view regarding a situation or event. It is also essential to treat everyone with the same degree of respect. This will not only help to create good and trustworthy relationships in the observation site, but also help to avoid being 'taken hostage' by any particular sub-group and help you to be socially mobile among all the factions composing the research milieu.

RECORDING INFORMATION

As you chose your observation site, negotiated your entry, started developing relationships with participants, you were gaining a lot of information about the way this milieu works, the alliances within it, the formal and informal norms that govern it. These are all field information that you should have recorded in your fieldwork journal. Now that those initial steps are accomplished, you are ready for full recording mode (Laperrière, 2003; Peretz, 1998).

If it is possible, early on, get a general idea of the observation site, what Spradley (1979) has called the big picture. Start from the general and proceed to specific situations and activities that inform your research question (Figure 4.4).

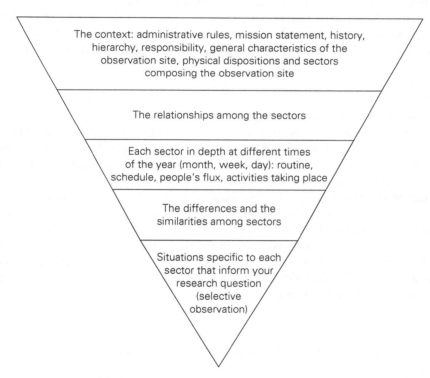

The context: administrative rules, mission statement, history, hierarchy, responsibility, general characteristics of the observation site, physical dispositions and sectors composing the observation site

The relationships among the sectors

Each sector in depth at different times of the year (month, week, day): routine, schedule, people's flux, activities taking place

The differences and the similarities among sectors

Situations specific to each sector that inform your research question (selective observation)

Figure 4.4   Observing: from the general to the specific

This progression from the general to the specific will lead you back to the sampling you devised earlier on. As you get to know your observation site better, you might have to revise your initial sampling to adapt to the reality of your fieldwork (emerging opportunities, unplanned constraints).

But what exactly do you record? While it is essential to get into the groove and let oneself be surprised by the 'strangeness' of the observation site (Silverman, 2013), one has to have a plan! In the case of observation, the plan is called an observation grid.

DESIGNING YOUR OBSERVATION GRID

In an open type of observation, the first sessions are general and you should devise an observation grid that reflects your need to grasp the 'gist' of the place. As you get to know the milieu, you will want to create a more systematic observation grid. At this stage, your decision to conduct a structured or an open observation will be determinant. In the first case, your observation grid will be detailed and stable. In the latter case, your observation grid will be a changing, organic tool, a work in progress that will reflect your questioning and interests as your fieldwork evolves. Think of your observation grid not as a table to fill out but as a list of items you need to have in mind to direct your attention when you are in the field conducting an observation session. Figure 4.5 shows a general observation grid designed by Peretz (1998: 84–5) to conduct an observation in a religious setting.

You do not even need to bring your observation grid with you in the field. You have to prepare it in advance, ponder it and assimilate it. It will counteract your being guided solely by common sense or curiosity for the atypical elements.

NOTE TAKING

Filming, taking photos, recording the sounds of the site are all possible with the permission of the participants. It is equivalent to bringing an 'intact' portion of the fieldwork back home. While it might be comforting to rely on those possibilities, they also have their drawbacks: used indiscriminately (because we can, they are there, accessible, easy) visual or sound recording devices can quickly generate an enormous quantity of material that will require us to watch and listen to again as well as proceed to a final selection of 'scenes'. This selection a posteriori, rather than on the spot, might be a good thing to do; you might become aware of elements you had not noticed during the event (Martineau, 2005). But depending on how they are used, video cameras and audio recorders can actually add to the work and dull our sense of observation while in the field because we are confident we can observe again after the event.

Peretz (1998: 93) gives us advice on writing field notes:

- Write using the active voice and the present tense. For example, 'I am in the red hallway of the Casino and I see …' It will likely help your memory relive the experience and make your notes more precise and lively.
- Beware of generalized descriptions. Try to be precise. Rather than: 'A man approaches the table' it might be more accurate to write 'A six foot tall man is approaching the blackjack table.'
- Use the language that is used by the participants if you know it. For instance, in the Jewish Ashkenazi community, people are not orthodox; they are 'frum' (a Yiddish word that means pious). This will not only transmit the flavor of the field, it also helps to depict the worldviews of the participants in their own terms.

- Do not forget to describe the verbal interactions you witness or have with people. These are important parts of the observation.

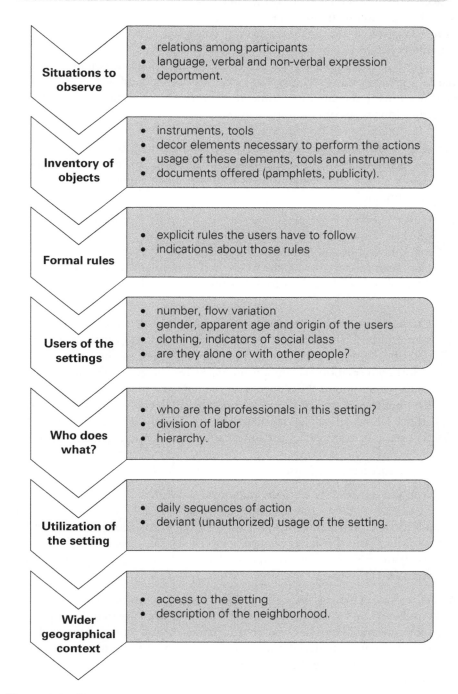

Situations to observe
- relations among participants
- language, verbal and non-verbal expression
- deportment.

Inventory of objects
- instruments, tools
- decor elements necessary to perform the actions
- usage of these elements, tools and instruments
- documents offered (pamphlets, publicity).

Formal rules
- explicit rules the users have to follow
- indications about those rules

Users of the settings
- number, flow variation
- gender, apparent age and origin of the users
- clothing, indicators of social class
- are they alone or with other people?

Who does what?
- who are the professionals in this setting?
- division of labor
- hierarchy.

Utilization of the setting
- daily sequences of action
- deviant (unauthorized) usage of the setting.

Wider geographical context
- access to the setting
- description of the neighborhood.

Figure 4.5 Observation grid (adapted from Peretz, 1998: 84–5)

Written notes remain the usual way to proceed. These can be taken as the action occurs, whether during researcher 'writing breaks' or after completion of the observation session altogether. Such decisions are made in light of what is acceptable and convenient at the time. Furthermore, each observation session should result in an observation report made from two kinds of interwoven notes: descriptive and analytical. For pedagogical reasons, we present them separately here.

Descriptive notes are vivid depictions of the situations you observe written in a precise and descriptive language (Deslauriers and Mayer, 2000). The goal is to make the situation come alive on paper. Laperrière (2003: 283–4) identifies four types of descriptive notes:

1. 'On-the-fly' notes are written as the situation is unfolding. Sparse notes are taken quickly, discreetly, often in the form of key words, markers, points of reference. Such notes would look like: 'Upper–lower class clash about work.'

2. Quick overviews are produced during a writing break. A short scene is quickly written that fills up the missing elements among the keywords, markers and points of reference noted on the fly. Such notes would look like: 'Jean [upper class] came to the coffee shop and when she heard that Sharon [lower class] had found work, she gave her a lecture about the intensity of work.'

3. Extensive reports are written as soon as possible after the observation session and with the help of the 'on the fly' notes and quick overviews. It describes with accuracy and details the unfolding of the events. As you report conversation, use quotation marks for the verbatim you remember. At the beginning of the report, note the date, the place of the observation, the time, the length, list the actors present and the activities observed. Most ethnographic articles or monographs are full of excerpts of observation reports. For example, in her observation of the way regular women customers at a coffee shop 'do class', Yodanis uses excerpts of her observation to support her assertions. Those excerpts look like this one:

    Jean [an upper-class woman] came into the Coffee Shop. Sharon was sitting at the counter and said that she had worked 13 days in a row. Jean asked in a very condescending way, 'So you got a job? Where are you working?' and then after Sharon answers, she said, 'Now you finally have work and now you are working too hard … You jumped right into it. You went from nothing to overtime.' (2006: 350–1)

4. Observation indexes are written after a few observation sessions have been conducted and a few extensive reports have been written. Producing an index means identifying the broad themes or key words associated with the observation material and noting where the observation notes can be found on that theme. For example, 'Conflict between coffee shop customers: report April 4, p. 13; report May 15, pp. 20–4.'

Analytical notes are comments written to oneself that were generated by being in the field and interacting with participants (Deslauriers and Mayer, 2000). They are an essential part of the extensive report for each observation session and we suggest you put them in brackets to distinguish them from your descriptive notes. Those notes are the same whether you conduct observation or interviews, or else analyse documents. You will find examples of analytical notes in Chapters 7 and 8 in this book. Laperrière (2003: 285–7) identifies four types of analytical notes:

1. Memos: analytical thoughts on the fly. For instance, after having witnessed a subway worker answer in an abrupt manner to a young black man, you note: [stigma?].

2. Data analysis notes. These are made of nascent interpretations, linked with concepts and readings, comments on the variations observed, hypotheses to be documented in further observation sessions. Like the memos, they are included in the extensive report.

3. Personal matters and **reflexivity**. Keep a second fieldwork journal where you can log your personal feelings and reflections on the research process, your impressions, your fears, your confusions, your joys and angry feelings. This is a good tool to help you become aware of the relationship you are developing with the observation milieu. For example, from an observation in a blue collar environment: [I am afraid I am losing touch with a clique in the factory for Allan, the 'leader', does not sit with me during breaks anymore, he barely says hi. I feel lonely, even more of an outsider. He was my main anchor in this group. What should I do? Should I address this issue head on with him or should I try to develop other stronger alliances with other people in that group?] This journal is also the best place to generate and record your analytical comments as they occur to you.

4. Planning notes. Those refer to methodological comments to yourself for the next observation sessions: what situations you should focus on, conversations you want to have with this or that person, what is still left to be observed and the like. Those planning notes are a source of the changes you progressively make to your sampling and observation grid.

ANALYSING THE INFORMATION

Chapters 7–9 will help you to analyse the material you produce so we will not cover this topic here. However, we want to mention one essential thing: do not wait to exit the field before you start analysing your material. Try to devise a schedule that will allow you to share your time equally between generating your material and analysing it.

This is crucial if you want to make your fieldwork as useful as possible and to generate information on topics that emerge as the analysis proceeds.

You cannot wait until later to 'think'. The material you generate will be richer and better suited to help you answer your research question if your analytic brain is already in motion.

INTERVIEWS

The popularity of interviews comes from the clinical world where they serve therapeutic functions. The first traces of interviews being used as research tools come from Charles Booth's (1840–1916) extensive study on the life of working-class Londoners. The fieldwork was conducted between 1886 and 1903 and involved observation as well as a multitude of qualitative interviews (Laperrière, 2003).

> Field notes from Booth's studies, a pioneer of fieldwork research, are still available today in a series of digitalized handwritten notebooks. Visit the following website: http://booth.lse.ac.uk/

With the new Chicago school and the work of authors like Goffman (1961) and Becker (1963) in the 1960s, interviews, as well as qualitative research in general, regained the status they had lost in the previous decades when quantitative methods were the dominant option (Poupart, 1993). Today, in this era of methodological diversification, their use is widespread.

The richness of the material generated by qualitative interviews is without doubt a reason for their popularity. Beyond factual information (characteristics, routine), interviews are used to uncover individual as well as collective practices, habits, trajectories, processes, dynamics, rationales, values, opinions and representations. Moreover, interviews are interesting not just for their content but for their structure as well. Indeed, as shown in the previous chapter in the section on narrative analysis, the way a participant organizes his or her story is worth analysing in itself.

DEFINITIONS OF INTERVIEWS

While it is practical to think and speak of qualitative interviews as if there is an agreement as to their nature, doing so hides the variety of definitions attributed to this data producing tool. The typology of interview definitions we present here (see Figure 4.6) is based on the chosen research paradigm (see Chapter 1).

The first definition corresponds to the realist paradigm, the second to the constructivist paradigm (Savoie-Zajc, 2003) and the last to the postmodern approach in social sciences (Fontana, 2001). These three definitions are also situated along a continuum that emphasizes the importance of the technical aspects in conducting an interview or the importance of the connection between the two people engaged in the interview process (Roulston, 2011; Savoie-Zajc, 2003; Warren, 2012). Depending on the way you define what an interview is in your research, your analysis will focus on the informational content and therefore essentially the participant's answers to your probes (definitions 1 and 2). Or it will also embrace the interactions with and the contributions of the researcher (definitions 2 and 3).

Developments in social media have opened up possibilities for field-work and especially for interviews (James and Busher, 2012). For example, they can now be conducted by phone, chat, email or Skype. The techno-logical mediation has an effect on the type and quality of the rapport created between the researcher and participant – sometimes in a very posi-tive way. An experienced researcher shared with us the fact that when she encountered problems recruiting clients of sex workers for interviews in person, she switched to phone interviews and was much more successful. Not only could she get participants that way, but she also noticed that the phone mediation made it possible for participants to tell their story at

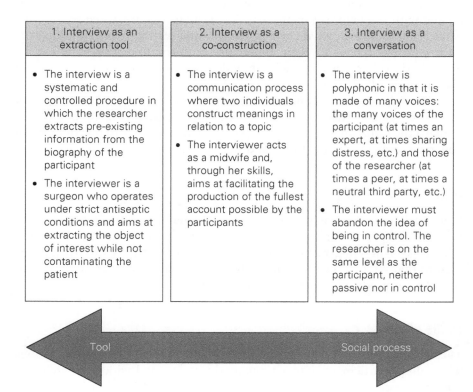

Figure 4.6 Typology of interview definitions and associated researchers' roles

length, with ease. The lack of visual contact with the researcher added a level of perceived anonymity that was conducive to richer interviews than the ones conducted face to face. The same intimacy effect has been found when using online interviews and even for topics that are less sensitive. This has led researchers to privilege a mix of *in vivo* and technology-mediated interviews to maximize the reach and quality of the fieldwork (Murthy, 2008: 842). Adapting to the needs and possibilities of the fieldwork remains a key principle in research.

The same goes with combining arts and science. Indeed, hybrid forms of interviews have developed over the last decade. Artistic forms of expression are combined with oral interviews to widen the span of expression of participants and increase their level of involvement and control in the research. Photos, collages, story writing, sculpture, drawings and films have all been combined with interviewing to transform it into a complete performance (Springgay et al., 2005). For example, 'photovoice' projects ask participants to take pictures of their reality and to express what they feel is relevant for them to explore their story (Wang and Burris, 1994). There are many ways to use it, but a frequent pattern is to lend or give a camera to the participants (or ask them to use their camera phones) who, for a period of time, take pictures of their lives. The interview is then conducted with the help of the photos. The participants are asked to describe what a photo means, what their intentions and feelings were in taking the photo, how it relates to their experience, and the like. The same can be done with other media, such as video diaries and films (Rosenfeld Halverson et al., 2012).

With these options in mind, although it can change the rapport between researcher and participants, technological or artistic mediation has not changed the forms and types of interviews that are available to researchers. We now turn to defining these forms and types of interviews.

FORMS OF INTERVIEW

Individual interviews are the classical form of interview in qualitative research in that they have a long history and are used widely. Nevertheless, some disciplines, like marketing research, use focus group interviews extensively. For reasons that are both practical and substantive, focus groups are an option to consider for producing your empirical material.

FOCUS GROUP

The term 'focus groups' or 'group interviews' refers to interview situations where many participants interact among themselves and with a researcher or a team of researchers. The goal is to create a group dynamic where participants think out loud, more or less collectively, react to others' assertions and where they discuss with each other (Flick, 2006). This interactive situation is often favored to deepen the substance of the material gathered. Sometimes, the constraints of the research milieu demand that the researcher produce the research material in concentrated blocks of time. We could imagine that, in a shop where the work of one person is highly dependent on the work of another, employers might be reluctant to let you interview five of their employees individually during a work day since each interview is likely to disrupt the work flow of the whole unit. However, they might be willing to let you gather the employees together for a couple of hours. Sometimes, the participants ask for it because they enjoy each other's company (Creef, 2002). In research on Internet privacy conducted with teenagers about their data sharing habits, an experienced researcher shared with us the fact that focus groups were ideal for inducing young people to communicate their experiences. Focus group interviews can also be organized around an expressive medium such as collage or choreography.

The interviewer in a focus group has an additional task that an interviewer in an individual interview does not have: managing the group dynamic or, said otherwise, acting as a moderator (Flick, 2006; Mayer and Saint-Jacques, 2000). You have to be careful to solicit the participation of all the interviewees and to create a respectful atmosphere where all participants feel that they can and are welcomed to participate. Some shy people might be hesitant and have difficulty finding their place in the group dynamic. You will have to invite them to speak. Some vocal people might take more time than their share. You will have to subtly intervene in those cases too. As a researcher, it is also important that you give serious consideration to power relations that might exist in a particular group or that might surface during the interview process.

As such, consider the following suggestions when preparing to do interviews:

1. Set a reasonable time limit and stick to it. It might be inefficient to hold people's attention for more than two hours.

2. Limit the number of participants to 10 or so. You want to make sure everyone can participate in the discussion.

3. If the discussion gets chaotic, think about using an object as a prop and set a rule according to which only the person in possession of the prop can speak.

4. Enlist the help of a colleague and share the interviewing time. While you prompt and manage the group, your colleague can take notes about promising topics that were not fully explored by the group. At mid-point, switch positions with your colleague so he or she becomes the interviewer and you become the note taker. Your colleague can then go back to the unexplored topics he or she noted while observing.

Most of the following considerations about individual interviews apply to focus groups as well.

INDIVIDUAL INTERVIEW

Individual interviews refer to situations where a researcher interviews one participant at a time. Depending on the research question, individual interviews can pertain to the actual situation of the participant or else aim at eliciting his or her life story. These types of retrospective interviews, where the researcher needs a detailed and complete life history, a detailed account of a specific life episode (youth, transition from bachelor to married status, etc.) or a complete topical life story (a chronological portrait of one sphere of the person's life like their work, love life or medical history, etc.), are best suited for individual interviews (Bertaux, 2010). When possible and useful to do so, repeated interviews can be conducted at different times with the same participants.

In individual interviews, the researcher fully concentrates on the relationship that is developing with the participant and on the content that is shared. Contrary to the therapeutic context, the objective of the research interview is not to provoke some thoughts or fuel changes in the participant, but to understand the world. Despite the idiosyncrasies and specific identities of the participants, we are interested in them as representative of a larger category: a member of an age group, gender category, profession, etc. Nevertheless, it is worth noting that participants engaging in an interview might benefit or at least be impacted by having talked about themselves at length to a receptive audience. After an interview on her rapport with health and medications, a woman wrote to thank one of us for the interview that had been, for her, an occasion to sort out her own thoughts. She said that, as a result, she found the energy to solve a latent conflict she had in her marital life. Research relationships sometimes have mysterious outcomes.

As we mentioned above for focus groups, individual interviews can be organized around another expressive medium, such as writing. In such a case, a series of interviews can be transformed into a co-writing project between the participant and the researcher (Ellis and Rawicki, 2013).

TYPES OF INTERVIEWS

Individual interviews, and to some extent focus groups, come in different types (Flick, 2006; Mayer and Saint-Jacques, 2000; Michelat, 1975). They can range along a continuum from most to least directive (Figure 4.7). Direction refers to the amount of control exercised by the interviewer as well as the strictness of the interview format as determined by the interview guide. The degree of direction translates into the degree of homogeneity that is expected to be found in the structure and topics covered from one interview to the other in the same research project. The continuum from most to least directive also reflects the position the researchers adopts vis-à-vis expertise. Indeed, if

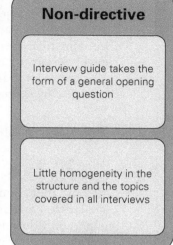

Directive	**Semi-directive**	**Non-directive**
Interview guide takes the form of a series of open-ended questions	Interview guide takes the form of an opening question and a short predetermined list of topics	Interview guide takes the form of a general opening question
High degree of homogeneity in the structure and topics covered in all interviews	Some homogeneity in the structure of the interviews (in the beginning of the interview) but little in the rest of the interview and in the topics covered in all interviews	Little homogeneity in the structure and the topics covered in all interviews

Figure 4.7 Three types of interview

researchers conceive of themselves as experts on a topic, they will be comfortable with designing and using a strict interview guide to extract information from participants. However, if the participants are seen as experts, then it might be more congruent to let the participants define their own field of expression and adopt a semi- or non-directive type of interview.

DIRECTIVE INTERVIEW

The interview guide prepared by the researcher before the fieldwork begins takes the form of a series of open-ended questions, the equivalent of a qualitative questionnaire (Mayer and Saint-Jacques, 2000). This type of interview is suited to research on opinions. The questionnaire often remains identical for the duration of the fieldwork and is used with all the participants in the same manner. The idea is to expose all participants to the same 'stimulus', meaning the same wording, phrasing and question order. This protocol is believed to neutralize the researcher's effects on the participants or at least subject all the participants to the same effect. It then becomes easier and, some would say, more legitimate to compare the participants' answers.

One of the clear advantages of the directive interview is the relative ease and speed with which answers from many participants can be located within the recording or transcript and compared. For example, one could simply extract the answers given by all female participants to question number 2 on their opinions regarding the usefulness of their university degrees in the job market and compare them for patterns. On the other hand, this type of interview might not yield the depth of a non-directive interview for it determines in advance the topics and even the questions that matter in order to investigate the research subject. There is little room for the researcher to improvise according to the answers given by the participants, and researchers have little freedom to explore themes that might emerge during interviews and that might appear to be of interest to the research project.

To better grasp their respective specificities, we will contrast this type of interview by shifting our discussion to the non-directive interview.

NON-DIRECTIVE INTERVIEW

The interview guide takes the form of a single general opening question (Kandel, 1972; Mayer and Saint-Jacques, 2000; Michelat, 1975). For example, 'Tell me about your entry into the job market.' The opening question is often similar from one interview to the other but does not have to be identical. An important principle in non-directive interviews is adapting to the participants and the requirements of the situation. From the initial story told by the participant, the interviewer identifies the important topics to be investigated further to gather a complete picture of the participant's experience (Kandel, 1972; Michelat, 1975). It means that the prompts the interviewer uses are not prepared in advance but rather improvised on the spot, depending on the account in progress.

While not predetermining a list of questions in advance might appear scary for an interviewer, it has important benefits. First of all, it ensures the complete availability of the interviewer; in other words, it keeps us on our toes! One has to listen intently, be on the lookout for topics that are merely brushed upon, assumptions, implicit references that need to be further explored, and use them as prompts later. Second, it not only means that the interviewer adapts to the vocabulary of the participant, but also allows the latter to control the shape and substance of his or her story. All the prompts to further explore a topic will have been anchored in the participant's wording and the material contributed to the interview. The idea of co-construction that was brought up earlier clearly resurfaces here. While it is called non-directive, this type of interview might be better described as having a non-directive inspiration rather than pure non-directivity. It is impossible for the interviewer not to influence the telling and content of his or her story by the participant (Mallozz, 2009). Behaviors as banal as the way the interviewer listens, nods, sighs, prompts and smiles are all likely to be interpreted by the participant as an indicator to elaborate more here or cut short there.

Non-directive interviews lend themselves to the telling of experiences, exploration of representations, life processes and topical or complete life stories. While the prompts are clearly the contribution of the researcher, these are inspired by the participant's story rather then decided a priori. This feature is supposed to make the interview more organic to the participant's experience. Therefore, there can be few expectations of homogeneity in the structure and topics from one interview to the next in a research project. But while such interviews might allow delving in depth into the participant's experience, they represent a challenge when the analysis phase comes for they are quite different, in form and substance, from one another (Daunais, 1992).

SEMI-DIRECTIVE INTERVIEW

Semi-directive interviews strike a balance between the two previous types (Mayer and Saint-Jacques, 2000). The interview guide takes the form of a general opening question to which is added a short list of topics that the interviewer wants to cover in every interview (Mishler, 1986). When all the avenues and topics from the participant's answer to the opening question have been explored, the interviewer can use the prepared list of topics to formulate prompts. This ensures that important subjects, according to the conceptualization and research question, have not been forgotten. The list of predetermined topics can be added to as the interviews accumulate and new areas of inquiry emerge.

In response to a wide opening question, the participants decide on their field of expression, that is the contours and substance of what is important to them on a certain subject. On the other hand, the prepared list of topics ensures that the interviews still have some degree of substantive homogeneity. Nevertheless, the structure of those interviews is often quite variable. Semi-directive interviews, like non-directive ones, are useful for allowing the participant to describe experiences at length, to explore representations and document life trajectories. The medium allows participants and researcher to share some control in the production of the narrative.

Two basic principles guide how interviewers conduct non-directive and semi-directive interviews. First, interviewers act as facilitators in the interview process. To do so, interviewers have to come to terms with the fact that they do not need to unleash a barrage of questions. Indeed, as we will suggest shortly, listening actively and mirroring the words of the participants might be enough to get them going, to think out loud about their lived experiences. Second, the interviewers have to help the participants explore their own minds and personal experiences. The goal is to produce an 'I' account, an account told from the point of view of the participant, about his or her lived experience.

Even more than with directive interviews, where questions are phrased in advance and asked in a homogeneous manner, with non- and semi-directive interviews the quality and extent of the material gathered are highly dependent upon the abilities of the interviewer (Savoie-Zajc, 2003) (See the companion website https://study.sagepub.com/gaudetandrobert for the transcript of an interview with Jodi, an activist.) To develop one's listening capacity and one's skills at identifying interesting leads offered by the participants, there is nothing like experience. Listening is a faculty and the more we use it, the better we get at it. And there is no need to be in a research context to practice! Everyday life offers many opportunities to improve our listening skills. Sharpening our main working tool, our ability to listen, is what makes it possible to see the world through the participants' eyes and limit our tendencies to impose our own categories upon them, our own sense of what matters, our own frame for them to tell their stories.

CONDUCTING INTERVIEWS STEP BY STEP

The following are suggestions regarding the interview process. Interviewing starts well before the opening question is posed to your interviewee. It requires preparation. It also finishes well after you turn off your recording device. As with any other tool proposed here, the steps and suggestions we lay out below are to be adapted and modified depending on your fieldwork situation.

BEFORE THE INTERVIEW IS SCHEDULED

Interviewing requires thorough preparation. It starts even before you contact your first participant to schedule an interview (Daunais, 1992; Mayer and Saint-Jacques, 2000; Savoie-Zajc, 2003).

Start by revisiting your research project. Indeed, reread, again, your literature review (whether you just wrote reading notes or a detailed synthesis of the literature on your topic) as well as your theoretical framework (whether you chose to keep things flexible by electing a few sensitizing concepts or you follow a definite theory). Reviewing this conceptual work will give it a new life in your memory and will likely help you grasp all the fruitful prompting avenues during the interview. It will also help you 'read' the interview analytically as you conduct it, above and beyond the factual information that is shared with you by the participant. Keep the research question in your mind at all times, even more so during the interview. Reread, again, the methodology section of your research protocol. Remind yourself what type of interview you chose, why you did so and what are the characteristics of this type of interview. Refreshing your memory on the rationale behind those choices is likely to help you abide by them and not transform a non-directive interview into a questionnaire out of nervousness (though it may happen with the first interviews!). Reread, again, your research objectives. Hopefully, this will help you strike a balance between producing meaningful material rather than just satisfying your curiosity by prompting the participants on topics that are clearly unrelated to your main research interest.

Then, think about your accessories. Choose your recording device and become familiar with it. Will you make handwritten notes, computer notes, or will you record the interview? If so, will you use your phone, an audio recorder or a video recorder? Choose what is most appropriate for your research needs and what is least invasive for your participant. You will have to notify your participant in advance of your choice in the matter.

Moreover, prepare and write your introductory text. While it may seem a bit artificial, we highly recommend that you take the time to write down the paragraph you will use when first contacting your future participants to inform them of your research and convince them to participate. This paragraph, especially if it is your very first contact with a participant, is central to setting the tone of your relationship with this person and to give them confidence and enthusiasm enough to help you with your research. Your introductory text should contain at least the following elements (Daunais, 1992; Mayer and Saint-Jacques, 2000: 127):

1. Your identity.

2. Your intermediary: the person who gave you the idea of contacting the participant.

3. The topic of your project and the reason this person is a good participant for your project.

4. The type of participation you require. Explain the type of interview you have in mind and be realistic about the time it will require.

5. Dispel potential misconceptions or misgivings even before they surface. For example, emphasizing that there are no right or wrong answers, that this is not a questionnaire, etc.

6. The request to record the interview and why it is important.

7. The participant's rights.

8. Ask if the person has questions.

Prepare and write down your interview guide. It will vary in length depending on the type of interview you choose to conduct. It will take the form of a list of open-ended questions for a directive interview, an opening question and a list of topics (keywords) for the semi-structured interview or, simply, an opening question for a non-directive interview (Mayer and Saint-Jacques, 2000; Savoie-Zajc, 2003).

1. Your question(s) should be simple and suited to the topic and the interviewee's language. Your question(s) should focus on the participant's personal experience.

2. Your question(s) should avoid pre-structuring elements such as suggestive words; they should be as open as possible.

3. Especially for semi- or non-directive interviews, think of your opening question as the spinal cord of your interview; it is not just a simple question, it is a signal about the territory you want to cover with your participant.

4. Write down many versions of the question(s) and select the widest but most concrete.

5. If you can, test it with colleagues or, at least, show your question(s) to them to get their reactions and suggestions.

Prepare your face sheet (Esterberg, 2002). A face sheet is list of factual information about your interview (Part A) and your participant (Part B). It is a record about your interview. It comes in handy when you want to describe the sample of participants you have gathered and the time span and context when the interviews were conducted. You should fill out one face sheet for each interview you conducted.

Here is a fictional example of a face sheet that could be used in research with doctors doing home visits on their relationships with residents of different neighborhoods:

A.   Information about the interview:

   a.   Date:

   b.   Time:

   c.   Place:

   d.   Length:

   e.   Recording technique:

B.   Information about the participant. Social characteristics and other pertinent information:

   a.   Pseudonym:

   b.   Gender:

   c.   Origin and nationality:

   d.   Place of residence:

   e.   Family situation:

   f.   Training and highest diploma:

   g.   Years of experience:

Review your consent form (we discuss this in depth in Chapter 5 and give an example on the companion website https://study.sagepub.com/gaudetandrobert) and make sure you have two copies of it ready for your interview. Again, test the recording device: check and test all its features in the calm and comfort of your home so that it becomes second nature to you.

DURING THE INTERVIEW

It is time to start the interview: breathe deeply, relax and adopt an open attitude. If you chose a semi- or non-directive type of interview, remember that your role is to help the participant explore his or her own experience and, to do so, you do not have to question the participant incessantly, you have to listen actively. Concentrating, listening and showing that you are listening by nodding and keeping eye contact are essential parts of this process. So is respecting full silences, those moments when the participant thinks and revisits some portions of his or her experience before speaking about it.

Especially for semi- or non-directive interviews, as your participant speaks, be sure to take note of elements you identify as important avenues to explore later on. Do not write frenetically, just use keywords. You might also want to make notes of non-verbal cues that help you interpret what the participant is saying. For example, if the participant rolls his or her eyes when talking about work, it is worth noting.

At some point, when the participant has finished talking, you will have to intervene. If you chose a directive interview, you will already have prepared your next question. But, if you chose to conduct a semi- or non-directive interview, you will rely mostly on reiterations and, to a lesser extent, on open questions that you improvise. A reiteration is an interviewer's intervention that consists of repeating, in a concise and clear way, what the interviewee just shared. The point of this kind of probe is that by reiterating the participant's words, the interviewer does not add anything new or different in the interview. Reiterations will, hopefully, encourage the participant to elaborate on what he or she has just said. Questions are open when they avoid any structured elements that could lead the participant in one way or another. Let us borrow a categorization and an example inspired by Blanchet (1987; 1989). Suppose that you are conducting an interview with a nurse working in a dermatology department in a hospital about the changes he has experienced over his career. He talks about a phenomenon he has encountered more often in the recent past: complications related to full-body tattoos. He talks about his experience with them and says, 'People who get full-body tattoos are courageous ... but I think they are thoughtless' and he stops there. Figure 4.8 shows your possibilities in terms of probes and follow-ups.

Register	Reiterations	Questions
Referential Prompts about the content of the participant's statement, topic	**Echo** 'They are unconscious?' or 'They are courageous but unconscious?'	**Referential question** 'In what ways would you say they are courageous?'
Modal Prompts about the participant's position, beliefs, desires	**Mirror** 'You think they are courageous?' or 'You think they are courageous but unconscious?'	**Modal question** 'What do you think about their consciousness level?'

Figure 4.8 Types of follow-ups and probes in an interview (adapted from Blanchet, 1989: 371)

An echo repeats the last words the participant just said, emphasizing the content of the statement (they are …), while a mirror repeats the participant's statement while emphasizing the participant's position (*you think* they are …). These two types of follow-up might seem artificial to you at first, but try them in a daily conversation and you might be surprised by the encouraging effect it has on your conversational partner. Of course, an abuse of reiterations, whether echoes or mirrors, will feel bizarre and should be avoided. Try to vary your follow-ups and prompts so as not to appear to be on autopilot.

Referential questions, those about the content of what the participant just shared, are another option. Like echoes, they emphasize the content of the participant's statement and ask for additional information ('In what ways would you say they are courageous?'), while modal questions emphasize the participant's state of mind or attitude ('What *do you think* about their thoughtlessness?').

Otherwise, if you are asking questions, keep them open; that is, avoid factual, yes–no or either–or questions. Favor questions like 'Can you tell me more about this?' or 'Can you expand on that?' They are always good fallback follow-ups.

If you chose a semi- or non-directive interview, make sure you covered the topics that you prepared in advance (semi-directive) and identified in the course of the interview and jotted down (semi- and non-directive). When all the topics have been covered and the interview is coming to an end, conclude by synthesizing the content of the interview or at least the main elements covered (Daunais, 1992). Make a broad closing reiteration. The beginning of this reiteration might sound like:

> Ok, so if I understood you well, you have been working in the dermatology department of many hospitals over the past 15 years. You told me that you specialized in dermatology because the skin is one of the largest and most intriguing organs in the human body. We have talked about the fact that, over the course of your career, technology, pharmaceutical products and ethics have changed the modalities of your work. You told me that you encountered recently more cases of people having complications with full-body tattoos, etc.

This synthesis of the interview is a great time for you to evaluate whether you are clear on everything the participant said. But, even more important, it is the opportunity for the participant to correct, nuance and add to what he or she has said. Indeed, a closing reiteration can give a second wind to an interview.

Once your understanding has been confirmed by the participants, you might want to ask if there is any other thing you should know in order to understand your topic. The participants might suggest other categories of participants to interview or other topics that they deem relevant. All these suggestions, even if you do not follow them, will help you 'get' the participants better. Once the interview is finished, you can keep the recording device on and fill out the face sheets with your participants.

If telling their story brought up intense feelings in your participants, especially if you interviewed someone who is fragile or marginalized in any way, do not leave the premises before you know that they are feeling well. It is essential that you provide participants with contact information for pertinent helplines or support organizations.

AFTER THE INTERVIEW

You are back home after your interview and you feel like your work is done. There are, however, a couple of things you should take care of right away. Indeed, before the memory of this privileged moment fades away, we suggest writing a preliminary report (Mayer and Saint-Jacques, 2000).

Just after you have conducted each interview, write up the vivid information that comes to mind: describe the physical context of the interview, the neighborhood, the house and the room where the interview took place. Try to create images with your words.

Describe the interview process: How did it go? How comfortable did your participants seem? How comfortable were you? Describe the rhythms of the interview: how long did it take to break the ice? Were there interruptions, breaks? How did they affect the interview process?

Synthesize the content of the interview. Try to summarize the content of the interview in chronological order. What seems especially striking to you? If it is not the first, what seems to stand out compared to the previous interviews you conducted for your project?

Reflect on how you conducted the interview. As an interviewer, what were your strengths and weaknesses? What would you change for the next interview? Look at the guide in Figure 4.9 to help you think about the conduct of the interview, especially if you chose a semi- or non-directive type of interview.

Jot down your analytical remarks: How does the content of the interview confirm, nuance or contradict the results of previous studies on the topic? Do you see links with your conceptual constructs and the interview? What processes seem to be at play in the participant's story? What interpretative insights does this interview generate?

The preliminary report is a long memo to yourself, an exercise to help you think, a way to involve yourself completely in your research and get the most out of your fieldwork. It would be an error to bulldoze through the data producing phase and wait until the end of it to engage the analyst in you. We recommend you write a preliminary report after each interview, to get your methodological and theoretical mind fully engaged.

The next task following your preliminary report is to transcribe the interview itself. We recommend you transcribe it verbatim, meaning word for

Was the interviewer capable of creating an atmosphere conducive to self-exploration by the participant?

- Was the interviewee given the power and the space to tell his or her story?
- How was the non-verbal communication of the interviewer?

Quality and quantity of follow-ups and probes

- Analyse the opening question. Was it conducive to 'launching' the interview? What would have been a better opening question?
- Was the interview semi-or non-directive as planned?
- How were the prompts and follow-ups of the interviewer? What types were they: reiterations, interrogations?
- Did the interviewer pre-structure the interviewee's account through follow-ups?
- Were the prompts related to what the interviewee shared?
- Was the interviewer able to adapt to the vocabulary and language level of the interviewee?
- Was the interviewer able to respect the full silences and reiterate to break empty silences?

Did the interviewer get the information needed?

- Was the interviewer successful in getting the information needed or were long passages of interview unhelpful?

Did the interviewer identify and follow the leads suggested by the participant?

- Did the interviewer get more than needed?
- Was the interviewer able to follow the leads in the interviewee's narrative and explore them; was the interviewer flexible enough to clue in and dig out the essential elements offered by the interviewee?

What effect did the interviewer have on the participant and vice versa?

- How did the participant feel during and after the interview? Worried? Regretful? What did the interviewer do to reassure him or her?
- What was the quality of the rapport between the interviewer and the interviewee?

Figure 4.9 Guide to commenting on an interview process

word. While it might seem tedious at first, you will gain speed with each interview you transcribe. Technology can be helpful at this stage. Since we use a digital audio recorder, we are particularly fond of software that allows the user to control the speed of the speech on a recording. Transcribing an interview at 50 per cent of its original speed is much easier that at the regular speed! People have developed elaborate transcription conventions (Jefferson, 2004) and problematize the work of putting speech into words on paper (Lapadat, 2000), showing that transcribing is always an interpretative work.

> Consider software such as Express Scribe to help the transcription process (www.nch.com.au/scribe/index.html).

Transcribing is a great way to generate thoughts and conceptual insights from your interview, so be sure to note your reflections as they come to you while transcribing. This is precious! Your analysis started while you were doing this apparently mechanical work. Moreover, transcribing your interviews will ensure that you have an in-depth knowledge of your material. This will help when the next stage of analysis begins.

When the transcribing is done, you are ready to apply your analytical strategy to the material. The aim of Chapters 6–9 is to accompany you in this endeavor.

DOCUMENTS

In order to limit the overlap with previous sections, we will leave out direct references to documents produced by participants for the purpose of the research or 'reactive documents': that is, journal entries that the researchers ask participants to write as part of their research participation, photographs taken as part of their participation in a photovoice project, and the like. We will concentrate here on documents produced by participants in the course of their 'natural' experience, which is often referred to as unobtrusive research or non-reactive research.

DEFINITION OF DOCUMENT

For the purpose of this chapter, 'Documents' refers to all kinds of material or electronic artefacts that reveal something about a culture – be it a moving or still image, a plan, a monument, a building or, indeed, a text. We will restrict our discussion to documents that contain written traces (for documents that emphasize audio or images, see especially Burri, 2012; Carrabine, 2012; O'Toole and Were, 2008).

Ethnographic methods were developed for societies that relied mainly on oral culture (Atkinson and Coffey, 1997: 45; Prior, 2004b). Nowadays most research takes place in literate environments where the social actors produce documents about and for the organizations or groups they belong to or for themselves: namely, workplace websites, social media pages, transcripts, commercials, rules and regulations codes, training manuals, history of the organization, annual reports, scrapbooks, family photo albums and other similar documents.

These are 'self-descriptions' that settings, organizations and people produce to represent themselves to themselves and often also to the world (Atkinson and Coffey, 1997: 45). They are therefore a rich source to take into account. Besides the self-presentation documents, there are documents produced and consumed as part of the working of the organizations or groups. Those documents are all the internal tools developed to coordinate the activities of the social actors on a site: records, procedures, forms, invoices, evaluation scales, clients or patients' files, memos, grocery lists, calendars, lists of tasks, etc.

Documents accomplish a lot of work:

> Contractual commitment, ratifying work, facilitating work, record-keeping, persuasive work, identity-establishing work, and so on. In fact, one might suggest that virtually every recognizable activity in our society has its textual aspects, involving and incorporating people's monitoring of written or other textual 'signs' – texts that, in a wide variety of ways, help us to orientate ourselves to that activity, occasion or setting and to make sense of it. (Watson, 1997: 80)

Like observations and interviews, these documents can constitute the empirical basis of a study in itself or find their way into multi-method fieldwork. But they often do not or not as much as they could. As an authority on document analysis remarks about his own research practice in different organizations:

> Looking back on my work in such sites, I suspect that I tended to regard documentation as somehow peripheral to the nature of the research process (although I always acknowledged the presence of documents and documentation). Perhaps this was because, as with so many others, I felt that real data were only to be found in talk and interaction. Only with time and practice did I come to realize the significance of inscription in organizational settings. (Prior, 2004b: 346)

It is likely that your research topic lends itself well to research by documents. But then, how do you approach those artefacts? Are all documents of equal value and purpose? We will turn to these questions in the next section.

APPROACHES TO DOCUMENTS

The all-encompassing category of documents containing written traces must be unpacked. The French historian Arlette Farge justly reminds us that there is a world of difference between archives or manuscripts and the printed public word:

> The printed word is a text, deliberately given to the public. It is organized to be read and understood by many. It tries to present and create a world, to modify the flow of things by putting in place a story or a thought. It is ordered and structured according to systems that are more or less easily decipherable, and, no matter what format it takes, it exists to transform knowledge … Hidden or not, it is pregnant with intentions, the simplest and most obvious is that of being read by others. Nothing to do with archives that are raw traces that did not ask to be told and are constrained to reveal themselves … They share something that should never have been told if a disturbing event would not have happened. In many ways, they share the unsaid. (Farge, 1989: 12, our translation)

This distinction might not hold as strongly in the computerized and very public world in which we live since even school children are writing homework online and people are documenting electronic personal journals. But still, Farge reminds us that a document can have a different status based on whether or not it was meant to have a readership beyond the author.

Not only are there intrinsic differences between private and public texts, but also written documents can be conceptualized as different entities. Borrowing a powerful distinction that we introduced in the previous chapter and owe to Alasuutari (1995b), we can say that there are two broad approaches to documents as data: the factist and the specimen approaches.

In a factist approach, we see the document as a receptacle for content to be extracted. A document is conceived of as a reservoir of indicators or testimonies about a reality that interests the researchers. For example, one would study scrapbooks constituted over the years by parents as indicators or testimonies of their family life or their child's development. In this case, the scrapbooks are only a conduit to the object of interest: family life. Those indicators and testimonies are reflections and statements about family life that are more or less complete, straightforward and idealized. Therefore, the researcher has to be vigilant as to the power of these documents. The researcher has to ensure that the material makes the object of study as transparent as possible. Issues of triangulation, multiplying and diversifying the sources of material, become of the utmost importance.

On the other hand, a specimen approach concentrates on the artefact as such, not as a conduit to another reality. Following our example on family life, the questions can become: How are scrapbooks constructed and organized? Who participated in their creation? What found a place in them? When and to what effect were they used (e.g. family reunions)? Hence, when seen as an artefact, the form, structure, components, method of fabrication and uses of a document all become important. Here, the document is studied for itself.

This distinction between factist and specimen approaches ties in with the double status that researchers have attributed to documents: that of source or resource and that of agent or active social phenomenon (Prior, 2003; Watson, 1997). According to the type of research and the theoretical perspective adopted, weight is given more to one than the other (Figure 4.10).

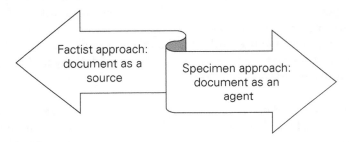

Figure 4.10   Approaches to documents

GENERATING DOCUMENTARY SOURCES STEP BY STEP

Not surprisingly, historians have a lot to teach social scientists on the issue of document as a source since it is often their only access to the phenomena that interest them. However, whether the document is old or current, the source will require a different treatment. Bowen identifies the wide range of documents that can be useful as sources in a research:

> advertisements; agenda, attendance registers, and minutes of meetings; manuals, background papers; books and brochures; diaries and journals; event programs (i.e. printed outlines); letters and memoranda; maps and charts; newspapers (clippings/articles); press releases; program proposals, application forms, and summaries; radio and television program scripts; organizational or institutional reports; survey data; and various public records ... These types of documents are found in libraries, newspaper archives, historical society offices, and organizational or institutional files. (2009: 27–8)

To those, we can add speeches (see the example of a transcribed speech on the companion website https://study.sagepub.com/gaudetandrobert) as well as the electronic version of all those types of sources to which we can add web pages, blogs, social networking sites, audio files, videos and films.

IDENTIFYING THE FUNCTIONS YOU NEED YOUR DOCUMENTARY SOURCES TO SERVE

Apart from the cases where documents are the main if not the sole empirical basis of a study, documents can play five complementary functions in a research (Bowen, 2009: 29–30). Documents can:

1. Provide contextual information: they can help document the context of the research participants, background information and historical insight. Documents can be used to contextualize material produced during interviews.

2. Act as sources to generate additional interview questions: to suggest questions to be asked and situations to be observed.

3. Serve as additional empirical material so as to supplement partial material from other sources.

4. Be the indicator to track change: this is doable when a series of the same document is available (e.g. annual reports) or when several drafts of the same document are available (e.g. a Bill that is discussed and rewritten until it becomes law.)

5. Corroborate evidence from other sources. Some would say that if results of the documentary analysis contradict previous findings from other sources, there is a need for further research (Bowen, 2009: 30). On the other hand, if the document analysis confirms the previous findings from other sources, then we can have greater confidence in them because the findings have been triangulated and validated (2009: 30). As we will see in the final section of this chapter, other methodologists are dubious that validation can proceed through the comparison of different data sources. The reasoning is that each data source has its own particularities and logic and cannot be expected to match another data source (Atkinson and Coffey, 1997).

Depending on the functions you need your documentary sources to serve, you will select and sample them differently. However, as part of this reflection, you want to make sure that you are aware of the potential and pitfalls of using documents as sources. Each document and each document type has its own characteristics, but the advantages and disadvantages shown in Figure 4.11 are often noted (Bowen, 2009: 31).

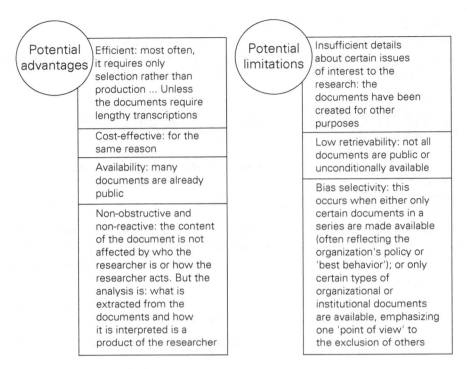

Figure 4.11   Potential advantages and limitations of documents as sources (adapted from Bowen, 2009: 31)

FINDING THE DOCUMENTS

While it is very possible to design a research project for a corpus of documents that we know is already available and waiting for us, it is often the other way around. The project is first thought about and then the hunt for documents begins. If that is your situation and you are not familiar with your documentary material from the start, we would urge you to begin on both tracks simultaneously. That is, find a topic of interest and explore the different documentary sources on this topic at the same time. By progressively designing your project around the documentary material that you find or know is available to you, you limit the risk involved in polishing a perfect research project that cannot be conducted for a lack of empirical material or an accessibility issue. Moreover, it keeps you flexible enough to later adapt your research project to the rich sources that you were initially unaware of.

What documents exist on your topic? A thorough research to find sources is necessary both online and on site through library catalogues, professional association websites, archives of organizations, governmental documentation centres. Think about all the possible points of view on your topic and list the actors involved. Then, think about the different spokespersons or associations that represent each of the actors you listed. Every one of them might be a good point of departure to trace the portrait of the phenomenon you are interested in.

For example, controversies about schizophrenia diagnosis potentially involve: psychiatrist associations, mental health organizations, associations of defense lawyers, journalists, families of patients' representatives, hospital ombudsmen, civil liberty associations, non-governmental organizations of psychiatric services users, pharmaceutical companies, Ministries of Health, etc. The broad categories of groups that we list here have their national, provincial, regional networks. All are possible avenues to map the information that exists on your topic.

Are those documents available to the public or at least for research purposes? Here, one might have to be convincing and persistent. For example, it is possible to get access to prison records but the research project must be deemed important and pertinent enough by the authorities for them to accept your request and go through the trouble of making each document respect anonymity rules. When dealing with official administrations, you might not be given an answer before submitting a full research proposal and an ethics certificate from your learning institution (see Chapter 5 on ethics boards). In many cases, if not directly, governmental information can be accessed through the Freedom of Information Act (Larsen and Walby, 2012).

SELECTING AND APPRAISING THE DOCUMENTS

Among the available documents, how do you choose which ones to keep and which parts of the selected documents you will analyse? You can go about it in two simultaneous ways: (1) refine the research question to be in sync with the nature of the information found in the chosen documents; and (2) sample your documents, that is take a diverse group of documents that are part of a large pool. The number of documents selected will in part depend on whether they are the sole empirical source for your project or supplementary.

In order to evaluate the quality of a document, or rather its usefulness to your research, it is important to understand the process of production that gave it life:

1. What is the context of production of the document (reactive document following an event, routine document produced serially, etc.)?

2. Who is the intended audience?

3. What is the purpose of the document (representing a group, getting funding, justifying actions, etc.)?

4. Who is the author of the document – is it an identifiable author or an anonymous author (as in many governmental publications)?

5. What is the author's general source of information?

6. Is it a primary source (does the author of the document have first-hand experience of what he or she writes about) or a secondary source?

All these questions help establish the credibility and the usefulness of documents as sources of information about a phenomenon and help you decide what weight to give the documents in the analysis you are producing.

If your documents are an archive, personal or organization documents that date back decades or centuries, establishing authenticity, accuracy and completeness is an essential part of appraising the documents. For this, you will want to get acquainted with historical methods (Cellard, 1997).

ANALYSING

The analysis and interpretation of the document when it is conceptualized as a source and mined for content will depend on the chosen analytical strategy. It can span from semiotic analysis (Atkinson and Coffey, 1997) to Foucauldian discourse analysis (Prior, 2004b) to thematic analysis (Bowen, 2009) to phenomenology (Angrosino, 2003). Some of these approaches were presented in the previous chapter. In all cases, whether it is conceived as static or whether we are interested in 'how document content comes into being' (Prior, 2008: 825), the content of the document will be the focus of analysis.

We want to bring your attention to another selection step that we include in the early stage of the analysis procedures. Despite the fact that you have already proceeded to the selection of documents, before you start the analysis per se, you might still have to do some skimming and selection within the chosen documents. Indeed, it might be reasonable to select portions, sections or chapters of documents that will be thoroughly analysed using your chosen strategy while other portions will only be read and summarized. The chosen topic, research question and objectives will orient this selection process within the documents. Hence, for example, from a United Nations Development Program, only passages related to the Human Development index and related data can be extracted and analysed because they fit your research question (Bowen, 2009: 36). Nevertheless, it is important to keep an open mind and look out for the importance of sections that seem, at first glance, meaningless at the beginning of the selection and can take on a different meaning as the analysis progresses.

But documents are not, or not only, interesting for their content. The next section turns to the very activities that documents accomplish.

STUDYING DOCUMENTS AS AGENTS ONE FACET AT A TIME

In line with institutional ethnography (Smith, 2002), some advocate the conceptualization of documents as agents and not just as sources. On the one hand, textual documents are active in that they predispose the reader to read them one way or another (Watson, 1997). On the other hand, documents are full agents, since 'they can influence episodes of social interaction, and schemes of social organization' (Prior, 2008: 822). As researchers, we can focus on the production of those agents or on their use; we can focus on the transcription work they accomplish, that is how they transform a reality into their own language, or on their circulation, the way documents pass through a network of users. These aspects often overlap.

DOCUMENT PRODUCTION

Some documents are points of reference for an entire organization or entire culture. They are pillars of policy-making. What is their status?

> In paying due attention to [documents], however, one must be quite clear about what they can and cannot be used for. They are 'social facts', in that they are produced, shared and used in socially organized ways. They are not, however, transparent representations of organizational routines, decision-making processes or professional diagnoses. They construct particular kinds of representations with their own conventions. We should not use documentary sources as surrogates for other kinds of data. We cannot, for instance, learn through records alone how an organization actually operates day-by-day. Equally, we cannot treat records – however 'official'– as firm evidence of what they report. This observation has been made repeatedly about data from official sources such as statistics on crime, suicide, death, education outcomes and so on. (Atkinson and Coffey, 1997: 47)

This quote begs the questions: how then are those documents constructed and how do they construct the reality they are supposed to portray? Tracing back their biography can be a monumental and worthwhile research project in itself. Taking the example of the *Manual of World Health Statistics* published by the World Health Organization, Prior (2004a) focuses on a category of mortality statistics found in the *Manual* – the suicide statistics – and follows each step that contributes to creating the related tables in the *Manual*. The research becomes an ethnographic study of how suicide statistics are produced. Indeed, the author's contention is that by studying each decision that presides over the making of these statistics, we will learn a lot about our culture and its rapport with self-inflicted death. There are a series of turning points in the generation of the final document (Prior, 2004a): How are the causes of death organized and classified? How does this classification change over time? How are decisions made to record one cause of death when multiple causes are likely? How do the decision-making rules evolve on that issue? How is the cause of death identified when someone passes away? Who is in charge of recording it and how does this person make the coding decision based on a coroner's report? Prus (2003) suggests a similar approach to studying policies in that he sees in them not simply inert documents, but a collective venture, in both their production and use.

DOCUMENT USE

We have to approach documents in terms of what they are used to accomplish (Atkinson and Coffey, 1997: 47). Documents make certain actions possible and humans use them to perform and justify their actions. In any school, health service, community organization, private workplace or government service, documents are mediators between humans. On the other hand, readers activate the documents in a certain way because reading is an active, interpretative process (Watson, 1997: 89). The use of a document refers to the way the document functions in real-life settings.

DOCUMENT AS TRANSCRIPTION DEVICE

Intake forms, registration documents, admission forms, police records, medical files, computerized records, ID cards, credit records, library files, usernames and passwords constitute what surveillance theorists call our 'data double' (Brown, 2006). Documents are what make the hybridization of people possible. We do not just exist as flesh and blood; we exist 'informationally' and sometimes even more so than physically. Records, and we notice when we are the object of a mistaken record, can take precedence over the physical person themselves (Los, 2006). Indeed, you can have the authorization to be on a securitized campus but if you show up in person, having forgotten your ID card, you might not be admitted. Your card, which holds information about you, seems more 'real' than the flesh and blood person. At least, it conveys more power in certain situations.

Documents work as 'transcription devices': they 'pack the world into words' (Latour, 1999: 24). In the process, they make things visible. Hence, a medical sociologist following the CAT scan of a patient in a hospital can show the ways the document is activated by health professionals with different priorities in mind (daily care, acute care, bed management). Moreover, a researcher can document how a transcription, for example a diagnosis of schizophrenia, takes on a reality of its own that makes the actual patients' experiences of their disease, if not irrelevant, at least of secondary importance (Prior, 2004a). This disconnection process between very potent documentation and marginalized lived experience has been shown in an institutional ethnography of restraining orders in the case of intimate partner violence (Adams, 2009). The account of the 'case' that is produced by the court system, formatting the experience in terms of institutionally pertinent categories, excludes the reason for resorting to the justice system in the first place and the main need of the service users, namely their security.

There have been studies dedicated to following these transcription devices and watching them in action. On the assumption that social coordination is accomplished textually, institutional ethnography studies shed light on how documents work in daily settings (Campbell and Gregor, 2002). Hence, in a nursing home, the daily routine is organized by documents and the work of filling in documents: nursing charts, nutrition records, restraints and positions forms. The whole workload of care-giving is here structured by carefully documented tasks (Diamond, 1992). Document production and document use is how the power of the institutional regime assumes control and how the institutional gaze is achieved. Studying a nursing home without considering the documents would mean missing an important part of how the organization produces and reproduces itself.

DOCUMENT CIRCULATION

Document circulation may be used to document social networks and networks of influence.

> In his conversations with Latour, Serres (1995: 161) refers to objects that trace or 'make visible the relations that constitute the group through which it passes, like the token in a children's game' (Prior, 2003: 171). The term that Serres uses to refer to such objects is 'quasi-object' – a term chosen to emphasize the fact that the world cannot be simply divided into objects and humans, for objects and people belong in an ensemble that is often difficult to unravel. (Prior, 2004a: 357)

In such research, the circuit of information by which a document travels is traced to establish the border of a network of influence as well as the vectors and nodes of force in such a network. When applied to information about a specific pharmaceutical innovation, such a mapping can help to show how the innovation comes to be adopted or not.

Hence, while we may be tempted to observe and speak to human actors, non-human actors, by themselves or in combination with their human counterparts, have a lot to offer a curious researcher. Their richness is often underestimated and we suggest you ask yourself if documents can represent a way to answer your research question. Ethically, it is a good idea to avoid requiring time and energy from people if you can get your answer otherwise, by 'interviewing' and 'observing' the non-humans around you.

CHAPTER SUMMARY

In this chapter, we first saw that fieldwork is directly connected to your epistemological position: you will either gather or produce the material basis of your study. We then delved into three different tools to produce your material: observations, interviews and documents. We described the approaches, forms and types those tools can take. We also presented, for each one, a step-by-step guide on how to proceed during fieldwork. The second half of this book will show you how to analyse this material once you have produced it.

Your project checklist

Now that you are more familiar with the three main tools used to conduct fieldwork in qualitative research, you can:

✓   Reflect on whether you conceive of your fieldwork as an occasion to gather information or produce empirical material. Adjust your vocabulary in consequence when writing your research project.

✓   Decide on the tool, or combination of tools, that would generate the best type of material to fit the project you are designing, including your research question.

✓   Read additional texts on the selected tool(s) to broaden your understanding of them and narrow your selection further. See the annotated list below for a start.

✓   Justify your final choice of tool(s), laying out the approach, the type and form of observation, interview or document best suited for your project and its feasibility.

✓   If thinking about using observations, identify potential sites as well as the people you would need to contact and the ways you would go about gaining access. Design a first observation grid.

✓   If thinking about using interviews, identify potential participants as well as the way you would approach them. Write a first introductory text, a face sheet as well as a first interview guide.

✓   If thinking about using documents, identify your potential sources or agents as well as the way to gain access to them. Decide on whether you are interested in their content, their production, their use, the translation they perform or the way they are circulated. Depending on your choice, you might need to introduce observations or interviews into your research design.

What you should read next

Alvesson, Mats. 2011. 'Rethinking Interviews: New Metaphors for Interviews', pp. 75–104 in *Interpreting Interviews*, ed. M. Alvesson. London: Sage.

•   This chapter is about the status of the speech and data generated in interviews. This text will sharpen your critical sense regarding the different layers of communications that happen in an interview and therefore the analytical richness of such a source.

de Montigny, Gerald. 2014. 'Doing Child Protection Work', pp. 173–94 in *Incorporating Texts into Institutional Ethnographies*, ed. D. E. Smith and S. M. Turner. Toronto: University of Toronto Press.

- This short chapter is an example of a youth worker doing institutional ethnography. This type of ethnography focused on following the production and circulation of documents in an organization. It shows vividly the way documents are translating a social interaction into their own logic.

Fontana, Andrea and James H. Frey. 2005. 'The Interview: From Neutral Stance to Political Involvement', pp. 695-727 in *The Sage Handbook of Qualitative Research*, 3rd edition, ed. N. K. Denzin and Y. S. Lincoln. Thousand Oaks, CA: Sage.

- This chapter briefly touches upon the history as well as the main forms and types of interviews. It covers the main debates regarding this tool and points to the future directions it is taking, namely the feminist engaged interview as well as the postmodern trend in interviewing. If you want a solid panorama on the topic, and also if your project borrows from feminist, postmodern, postcolonial literature, this chapter would be a good place to start.

Gubrium, Jaber F. and James A. Holstein (eds). 2001. *Handbook of Interview Research*. Thousand Oaks, CA: Sage.

- The 2001 version of the *Handbook of Interview Research* is informative from one cover to the other, but we want to direct your attention to Part II of the book that is dedicated to 'Distinctive Respondents'. Here, eight chapters are dedicated to the specificities of conducting interviews with participants of different age groups, gender category, races as well as interviewing elites and ill people. In this version and the more recent one (2012) of the *Handbook*, you will also find chapters dedicated to focus groups, in-depth interviewing and postmodern trends in interviewing.

Ocejo, Richard E. and Stephanie Tonnelat. 2014. 'Subway Diaries: How People Experience and Practice Riding the Train'. *Ethnography* 15(4): 493-515.

- This article is an example of the way ethnography can easily merge with document analysis and also of the way it is possible to transform ethnography 'participants' into 'co-researchers'. In this case, teenagers are asked to document their experience when taking the train by logging their travels. The journal they produce is a key part of this ethnography of youth in public places.

Prior, Lindsay. 2003. *Using Documents in Social Research*. Thousand Oaks, CA: Sage.

- This book is key reading if you are thinking about using any type of documents in fieldwork. Inspired namely by Foucault and actor–network theory, Prior is a refined analyst of documents, and his articles, chapters and books on documents are all worth reading.

Wacquant, Loic. 2004. *Body and Soul: Notebooks of an Apprentice Boxer*. Oxford: Oxford University Press.

- This ethnography of the way a French intellectual immerses himself into the boxing world in Chicago reads like a novel. It will give you a feel of how a participant observation unfolds and the richness of material and analysis such involvement can generate.

Woodgate, Roberta L., Melanie Zurba and Pauline Tennent. 2017. 'Worth a Thousand Words? Advantages, Challenges and Opportunities in Working with Photovoice as a Qualitative Research Method with Youth and their Families'. *Forum Qualitative Sozialforschung/Forum: Qualitative Social Research* 18(1): Art. 2.

- This article will introduce you to the way you can conduct interviews using photographs that your participants have taken of their own lives. This article is especially useful if you are looking for ways to engage your participants more fully in the research process.

Want more support and inspiration? The online resources are here to help! Get to grips with key terms using **glossary flashcards**, see methods in action with a **library of SAGE cases and journal articles**, and follow analysis step-by-step with full transcripts of the sources discussed in the book.

5

ETHICAL CHALLENGES IN QUALITATIVE RESEARCH

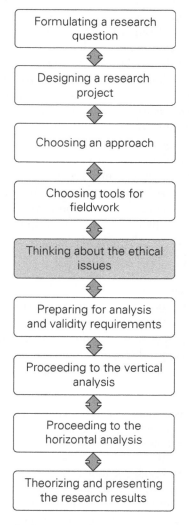

Figure 5.1 Where we are in the research process

IN THIS CHAPTER YOU WILL LEARN:

- To value and understand the three moral foundations of research ethics: the dignity of human beings, the integrity of people and the values of justice.
- To develop ethical arguments to defend your methodological choices.
- To write an application to your organization's Research Ethics Board.
- To be reflexive about ethical relation problems that can occur in fieldwork.

INTRODUCTION

Up to this point, we have taken you through all the options for assembling and writing your research project, from framing your question to choosing your data collection tools. But before you decide to interview, observe, film or photograph people, you need to consider the ethical issues that might affect your relationship with them. On a more formal level, many institutions also request a certificate of approval from an institutional board mandated to apply national laws regarding scientific research ethics. In this text, we will designate these boards as Research Ethics Boards (REBs).

This chapter is most important for those of you who would like to work with living participants. The first part of the chapter describes the three philosophical principles one needs to understand in order to respect the spirit of the laws regarding human protection in scientific activities. That is, integrity, justice and human beings' interests. The second part of the chapter focuses on the list of elements you need to take into account in order to respect the integrity of your participants. Finally, we will discuss three relational ethics issues likely to surface in your fieldwork. In this last section, we consider questions like: 'What if seduction begins to creep into the research relationship?' How does one react in the face of expectations created by the researcher working in a disadvantaged area?

PROCEDURAL ETHICS

Procedural ethics designate values codified in laws, codes or rules. In the late twentieth century, several occidental countries developed legislation to frame ethical issues related to scientific activities. Even professional associations such as the American Anthropological Association developed their own code of ethics. The various texts that were produced are often based on three moral foundations: the dignity of human beings, the integrity of people and the values of justice.

Kant is known as a philosopher of Enlightenment. He developed ethics based on reason instead of traditions or religion. His ethics are based on the duty that each human has to generalize its own moral decision in a universal law. For example, a person might think that lying in a specific situation – such as in a research project – has more positive moral consequences. For example, not telling the goal of the research to participants might have more benefits for science and the common good. For Kant, it would not be moral because it's impossible to universalize lying as a moral universal law applicable in all situations.

The principles that guide such documents often come from Kantian deontology and utilitarian theory. First, they are influenced by Kantian ontology which defines human dignity as a moral absolute. It is necessary to respect rigorously the notion of free and informed consent, as well as the right to anonymity. This way, participants are always treated as an end and never as a means, that is as merely an instrument for the achievement of the researcher's ambitions. It is considered extremely important that each human be treated in a fair way. Second, most policy statements are based on the utilitarian theory since it attempts to weigh benefits against potential harms that could stem from the research process. This is done in order to optimize the positive outcomes for individuals and for society. The moral objective is to protect participants from adverse consequences connected to their involvement in a research project, namely physical or moral suffering.

> John Stuart Mill is one of the founders of utilitarianism. He developed this moral philosophy in order to find 'rules' based on reason. For him, the rule of utility is defined as the pursuit of happiness. A moral decision should be based on the calculation of good and bad consequences and should tend to a maximization of good consequences.

Hence, in your application to the ethics committee of your university or in any other organization, your first task is to justify the risks incurred by the participants in your research project. You have to specify how the benefits of your research, such as additional knowledge about a particular population or issue, might surpass the risks incurred by the participants. You must also explain how you will respect the right to anonymity and informed consent during the key steps of the project: the recruitment, the data collection, the archiving of data and the presentation of results.

No one can be against virtue and, in theory, most researchers try to adhere to these principles. In practice, however, these principles are not so simple to apply. It is important to realize that the systematic consideration and supervision of ethics in research were first and foremost implemented in relation to clinical research, even though a progressive adaptation was made to qualitative methods (Greenwood and Levin, 2005; Van den Hoonaard, 2002). In fact, such laws in Western countries were modeled on legislation governing bioethics. The Nuremberg code of 1949 was the first modern landmark in this type of regulation (Van den Hoonaard, 2001). A tradition of governance of scientific research in the medical domain gave rise to an institutional discourse and to its technocratization, which has subsequently been transposed onto social sciences (Halse and Honey, 2007).

However, social science research creates significant ethical challenges that are ignored by most codes and the ethics regulations of clinical and experimental research. The difficulty in thinking about this area is partially explained by the diversity of epistemologies and methodologies used in the social sciences. Qualitative research projects, which often favor inductive reasoning, are varied. It is therefore often difficult to 'predict' situations that might cause moral dilemmas for the researcher. This is especially so because the process of research is iterative; fieldwork might take different avenues than those presented in your REB proposal.

In spite of this formal recognition, the culture of ethical regulation is solidly anchored in clinical research and qualitative researchers must continually justify their choices. It is important to understand this minority position within the majority clinical or experimental research culture when filling out the REB form. Each university has different forms; some are specially adapted to social sciences alone and others are used more broadly for clinical, experimental and social sciences. In the latter case, completing the form can become a real challenge because questions are intended for experimental researchers.

In the next section, we will introduce important issues requiring explanation and justification when making an application to the REB of your institution. In the last section of the chapter, we will discuss relational ethics issues.

MAKING AN APPLICATION TO THE REB

The role of REBs is to consider research proposals, as well as all of the research instruments that will be used and the documentation that will be provided to the participants. The objective is to regulate research practices that might involve negative consequences for participants and the reputation of the institution.

To obtain the approval of the REB before beginning your research, the board must analyse your project, the documentation that will be made available to the public or the participants, as well as a form in which you explain how you plan to conform to the principles of integrity and dignity of human beings, and the principle of justice, throughout the research process.

For this reason, you need to submit the research project (in whole or in part) to the REB to ensure that your data collection strategies are justified and fit well with your research question. All of the documents given to participants are also required at this stage: the recruitment posters, the text that will be used to recruit participants, the letters of presentation and informed consent forms, the interview guide and all the data gathering tools that will be used. These requirements will thus force you, in effect, to submit an advanced version of your research project, because the data collection tools will have had to be assembled and described by the time of the submission.

The forms that you must complete showing that you conform to the principles of justice, as well as the dignity and integrity of the person, vary from one institution to another. We have compared the features of different REB forms and identified the most common ones. We will now discuss the researcher's ethical obligations with respect to each one: assessing the vulnerability of the study population; the inclusion and exclusion criteria regarding research participation; the partial disclosure of the project; respect for free and informed consent; anonymity and confidentiality.

These last two items are at the heart of the ethical issues governing the researcher–participant relationship. For this reason, we will analyse their application during the key stages of the research: recruitment, first contacts with the participants, publication and archiving of the data.

EVALUATING THE VULNERABILITY OF THE STUDY POPULATION

Ethical issues are crucial while working with vulnerable people or communities. Thus, REBs also carefully assess the level of vulnerability of the people who will be participating in the research. A vulnerable population often refers to people living in precarious situations. For example, will you be working with children, people losing their autonomy, victims of violence or social disqualification? If so, you will have to persuade the REB that the benefits of the research outweigh the possible risks to those potential participants as well as the burden that may be placed on them. For example, it has become a lot harder to conduct research in schools because access to vulnerable people, especially children, is very restricted. For instance, if you witness any child abuse and neglect, you are obliged to break the confidentiality protocol and inform the local authority.

It is important to understand that vulnerable people are often in contact with several social workers or facilitators. Interviews, evaluations and all sorts of interventions are often experienced as judgmental and as a form of power and control relationship toward them. For this reason, each contact with vulnerable people must be taken very seriously. First, establishing a trust relationship might be difficult, and, if you succeed, you need to be careful and respectful. Any disruption of trust and confidence toward you might impact the relationship they have with other professionals supporting them.

If you are working with aboriginal communities, it will be important to show that you respect their customs and traditions. For example, some groups are based on certain social norms, notably the creation of relationships through gift giving. Researchers who want to participate as observers in such groups must therefore demonstrate that they too would like to contribute to that group. This situation is not without difficulty. Indeed, researchers must be sure that their contribution does not support any political agendas that could subject them to a conflict of interest between their allegiance to the group and the scientific rigor of their research. Second, several aboriginal groups have been the object of curiosity of Western researchers and refuse to be research objects any longer. Countries with important aboriginal groups such as Canada and Australia have developed ethical guidelines for researchers in order to respect these minority groups.

Research with aboriginals:
Australian guidelines: www.nhmrc.gov.au/guidelines-publications/e52
Canadian guidelines: www.pre.ethics.gc.ca/eng/policy-politique/initi-atives/tcps2-eptc2/chapter9-chapitre9/
US guidelines: www.nsf.gov/bfa/dias/policy/docs/45cfr690.pdf

CRITERIA FOR RESEARCH PARTICIPATION

In assembling your project, you will have established selection criteria for your population in order to identify the relevant people to observe, interview or gather documents from. REBs ask you to specify these reasons and, above all, to demonstrate how you will exclude people who might want to partici-pate in your research. Indeed, the principle of justice that is fundamental requires that the researcher explain the reasons for excluding someone who could potentially claim the right to participate. Researchers must be sensitive to the possibility that someone might feel aggrieved about being excluded from the research. It will be your job to think how you will manage such situations.

In our projects, we rarely exclude people who badly want to participate in the research. We meet with them without necessarily using their data in our research. We thus maintain good contacts with the group and everyone feels respected. In addition, these unexpected encounters often open the door to exciting questions.

PARTIAL DISCLOSURE OF THE PROJECT

Some researchers, especially in clinical or experimental research, might pre-fer to reveal only partially to the participants the objectives and subject of the research. This could be done in order not to influence the research results. The researchers would have to explain to the REB how the benefits of this partial **disclosure** outweigh the disadvantages. Indeed, a lack of transparency might be perceived as an infringement of their rights to infor-mation and their personal dignity as shown in Table 5.1. It is quite rare, within research projects inspired by a constructionist, constructivist or critical epistemology, that this posture is adopted. In such cases, the researchers accept that the relationship between the researcher and the par-ticipant results in a co-construction of the problem, the data and the analysis. It is often considered important that the participants understand the objectives and the research question clearly so as to enable them to share their expertise on the subject and their experiences. However, some situations, as explained in the section on observation in the previous chap-ter, require covert observation or partial disclosure. Lofland and his colleagues (2006) capture well the challenges that these types of observa-tions raise (see Table 5.1).

Table 5.1 Key ethical and relational aspects to consider when choosing an observation approach

Aspects to consider	Covert observation	Disclosed observation
Ethics and informed consent	The most sacred principle of research ethics is informed consent. Choosing a covert approach needs to be justified to the researcher's institution's ethics board. The case has to be convincing that the benefits outweigh the costs for the participants. The board might ask the researcher to consider alternative ways to proceed.	A consent form is presented and signed by the participants in a small scale and private or semi-private milieu (a classroom, a workplace, a youth center). They know what the research is about, can refuse to participate or withdraw at their convenience. In a large-scale or public milieu (shopping center, metro, etc.), the people in charge sign the consent form and the information regarding the research is shared with the rest of the relevant people in the milieu.
Affective issues	An undercover observer might develop relationships in a milieu with participants who feel betrayed when, at the end of the observation period, they learn that they were being observed. This might lead the researcher to 'burn his bridges' permanently with the milieu and embitter the milieu toward researchers, in general.	While at first it might be harder to develop close relationships with research participants when one presents oneself as a researcher, the relationships that develop are likely to be experienced as honest and can more easily last after the fieldwork is over. This is useful if the researcher wants to communicate and validate his or her research results with the participants later on.
Structural constraints	When conducting covert observation, one has to adopt a role in a milieu and behave according to what is expected from a person in that role. The role structures and limits the point of view of the observer and the information that can be accessed. Hence, following the code of the milieu, Marquart, as a correctional officer, was expected to keep his distance from the Latino prisoners and vice versa. As part of the subculture of the institution, the latter were behaving toward every correctional officer in a cold and distant manner. For this reason, in the final analysis, Marquart's experience of the carceral world lacked certain elements due to the necessary constraints that were part of the role he had adopted.	Research participants will not be surprised to see a researcher connect with everyone on a site and his or her status as a researcher, with a commitment to ethics and scientific rigor, might help him or her partake of everyone's point of view. Years later, when Marquart went back to the prison and replicated his observation, but this time in a disclosed manner, he was able to develop a relationship with the Latino prisoners and get their point of view on the prison experience. On the other hand, presenting oneself as a researcher might also mean that participation will be restricted to certain sectors or events, that participants will be on their best behaviors and that the researcher will be exposed only to what is presentable. Some researchers might counteract these reactions by staying in the field for a long time until the participants became used to their presence. Finally, in some cases, there might be attempts by the participants to 'use' the researchers in their internal or external battles, trying to co-opt the researcher as a spokesperson. Fieldwork requires discernment.
Information recording	The recording of information might be challenging when doing covert observation. Memory has to be trained, so frequent periods away from the setting have to be found to make notes or record observations.	A researcher is expected to record information, so having a notepad or even a digital recorder, as long as they are used respectfully and discreetly, will allow the researcher to record his or her observations at length.

CONSENT AND ANONYMITY

Consent and anonymity are two key elements of human integrity. Any REB will put much emphasis on those two aspects of the research. Throughout the research, you will have to be sure that the participants freely consent to participate and that you protect their anonymity. We will discuss five critical stages in the research where you have to respect these principles.

RECRUITMENT AND FIRST CONTACT

For researchers using interviews, the recruitment period is an essential and often difficult phase. Difficulties in recruiting and research deadlines can lead some researchers to coerce people into participating. Remember: it is important that people are, and feel that they are, free to refuse participation in your research. For this reason, when you are soliciting participants, you have to avoid pressuring them.

Recruitment is also an important time to clarify expectations. If you are planning to offer financial compensation, it is important to mention that fact in the recruitment posters or recruitment letters. If you are not planning to offer financial compensation, make that clear – so as not to have the participants feel they have been deceived or 'used'.

In the case where part of your recruitment is based on **snowball sampling**, it is important that the interested person communicates directly with you. That technique refers to when a first participant introduces a second participant to you, and so on. For example, if, during the course of the interview, an interviewee gives you the contact information of someone from his or her network, you cannot accept that information. This would be considered personal information transmitted without the consent of the person concerned. Instead, you would have to leave your contact information for the interested person.

> In order to respect participants' freedom, researchers are not allowed to recruit participants directly. This rule is meant to protect participants from possible social pressure. It has happened that researchers and students were so desperate to conduct their research that they put pressure on people and participants felt obliged to participate or guilty to refuse! Thus, in a snowball sampling strategy, contacts' personal information must be given by a third party. The third party needs approval from the contact to give its personal information to the researcher.

In the case of interviews or observations, the first contact is often made through a phone call. Thus, it is important to prepare a text to give essential information about the ethics of your research. Here is an example of the first conversation you could have with a participant who contacts you.

This is an example of a conversation between a future interviewee and the researcher.

I: Hello, Ms. Robert. My name is Michael. Mister Daly give me information about your research on ayurvedic medicine. He told me you were looking for interviewees.

R: Hello Michael. Thank you for calling. I am Dominique, Professor at the Faculty of Social Sciences at the University of Ottawa. [PRESENTATION OF THE RESEARCHER]

I: What is the project about and what kind of participant are you looking for?

R: The project is on the use of alternative medicines and I am looking for people who are familiar with alternative medicines, others who are less so and participants who do not take alternative medicines because they do not want to or because they do not feel they need them. [THE RESEARCHER PRESENTS THE CRITERIA TO PARTICIPATE IN THE RESEARCH]

I: I am interested, I have been using ayurvedic medicine for several years and I will be happy to talk about it.

R: If you agree to participate, I will require between one and two hours of your time. I would come to your place or another location, as long as it is quiet enough, and we could chat about your experience with ayurvedic medicine. It is a moment where you could tell me your story, what you know about ayurveda, what it means in your daily routine, things like that. This type of interview is more like a conversation than a questionnaire. [THE RESEARCHER EXPLAINS MORE SPECIFICALLY ABOUT THE PLACE WHERE THE INTERVIEW COULD BE HELD, THE TIME REQUIRED AND THE QUESTIONS THAT WILL BE ASKED]

I: Looks great. We can meet at the public library in my neighborhood. We will find a quiet place to chat.

R: Because I will need to concentrate fully on your story, I would need to record our interview with an audio recorder. This will ensure that I do not forget portions of what you tell me but also that I portray your experience accurately. Does that suit you? If, at some point, there are things that you want to tell me but would rather that they were off the record, I can temporarily stop the recorder – no problem. [THE RESEARCHER INFORMS THE INTERVIEWEE ABOUT THE RECORDING]

I: No problem.

R: My university authorizes me to conduct the research as long as I respect the anonymity and confidentiality of my participants. I will explain to you how I will protect these two aspects when we meet. I know I gave you a lot of information at one time. Are there issues that come to mind, hesitations you might have about my research project? [THE RESEARCHER INFORMS THE INTERVIEWEE ABOUT THE CONFIDENTIALITY AND ANONYMITY AGREEMENT]

THE INTERVIEW AND THE REQUEST FOR CONSENT

Consent is based on a 'mutual understanding of the project goals and objectives between the participants and the researcher' (*TCPS* 2, 2014: 140). Free and informed consent requires that the participants be informed of the research objectives and of the consequences of their participation. It also requires that they confirm that they understand the agreement and are willing to participate. This withdrawal must take place immediately and be communicated to them verbally and in writing without any attempt to convince them to change their minds.

> It must also be clear for the participants and the researchers that consent is a process. Indeed, the participants may, at any moment, withdraw their consent.

It is important that, once you have arrived on location and before you begin the interview, you go through the information already shared at the first phone contact. After the greetings and the usual chit chat, once your participants and you are ready, briefly go over your research project again and remind the participants of the kind of interview you are expecting to conduct as well as the time you estimate it will take. Remind the participants of the reason they have been chosen: they have a unique experience about the topic you are investigating. For this reason, their contribution is important to your project. What you are interested in is their point of view and experience.

Go over the consent form with your participants and confirm the confidentiality and anonymity that you guarantee them. Also, confirm the following rights of the participants: the right to have an answer to their questions regarding the research project and what will become of the interview; their right to refuse to respond to some questions for reasons that they do not have to justify to you; the right to conduct the interview at their own rhythm and to take pauses if they so wish. Make sure you remind the participants that you would like to have their authorization to record the interview. Sign both copies of the consent form and make sure your participants sign them both as well. Your participants keep one copy and you the other.

The consent form is a letter co-signed by the researcher and the participant. An example is presented in the companion website https://study.sagepub.com/gaudetandrobert. Note that this very formal type of agreement can be considered standard procedure but may not be suitable for all situations or all participants, some of whom might feel threatened by such an approach. If you have good reason to believe that a signed agreement might threaten the bond of trust with your participants, you could explain to the REB that you would prefer to opt for another method. Such decisions must be carefully explained and justified, much like any other choice you make throughout your research project.

If you engage in ethnographic fieldwork or participant observation, your participants would probably have a negative perception regarding the signing of letters of consent. In this situation, verbal consent registered in your field notes or a voice recording could be considered entirely acceptable by your REB if well justified. Procedures used to seek and confirm consent need to be documented.

It can also happen that researchers connect with the participants or milieu before completing their project. Researchers can observe and even interview people before writing a research project and after submitting a request to the REB of their institution. However, if they wish to use the data, they need to explain their exploratory fieldwork in their research proposal, and include their strategy to seek consent from those interviewed.

If you carry out **covert observation** and do not infringe upon the privacy of the observed people, you are not obliged to make an application to the REB of your institution. Note that it is difficult to not infringe upon the privacy of people if you are observing small groups. For example, following an evangelistic religious assembly that is identified with a particular ethnic group can easily infringe upon privacy because the people being observed can be recognized and recognize each other even if you are in a public space.

When you conduct interviews, the preferred format will be two copies of a letter signed by the researcher and the participant. The participant keeps one signed copy, the researcher the other. In this case, it is easier to explain the objectives of the research, the implications for the participant and the techniques that you will be using to protect the anonymity of the participant at all stages of the research. It should also be noted in the letter that the participant is free to withdraw fully or partially from the research, and this means that he or she can end the interview at any time or withdraw any remarks.

DATA COLLECTION AND ANONYMITY

Participation in a research project can have many negative consequences for people if they can be recognized by people in their work environment, their community or their family. The best way to protect them is by protecting their anonymity.

In some circumstances, anonymity is impossible, especially when it involves interviewing people who hold important positions, for example the mayor of a municipality. In such cases, participants are speaking as representatives of their organization and reveal information of a public nature.

In other circumstances, people might not desire anonymity. In some cultures, it is perceived as a lack of courage. For some, participating in an interview is a form of social recognition, and they might insist on revealing personal information. A researcher could accept this demand of disclosure from participants if such a waiver does not have negative consequences for their community or other participants.

In order to maintain anonymity, care must be taken to use a system of symbols or pseudonyms to identify all participants in all of the collected data. This may include verbatim comments, face sheets, calendars, short questionnaires, and so on. For example, we could use a letter and a number to identify the documents from a multi-site research: 'M1' for the first interview with a resident of Miami and 'C2' for the second interview with a resident of Cleveland.

STORAGE OF DATA AND ANONYMITY

It is important to protect the anonymity of your electronic data. Working with a hard encrypted disc is the most secure way to protect data. When working with a team, it is easier to use cloud storage such as Dropbox. However, make sure that all the documents are anonymized and try to file as few documents as possible to avoid cross-reading identification of interviewees. Consult your institution policy regarding cloud data management. For a paper file, make sure to store it in a different folder from the consent letter which contains the name of the interviewee and his or her file. You will need to ensure that you have a locked storage site and a computer and a hard disk drive with a password.

PUBLICATION OF DATA

It goes without saying that publication is a moment when you must take special care to protect anonymity because portions of the data are then widely available. You must, therefore, alter information about places or people when you use verbatim or observation notes, without depleting the informative value of the data you are using.

CONCERNS AT THE HEART OF RESEARCH RELATIONSHIPS

The implementation of heteroregulatory moral norms – such as those of national laws regarding human security in scientific research and their various interpretations by the REBs – will not ensure the dignity and integrity of the participants if researchers do not engage in self-regulation. By this, we mean their self-reflective capacities exercised in the application of ethical principles during the course of the research. The implementation of these principles is based on knowledge and competence in applied ethics and not just on 'good intentions'.

This knowledge requires that researchers develop their ethical concern: a capacity to understand the values and issues involved and to take action in accordance with them. This ethical concern must focus not only on the aims of the research (questioning discourses and systems of power), but also on process (development, types of questions and their form, flow of questions, etc.) and all the symbolic aspects which come into play in the relationships with participants (Lincoln and Cannella, 2009).

For example, action research and collaborative researchers are analysing the relationship between participants and researchers, deconstructing their epistemological divide (Monceau and Soulière, 2017; Fontan and Heck, 2017). Asking questions such as: Can we work with participants instead of 'on them'? What does it mean for data restitution? Or, how can we mix a diversity of viewpoints (practitioners, scholars, and participants) in a social science knowledge production manner? Even researchers working with documents will have ethical issues regarding the relationship they have with (often passed-away) participants (Perreault and Thifault, 2017). Should we publicly disclose personal archives (medical records, personal letters) of mentally ill women of the early twentieth century knowing that their family will be able to read them?

In the next sections, we will explore some situations in which researchers and apprentice researchers might stumble.

LEAVING THE FIELD

Many ethical concerns have arisen related to the first contact and entry in the field. However, many forget about the importance of the relationship while leaving it. Here, all the rules of politeness apply – and a bit more. When your fieldwork is over, consider the following situations:

- Not only do you want to show your gratitude to your participants for the time they shared with you, but also you wish to test the possibility of conducting other interviews later with some of them. Ask them if they would agree to being contacted by you in the future for other projects (Arborio and Fournier, 1999).

- In the case of ethnography, you also want to know if the people with whom you negotiated your entry into the fieldwork (the gatekeepers) would let you return shortly if the analysis reveals shortcomings. Let them know that you might want to come back and see how they feel about this possibility (Arborio and Fournier, 1999).

- Remember what you asked for and what you promised when you negotiated entry to the fieldwork (Peretz, 1998). Honor your commitments. If you promised or were requested to share or validate your research findings with your participants, determine the best way to do so: a short report to be distributed to all participants, a lengthy report to the head of the organization, a talk by the researcher on the premises, etc. Be ready to commit to an approximate date for delivering on your promises to the gatekeepers if you are doing ethnography.

- Keep in touch with your interviewees, key participants and gatekeepers to inform them of the progress of the research. If you were given permission to publish, as a courtesy send them a copy of your publication.

THE POWER RELATIONSHIP BETWEEN THE RESEARCHER AND THE PARTICIPANT

Sometimes, working with vulnerable people might induce a power relationship between the researcher and the participant. In such a case, the participant might feel an obligation to provide information in order to access certain resources. Here, the relationship would mimic the relationship between a professional and a service user – a type of relationship common in the life stories of some vulnerable people. This is a situation that the researcher must be aware of. It is thus important to clarify all ambiguities regarding the consequences of the research. It is the responsibility of the researcher always to protect the participant from any possible adverse effects that might develop during the study.

In most laws regarding human security in scientific research, the relationship between a researcher and a participant remains a priori asymmetrical. Because of their status, researchers may have power over the participants. Yet the position of victim, which we might consequently associate with the participant (which might be true in a context of experimental research), does not reflect the complexity of research situations in the social sciences.

In some cases, researchers are also used by participants, either for tangible (access to resources) or political ends (to be heard). For example, a student who is interested in the involvement of fathers can easily be co-opted by masculinist groups. The same goes for studies conducted in collaboration with organizations. It would be naive to believe that the researcher is always in a dominant and superior position vis-à-vis the participants.

THE THERAPEUTIC VALUE OF THE BOND BETWEEN RESEARCHER AND INTERVIEWEE

Researchers conducting interviews or participant observations develop very unique relationships with participants. They share a great intimacy with the interviewees and learn a lot about them. As such, they can develop a relationship that is both friendly and professional. It is not unusual for interviewees to feel that their relationships with researchers have a therapeutic value (Birch and Miller, 2000). Interviewers must understand this latent reality in order to avoid any symbolic traps such as creating unrealistic expectations in the participants.

Researchers and students must sensitize themselves to this type of situation. People who are psychologically fragile can feel 'abandoned' or 'betrayed' by a professional who enters into their lives and shows an interest in their problems without offering any support or solutions afterward. In these cases, researchers need to be able to listen while still setting clear limits on the relationships. They must also be able to provide a list of resources like telephone numbers and hotlines that can assist the participants in case of need.

THE SEDUCTION DYNAMIC

At the recruitment stage, some ambiguities may occur between the researchers and the participants. In this phase, the researchers try to persuade people to participate in their research. In attempting to influence, they also sometimes try to seduce. The line between a seductive argument and sexual seduction can often be unclear in the minds of interviewees. It is often crossed in the minds of (male) interviewees, especially when the recruitment phase is being conducted by young women.

For example, a female student recounted that during her research in a working-class neighborhood in Montreal, she had to respond to a declaration of love made by a participant who interpreted her request for an interview as an amorous advance. Indeed, for some men, an interest expressed in organizing a meeting for the purpose of a research interview could be understood as a gesture of romantic interest. For this reason, it is important to clarify the limits of the relationship and even to end the relationship if its nature is not correctly understood by the interviewee. In some situations, an implicit relationship of seduction develops where participants share a lot of themselves as a way to get closer to the researchers. Again, there is an asymmetrical connection that forms where researchers must refrain from exploiting the situation by using their seductive influence to access more information.

REGRETS AND CONSENT

Often, participants will not have had much research interview experience. Indeed, it may be their first such experience. In such situations, participants might reveal more than they would have wanted to. It is, therefore, important to remind the participant, at the end of the interview, that he or she can ask the researcher to remove some information, even though a consent form has been signed.

CHAPTER SUMMARY

In this chapter, you learned how to ensure anonymity and integrity for your research participants. Indeed, you were introduced to the moral foundations of research ethics: the dignity of human beings, the integrity of people and the values of justice. You were also shown how to develop ethical arguments to defend your methodological choices. You learned what an application to your organization's Research Ethics Board looks like. Finally, beyond and above procedural ethics, you were also sensitized to reflect upon the different ethical issues and the complexity of research relationships that you might face during the course of your fieldwork.

Your project checklist

Now that you are more familiar with research ethics and Research Ethics Boards, you can:

✓ Justify the positive consequences of your research project and explain how you will minimize the impact for your participants. Ask a colleague for his or her comments on your rationale.

✓ If you conduct observation or interviews, write a consent form based on your organization template.

✓ Write down the solicitation text for your research if it applies to your project. Identify places where you could post it (Facebook, a clinic, a school, a community center).

✓ If it applies to your project, write down the information you will give to the people you are trying to reach for an interview. Ask a colleague if it could be improved upon.

✓ If you interview people, write down a list of support groups or resources that the participants can contact after their interview if they feel emotionally distressed.

✓ Spot quiet places in your city, university or organization if you need to interview people. The place needs to be secure for you and needs to protect the anonymity of the research participants.

✓ Fill out the REB form and complete the package that you have to send to the REB of your organization if needed.

What you should read next

Aluwihare-Samaranayake, Dilmi. 2012. 'Ethics in Qualitative Research: A View of the Participants' and Researchers' World from a Critical Standpoint'. *International Journal of Qualitative Methods – ARCHIVE* 11(2): 64–81.

• In this article, the author confronts the ethical challenges faced by the participants and the ones lived by the researchers. He presents ethical issues around a photovoice project and research projects with vulnerable people. He raises issues of power and asks ethical questions such as: how do we present our research participants so they do not feel disempowered, oppressed and vulnerable to emotional stress in our writing?

Sanjari, Mahnaz, Fatemeh Bahramnezhad, Fatemeh Khoshnava Fomani, Mahnaz Shoghi and Mohammad Ali Cheraghi. 2014. 'Ethical Challenges of

Researchers in Qualitative Studies: The Necessity to Develop a Specific Guideline'. *Journal of Medical Ethics and History of Medicine* 7: August (www.ncbi.nlm.nih.gov/pmc/articles/PMC4263394/).

- This article is interesting for people doing qualitative research in a health care context. It presents the ethical challenges of research when the researcher is also a practitioner. It goes through many relational challenges that a researcher needs to look at before starting fieldwork.

Website: http://guides.ucsf.edu/c.php?g=100971&p=654838

- University of California San Francisco presents a complete web page on ethical challenges in qualitative inquiries. It suggests blogs, several codes of conduct and an online course.

YouTube: https://www.youtube.com/watch?v=Zbi7nIbAuMQ

- In this presentation, Chris Flipp presents the basics of research ethics. A few slides are dedicated to the Belmont Report, which is a fundamental piece in bioethics.

Want more support and inspiration? The online resources are here to help! Customize your own **consent form template**, get to grips with key terms using **glossary flashcards**, see methods in action with a **library of SAGE cases and journal articles**, and follow analysis step-by-step with full transcripts of the sources discussed in the book.

6
PREPARING FOR ANALYSIS AND VALIDITY REQUIREMENTS

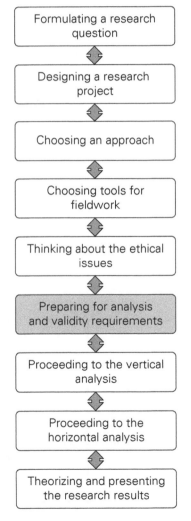

Figure 6.1   Where we are in the research process

IN THIS CHAPTER YOU WILL LEARN:

- To develop a global view of the data analysis phase through the metaphor of the palimpsest.
- To prepare for a three-layer analysis: vertical, horizontal and theoretical analysis.
- To understand that each step of the analytical layer is a condensation of information.
- To understand quality criteria related to each of the analytical layers in order to support the validity of your process.
- To understand the issue of sampling as validity criteria related to the horizontal analysis.

INTRODUCTION

You have received the approval of your research committee to begin your field-work. Here the analysis stage begins. It would be a serious mistake to wait until you have accumulated all of your material before beginning. Each visit to the fieldwork site where material is generated deserves your immediate attention because it will help you to better organize further fieldwork visits and ensure a coherent analysis as the answer to your question evolves. The goal of this chapter is to provide you with an overview of the three stages of the analytic process (vertical, horizontal and theoretical analysis). The subsequent chapters will present an in-depth description of each of these key stages in the analysis.

THE PALIMPSEST AS A METAPHOR FOR PRINCIPLES OF ANALYSIS

The word 'palimpsest' is Greek for 'scraped again'. It refers to manuscripts that had been written on parchment which had already been used. This method, used mainly in the Middle Ages, consisted of rubbing out existing writings on parchment with a pumice stone in order to write over them, thus saving paper and canvas. Archeologists have discovered manuscripts containing hundreds of such overwritten layers through the course of history. The palimpsest thus suggests the idea that a new creation can arise from original materials that had been repeatedly deconstructed and reconstructed.

The image of the palimpsest is used here because it helps us understand how an analysis deriving from original material can then be enriched through layers of readings and rewrites of memos, categories, themes, codes, narratives and field notes during the labor of analysing qualitative data. On that very issue, for many researchers, the rewriting of data is a mode of analysis (Paillé and Mucchielli, 2010). We wanted to present a metaphor and a method of analysis that could be applied to all materials (texts, photos, documents, verbatim interviews, etc.) and to most types of analytic strategies (grounded theory, discourse analysis, narrative analysis, etc.). In order to make our explanations even more precise, we use the idea of strata to identify the highlights of these different layers of writing and rewriting necessary to construct the analysis.

The image of the palimpsest and analysis through strata will guide our explanations throughout the second part of this book. This image is rich because it simultaneously symbolizes the idea of semantic depth and the interdependence of each of the strata. Indeed, the analysis begins with the study of the raw material upon which all of the other strata depend. We can even say that this raw data is built on previous layers of meaning resulting from the literature review and epistemological and theoretical constructions. It consists of the first stage of analysis, which we label **vertical analysis**. It involves interrogating the material in its 'totality', each source being a situated world of meanings. Following this is **horizontal analysis** – an analysis through which we compare the different sources of information. Lastly, **theoretical analysis** – also named as analytic generalisation – represents the final strata, which allows us to link the pertinent ideas we have discovered as well as answer our research question.

It is very difficult to discuss the process of analysis in a theoretical manner. We have made the pedagogical effort to dissect the cognitive process of analysis. This work follows other types of insightful studies regarding the process of analysis done by earlier researchers, especially the works of Glaser and Strauss, Miles and Huberman, and Paillé. Our explanation of the analytical process is certainly part of the approach emphasizing induction that was developed by these researchers.

VERTICAL ANALYSIS: THE FIRST STRATUM OF THE PALIMPSEST

We can illustrate the vertical analysis as the contextualization and synthesis of one piece of the palimpsest layer (Figure 6.2).

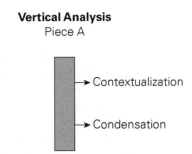

Vertical Analysis
Piece A

→ Contextualization

→ Condensation

Figure 6.2   Vertical analysis

The vertical analysis will focus on two main tasks: (1) the contextualizing condensation that documents the context of the production of the source; and (2) the semantic condensation which focuses on the symbolic content of the source.

The work of qualitative analysis requires first that we condense information that is relevant to our research question. This work includes its share of risk. Indeed, condensing information inevitably results in the dropping of some elements from the initial material. However, the richness of inductive qualitative analysis rests above all on its capacity to comprehend the complexity of a phenomenon.

It comprises one of the criteria of research validity. We therefore need to find the fragile equilibrium between the process of condensing information and that of respecting the richness and complexity of the initial material. This task must be performed methodically and in a spirit of research – that is to say, with a constant effort to question our own reasoning. Here, the rigor and consistency of the researcher will be put to the test. Vertical analysis is the preparation of the material that will guarantee this delicate balance. The condensation of information at the time of the vertical analysis will focus on two main tasks: (1) the contextualizing condensation that documents the context of the production of the source; and (2) the semantic condensation which focuses on meaning, that is to say the symbolic content found throughout the source.

CONTEXTUALIZING CONDENSATION

The first stage of vertical analysis is to read the material many times in order to absorb it. Then, the task of rewriting begins. This allows the researcher to summarize the information to better classify it and take a long look at the context of information production (Richards and Morse, 2012). It is divided into two stages: the identification of material and the documentation of the context of its production.

IDENTIFICATION OF THE MATERIAL

This condensation is purely descriptive. It involves attaching labels or codes to our sources, as we would with jars of jam to identify their contents. The condensation should correspond in some way to the criteria from our face sheet (see Chapter 4). For example, we can give a pseudonym to each of the participants and identify their place of residence, age group, etc.

DOCUMENTATION OF THE CONTEXT OF PRODUCTION

This step consists in using the information in our possession to identify and describe the context of the production of the source. For example, if we analyse an interview, we must be capable, at the stage of the contextualizing condensation, of describing the influence of the interview's context (location, people present, dates, presentation of self to people present) upon the substance and form of the document. Thus, we could describe the influence of a novice interviewer over the course of the interview.

Note that these contextualizing condensation notes become additional material to be analysed in the next stage: the semantic condensation. It is here that the image of the palimpsest assumes its true importance because our own work becomes part of the material to be analysed – another layer that is superimposed upon the raw material that is the talk or the interview.

THE SEMANTIC CONDENSATION

Semantics refers to the study of meanings of words or of signs. When we speak of semantic condensation, we are referring to the operation by which we reduce the material based on the different meanings it assumes in light of our research question. For each source, it is possible to condense the main information that it contains. The first stage of semantic condensation consists of soaking up the material through multiple readings. This 'creative' reading allows us to identify, following the analytic strategy we have adopted, the themes, codes, narratives, discursive repertoires, etc. It also allows us to make connections with readings we have done, to highlight interesting contradictions, to formulate questions. This also adds another layer to our palimpsest because this impressionistic semantic analysis is often very important in constructing a typology for theoretical analysis.

It may also involve identifying the structure of information – how it is presented if it is relevant to our research question or our conceptualization. If we are working with a life-story type of interview, it is important to identify its narrative line. Why does the interviewee begin the interview with one topic rather than another? What is absent from the interview? Each story is a mystery that the researcher must expose. The mystery does not necessarily have to be resolved, but our first obligation is to display that mystery as fairly as possible.

To suggest a parallel, the semantic condensation of a document corresponds to the floating attention of psychoanalysts. In their work, psychoanalysts do not need to focus on each element of the patient's discourse (or on each symptom) but rather direct their attention to the global meaning that they give to the structure or the connections between each of these symptoms. The focus on the structure rather than the content of the source is completely dependent on the analytical strategy that you choose to adopt.

This tension between the content of a document and its context must remain throughout the analysis, especially if you are working with software. Software is very powerful for 'dissecting' and comparing information. However, this exercise can become an obstacle to the validity of the research. Indeed, if the dissection is undertaken too quickly, the researcher can lose perspective regarding the context from which the information emerges. In inductive qualitative research, the contextualization or 'thick description' is the element upon which the scientific value of the analysis rests.

THE QUALITY CRITERIA RELATING TO VERTICAL ANALYSIS

The vertical analysis should be accomplished with two main preoccupations in mind. The first one pertains to the quality of the description of the units of meaning that you will decide upon. The second pertains to the rigor with which you will proceed to the condensation of each source.

QUALITY OF THE DESCRIPTION OF UNITS OF MEANING

Semantic condensation, although rooted in an analytic orientation, should not, however, reproduce the preconceptions of the researcher. The aim is to describe the content and not to evaluate or assess it. Preconceptions consist of theses, ideas or personal experiences that corroborate the document under consideration. Although standardization is impossible, the work of condensation consists of describing the practices of people, the social conditions of phenomena, the context of documents, their content, their structure and not an assessment that researchers might have of the phenomena.

RIGOR OF CONDENSATION

The validity of the research results rests in part on the rigor of condensation – but how to ensure that? First, depending on the analytic strategy adopted, the researcher must be able to give a clear and precise definition of all the categorizations created – whether they take the form of themes, codes or interpretative repertoires. For example, if codes are created, they must be easy to define according to explicit criteria of inclusion or exclusion. Thus, a researcher that works alone will not have any difficulties preserving coherence in the application of these codes. It could be different in the case of teamwork. In this situation, it becomes essential to reach a consensus so that everyone has the same understanding of definitions and tools of condensation.

HORIZONTAL ANALYSIS: THE SECOND STRATUM OF THE PALIMPSEST

In the construction of our palimpsest, horizontal analysis consisted of discovering and managing analytical threads that link documents together – analytical threads connected to our research question. If we return to Figure 6.2, horizontal analysis consists of comparing and differentiating the units of meaning that are present or absent in different documents. Horizontal analysis allows one to identify essential insights for understanding the phenomenon under consideration. More specifically, the diversity of the sample allows one to develop a more complex and nuanced comprehension of the phenomenon, of its analysis and of its explanation.

Horizontal Analysis

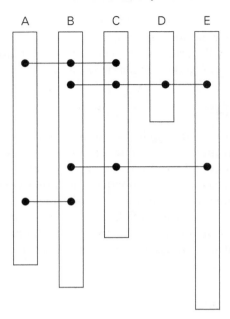

Figure 6.3 Horizontal analysis

In particular, the comparison of the different documents will allow us to answer the following questions: In what sequence does a process take place? In what context does a phenomenon appear? What are the characteristics of argumentation of this or that group? How does such a group of people become privileged? How does the historical and political context affect the phenomenon? What are the conditions of a situation? What are the common cultural characteristics of this group? In what ways are the actions and interactions of people part of some strategy for responding to a conflict? Are cognitive or linguistic resources mobilized by some groups in order to shape a phenomenon?

For example, in an interview-based study about parenting, its definition and its explanation will allow us to describe aspects that are common to situations with parents and their biological children, parents with adopted children, same-sex couples or significant adults who care for a child with unknown parentage. The diversity of the sample thus allows us to understand a phenomenon here: the parenting relationship, based on characteristics that are common to each of the interviews.

In other words, the comparison allows us to compare the social, cultural and symbolic conditions that allow us to understand the phenomenon under consideration. The comparison will probably take us back to the vertical analysis of each document, more precisely to the stage of information condensation, in order to consider the elements that we might have forgotten. As illustrated in Figure 6.3, the horizontal analysis implies the comparison of several sources. The researcher needs to identify common significations. As illustrated in Figure 6.3, a common theme or characteristic can be developed through sources A, B and C and another one through sources B, C and E.

In the work of comparison that is the core of horizontal analysis, it is necessary to understand that the quantity is not important. Indeed, some novice researchers sometimes make the mistake of eliminating a document that differs from others. However, a single document, with a different point of view, will generally allow us to better question our analyses. So we must not make the mistake of constructing an analysis based on the quantity of documents that underpin our ideas. In order to generate rich and accurate interpretations, comparison is essential, but it is important to find a fair balance between the comparison of similar and different cases – such as the next section on sampling suggests.

THE QUALITY CRITERIA RELATING TO HORIZONTAL ANALYSIS

SAMPLING

As in statistical studies, the validity of iterative research depends on the quality of the sampling. As we mentioned in the first chapter, an iterative process does not lead to the creation of statistically generalizable knowledge. This means that it is impossible to generalize our interpretation to an entire population. We must mourn the loss of 'representativeness' that is so dear to the positivist culture. In iterative research, the sample must be strategically constructed – also iteratively – in a way that provides the researcher with a source of information about the subject that has depth and range. These are the conditions that allow the researcher to theorize and theoretically generalize the knowledge produced. Several authors agreed to use the concept of transferability to describe this process of theoretical generalization.

For example, if we do work with homeless people in Paris, we cannot generalize our interpretation to all of the homeless people in France. We can, however, infer comparisons to situations that are empirically similar or develop a concept that allows us to interpret or reinterpret similar situations that would not necessarily apply to the homeless population. One can imagine, for example, that the concept of transitional space developed by Parazelli (2002) in his studies of Montreal's street youth could clarify the analysis of the residential trajectories of immigrants in large Western cities. This concept, deriving from a qualitative analysis, can be transferred to similar processes which demonstrate, among other things, the validity of the research.

Researchers need to develop sampling strategies in order to collect converging information about phenomena as well as a diversification of cases in order to enlighten the complexity of the observed topic. In qualitative studies, we always have **purposive sampling**, which is the opposite of random sampling. We choose people, documents or cases because they can help us to understand our research object. We need to justify this purpose in the methodology section of our report. The next section exemplifies homogenization arguments to support purposive sampling.

THE CRITERIA FOR HOMOGENIZATION

The validity of a theoretical generalization therefore does not depend on a random sampling method. Rather, it depends upon a strategic approach to the creation of empirical material for the study. First, each source (interviews, documents, cases) must be chosen based on its relevance in answering the research question. In the case of people being interviewed, they must be interested in the research topic, they must have the time, as well as an understanding and a profound experience of your topic.

It is necessary to choose sources that are comparable. This principle of homogeneity allows us to deepen our understanding of the phenomenon and answer the various research sub-questions. Sources that are too different will not allow us to achieve theoretical saturation. Theoretical saturation describes the point where the comparison of cases no longer reveals new paths of inquiry for the researchers.

For example, if we are interested in social integration in Denmark and we compare any type of immigrant, whether a political refugee, an economic migrant, immigrants accepted for familial reunification regardless of origin, it is very likely that we will have many difficulties comparing the various interviews. It will be difficult to understand the process of integration. At best, this type of information will allow us to develop some common themes.

The quality of the sample is closely tied to that of the research question. Too broad a question will inevitably lead to problems in determining the sampling criteria. At this stage of the research, the researcher is often going back to the question and reformulating it. It is when starting the fieldwork, producing the material and progressively conducting the analysis that the sampling criteria are likely to change.

THE CRITERIA OF HETEROGENIZATION

It is necessary to diversify the sources based on criteria that are relevant to our research. To diversify, we can base our choice on **stratified sampling, cell sampling, quota sampling** or **theoretical sampling** (Robinson, 2014).

- **Stratified sampling**: The researcher chooses categories he or she would like to compare within a population. They can be based on gender, geography, ethnicity, and the researcher develops a rationale for each of the categories of sampling. The number of interviewees is set in advance for each category.

- **Cell sampling**: The researcher chooses categories (or cells) to diversify the sampling. It is similar to stratified sampling but categories can overlap. The number of interviewees for each cell is set in advance. This strategy was developed by Miles and Huberman (1984).

- **Quota sampling**: This is similar to cell sampling but the number of interviews set in advance is a minimum quota. It gives more liberty to the researcher throughout the recruitment process.

- **Theoretical sampling**: The researcher has no beforehand conceived criteria for the stratification of the sampling. The sampling choices are made during the analytic phase. They depend on the theoretical saturation of analytic categories. This technique was developed by grounded theory researchers (Strauss and Corbin, 1990).

The choice of criteria for sampling will depend on our hypothetical propositions – on the temporary answers to our research questions, the literature review or our field experience. For example, for an inquiry into the transitions of young adults into university, the literature review would very likely lead us to want to compare categories such as gender, social class, type of university program chosen. In the case of ethnography, the same principle applies. Our research question leads us to create an observation grid based on certain criteria which would be comparable depending on the sources that we have chosen, whether they are personal interviews, documents or observations. These different sources should complement each other while possessing some homogeneity. Again, it is necessary to choose the sources while maintaining a difficult balance between heterogeneity and homogeneity.

> Recruitment is a key aspect of research. The validity of your data collection depends on the rigor of your recruitment strategy. If you plan to post recruitment ads, spot places in relation to your sampling strategy. Try to be imaginative because recruitment is always a difficult task. Snowball sampling is always a good option but beware of recruiting people in the same network!

THEORETICAL ANALYSIS: THE THIRD STRATUM OF THE PALIMPSEST

This stratum reflects a higher-order conceptualization based on a constant give and take between the research results of the first two layers of analysis and the literature review created for the development of the research project or protocol (Figure 6.4). We must not think that we stop reading thematic material once the research protocol has been written. In fact, the scholarly material must continue to inform the researcher throughout the iterative phases of the research.

At this stage of the analysis, going back to theories and to the scientific literature will allow for triangulation of the information. This triangulation will allow us to capture original observations made during the fieldwork that were not already empirically documented in the literature. At a more theoretical level, the process of reflection should lead you to confirm certain

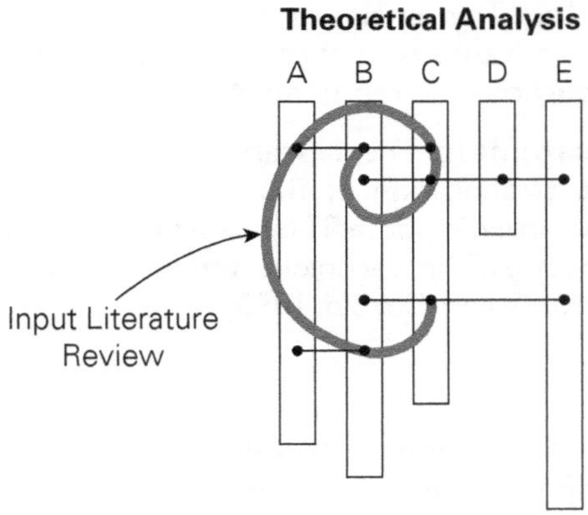

Theoretical Analysis

Figure 6.4   Theoretical analysis

hypothetical propositions (deduction), to highlight some details (induction) and to open other pathways of research (abduction) (see Chapter 1).

> Some students might think that the theoretical stratum is a strategy restricted to grounded theory researchers. This is not the case! Remember that the validity of research depends on its transferability, which is the possibility to theoretically generalize to other phenomena.

It is difficult to discuss such an abstract process without giving a concrete example and the following chapters will be aimed at doing just that. In the next section, we introduce you to a small research. In the following vignette, we present the project from which the material analysed in Chapters 7, 8 and 9 has been produced.

INITIAL PROJECT

Many observers note the disengagement of individuals from many forms of civic participation. Della Porta (2013) identifies four types of participation: electoral participation, participation in public action, protest and social participation. While we observe an increase in participation related to public action, encouraged particularly by the ideology of new public management, the other forms of participation seem to be undergoing profound changes. We see a decrease in the exercise of the right to vote among citizens of all ages and protest movements are increasingly the object of repressive surveillance. Social participation, originally perceived as a form of education and empowerment of the citizenry, is, on the one hand, in decline and, on the other hand, instrumentalized by governments so as to encourage individual responsibility and to empty collective actions of any subversive potential.

In this project, we will study more specifically the various forms of social participation and protest, because the other two forms have already been studied and we would like to focus on those forms that are the least institutionalized. Indeed, they allow more scope for the autonomy of citizens. Therefore, the required commitment stems from the duties connected to political citizenship, but mostly from the sense of engagement people experience vis-à-vis social conversations. The people so engaged invest not just in causes, but also their identities, emotions, and their material, social and symbolic resources.

In this project, we aim to understand the meaning of this social participation for different generations, especially in a world where social scripts multiply and centers of power become polymorphic. The theoretical and empirical objective of the project is to understand how forms of engagement have changed in relation to historical and structural transformations. By analysing these processes as they evolve through social changes, our results might possibly help inform the civic education of young generations. They might help to equip them for, as well as interest and involve them in, collective participation. The results of this project could be integrated into the citizenship curriculums found in primary and secondary schools to inform young people about the power of collective action, to analyse with them the various nodes of ideological and economic power; and arouse in them the desire to participate in collective issues.

CHAPTER SUMMARY

This chapter introduced you to the three layers of our palimpsest, the work of art made of necessary coats that, together, produce the final results. You learned that the first layer is the vertical analysis of each source that encompasses both the contextualizing and semantic condensation. The latter must be accomplished with finesse to ensure the quality of the description of a phenomenon, but also with rigor to ensure the validity of the analysis. We also told you that the second layer of the palimpsest is the horizontal analysis that pertains to the comparison of the results of vertical analysis of many sources. The horizontal analysis brings to the fore the importance of sampling carefully, aiming at a judicious balance between comparable but diverse sources. Finally, we introduced you to the last layer of the palimpsest, the theoretical analysis. This stratum of analysis is essential to ensure that your study goes beyond the mere description of your empirical material and achieves some explanatory power. Each of those layers of analysis will be dealt with in turn in the next three chapters and will be brought to life using the example of a research project on social participation that we briefly presented here.

Your project checklist

Now that you have an overview of qualitative analysis and validity criteria you can:

✓ Decide on a sampling strategy based on homogeneity and heterogeneity criteria. Write a text to explain and justify it to an external reader.

✓ Decide in advance how much snowball recruitment you will tolerate in your procedure. Write out this reflexion and ask a colleague to read it to test your rationale.

✓ Write a reflexive note about the pitfalls of the recruitment techniques you chose. As with the previous item, ask or discuss with a colleague to put your ideas to the test.

✓ Read several methodological articles describing the analytic process of different types of fieldwork. This way, you can get some inspiration for your own project.

✓ Look for free trials of qualitative software on the Internet to familiarize yourself with this tool prior to beginning your data collection. You do not have to work with these packages, but trying them out is a sure way to know whether you need them or not, and in the eventuality that you do, which ones fit you best.

What you should read next

Abrams, Laura S. 2010. 'Sampling "Hard to Reach" Populations in Qualitative Research: The Case of Incarcerated Youth'. *Qualitative Social Work* 9(4): 536-50. doi:10.1177/1473325010367821.

• In this article, the author explains the pitfalls of qualitative research. She focuses on the difficulties of recruiting vulnerable populations such as youth, aboriginals or homeless persons. She offers a reflexive analysis of the different challenges she went through while conducting research on incarcerated youth. She covers REB challenges, phone screening and gatekeepers.

Miles, Matthew B. et al. 2013. *Qualitative Data Analysis: A Sourcebook of New Methods*. Thousand Oaks, CA: Sage.

• This is a classic of qualitative analysis. It contains an extensive index of several techniques of coding strategies. Miles and Huberman are pragmatic researchers. They offer practical examples and strategies in order to pursue a qualitative analysis inspired by grounded theory. This third edition gives new examples of coding strategies from Saldaña.

Tracy, Sarah J. 2010. 'Qualitative Quality: Eight "Big-Tent" Criteria for Excellent Qualitative Research'. *Qualitative Inquiry* 16(10): 837–51. doi: 10.1177/1077800410383121.

- This is a must-read article for any student who needs to understand the common grounds of validity criteria in qualitative research. Tracy lists eight qualities a good qualitative research should respect: worthy topic, rich rigor, sincerity, credibility, resonance, significant contribution, ethical and meaningful coherence.

Yale YouTube Channel: Overview of Qualitative Analysis (https://www.youtube.com/watch?v=opp5tH4uD-w)

- Yale Global Health Leadership Institute offers modules on qualitative research for health care. Module 5 contains very good examples of the iterative process of research while entering into the analysis phase. Leslie Curry gives several examples of coding and presents the importance of qualitative software.

Want more support and inspiration? The online resources are here to help! Get to grips with key terms using **glossary flashcards**, see methods in action with a **library of SAGE cases and journal articles**, and follow analysis step-by-step with full transcripts of the sources discussed in the book.

7

VERTICAL ANALYSIS

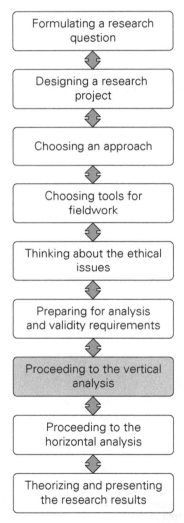

Figure 7.1 Where we are in the research process

IN THIS CHAPTER, YOU WILL LEARN:

* To identify what vertical analysis is and distinguish the analytical steps it entails.
* To proceed to the contextualizing condensation of each of your sources by identifying them and documenting their context of production. An example will be provided from the research project on social participation introduced in the previous chapter.
* To undertake the semantic condensation of each of your sources by using two different analytical strategies: discourse analysis through interpretative repertoires; and a mixed approach inspired by grounded theory and narrative analysis. Here again, we will illustrate the semantic condensation using one source selected from our research project on social participation.

INTRODUCTION

In this chapter, we will illustrate the stages of the vertical analysis we introduced in the previous chapter: contextualizing and semantic condensation. Contextualizing condensation is similar no matter what approach you choose. After showing you how the first stage is done, we will emphasize the second stage, that of semantic condensation, which is the most important and delicate part of vertical analysis. Moreover, since semantic condensation varies a lot depending on the chosen approach (see Chapter 3), we will illustrate this stage by using two approaches: (1) one school of discourse analysis, that is discourse analysis through interpretative repertoires; and (2) a mixed approach inspired by grounded theory and narrative analysis. To demonstrate concretely the stages of vertical analysis, we will analyse one source from the research project on social participation that we described in the last chapter.

CONTEXTUALIZING CONDENSATION

Contextualizing condensation is the first stage of the vertical analysis. As shown in Figure 7.2, it is itself composed of two discrete steps: identifying the material and documenting the context in which this material was produced.

IDENTIFICATION OF THE MATERIAL

In order to use the material you generated in an efficient and ethical way, your first task at the vertical analysis stage is to label it properly and ensure its anonymity. To illustrate how this is done, we will return to the project on social participation and more precisely to one of our sources: the allocution of Michael Parenti, an American writer, on how he became an activist. In the next

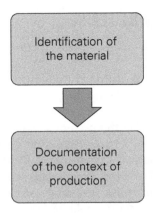

Figure 7.2   The two steps of contextualizing condensation

chapter, you will also be introduced briefly to our analysis of an interview transcript with Jodi, a Canadian communication specialist who is also an activist. You can find both sources on the companion website https://study.sagepub.com/gaudetandrobert.

> To help you follow the remainder of this chapter, we recommend that you pause and take a moment to read Michael Parenti's allocution.

At this stage, the task consists of attaching a code to each of our sources. This code allows us to grasp essential information about our sources and simultaneously assure the anonymity of the participant when necessary. In the case of our research, since it covers two countries with different dynamics and contexts, we need to capture this information. Also, the literature on social participation tells us that gender is a key element to understand people's trajectory of social participation. Therefore, we want our identifying code to capture these two pieces of information. For example, we assign the code USM1 to Parenti's talk. This classification identifies the material as a function of the geographic location of the participant (US for the United States and CAN for Canada) and gender (M for Male and F for Female) – two elements that are key to answer our research question. A Canadian woman would be identified as CANF1. The next identifiers would be USF2, USM2, CANF2, CANM3, etc., based on the number of sources.

DOCUMENTATION OF THE CONTEXT OF PRODUCTION

Once the source is identified, it is time to document its context of production. The goal is to identify the main characteristics of the source and the participant

USM1	Information on the source
	What type of source is it? Where or how was it found or generated? What are the main characteristics of the source: length, recording method, etc.?
	Information on the participant
	Main biographical information Characteristics of his or her social participation
	Our relationship and contact with the participant
	If the source is a document, how was it found and how was the permission of the author obtained to use the document? If the source is an interview, what was noteworthy about the interview, field notes and reflexive notes on the way the interview was conducted?

Figure 7.3 Questionnaire documenting the context of production for the project on social participation

and to reflect on the nature of the source and your rapport with it. To document the context of production of your sources in a systematic way, you can create a questionnaire that you fill out for each of the sources gathered or produced in your project. Figure 7.3 describes the questionnaire we created to document the context of production of our sources for the project on social participation.

When applied to the allocution of Michael Parenti, our source USM1, here is what our completed questionnaire looks like:

• **Information on the source**

'How I Became an Activist' is a 29-minute talk Michael Parenti (1933–) gave at Berkeley in California, United States, on June 6, 2003. The recording of this talk can be found in many locations on the Web. We came across it on the website of Alternative Radio (AR; www.alternativeradio.org), a weekly public affairs radio program that has been offered free to public radio stations in North America and Europe since 1986. The motto of the station is 'Audio Energy for Democracy'. On the website, we can read that 'AR provides information, analyses and views that are frequently ignored or distorted in other media.' Besides Michael Parenti, frequent speakers featured on the show range from Noam Chomsky to Howard Zinn and Angela Davis, to name but a few. AR offers the possibility to listen to the talk online and, for a fee, to download the audio file and the transcript of the conference. We did both.

- **Information on the participant**

As an introduction to the speaker, AR offers this description:

> Michael Parenti is a brilliant orator and one of this country's foremost independent political analysts. He has taught at major colleges and universities in the US and abroad. He is the author of numerous books including *Democracy for the Few*, *The Face of Imperialism* and *The Assassination of Julius Caesar*.

On other websites (e.g. www.radio4all.net/index.php/program/48855), where we also found the recording of the talk, he is presented in similar terms:

> Parenti now is an independent political writer and thinker and author of over 20 books. Invitations to speak come from all over North America. His topics are history, fascism, US Imperialism, globalization and terrorism. His writings have been translated into more than a dozen languages.

The content of the talk itself is summarized in this way:

> Parenti grew up in a poor, working class Italian community in NY City. He received his PhD from Yale in 1962 and was the success of his family. He risked and ended his academic career when he opposed the war on Vietnam. He authored over 20 books. (https://soundcloud.com/user-564548456/michael-parenti-how-i-became-an-activist)

Michael Parenti also has his own website (www.michaelparenti.org/) where more biographic information can be found.

- **Our relationship and contact with the participant**

While we became acquainted with the talk through the AR website, we contacted Parenti directly to inquire as to whether he would allow us to use his conference text for our research. Not only did he agree to our request, but also he insisted on reading the text of his conference over and made some editing changes to it so it would read better. Of course, since he is a public figure who told his story publicly, and, mostly, because we asked him for permission before using the conference text, we are not obliged to hide his name.

SEMANTIC CONDENSATION

In the following pages, we will show you how, concretely, the semantic condensation of Parenti speech unfolds whether we use discourse analysis through interpretative repertoires or a mixed approach inspired by grounded theory and narrative analysis. Each analytical strategy has its own list of steps.

DISCOURSE ANALYSIS THROUGH INTERPRETATIVE REPERTOIRES

As we saw in Chapter 3, discourse analysis is an umbrella term that covers many schools. The following section will summarize the mains tenets of the school we adopt here: discourse analysis through interpretative repertoires. We will then illustrate the four steps of semantic condensation using discourse analysis through interpretative repertoires as applied to Parenti's allocution. Note that in order to devise an operational analysis process specific to discursive analysis through interpretative repertoires, we borrowed from the series of analytical operations laid out by Wetherell and Potter (1986; 1988), Jorgensen and Phillips (2002), McMullen (2011) as well as Gee's (2005) introduction to discourse analysis. With the goal of identifying the ideological or discursive effects produced by words and language, discourse analysis through interpretative repertoires is entirely compatible with a **critical realist epistemology**.

TENETS AND MAIN CONCEPTS

Discourse analysis through interpretative repertoires stands on four conceptual pillars: construction, function, variation and repertoire.

CONSTRUCTION

Discourse analysis through interpretative repertoires conceives of language as a practice and a resource. Language does not reflect or does not aim to reflect entities it speaks of – whether actions, events or thoughts. Rather, people select certain linguistic resources, such as interpretative repertoires, as building blocks to construct their world (Wetherell and Potter, 1988: 172). As researchers, we ask ourselves: what are people doing with words in such and such a particular instance?

FUNCTION

Aside from the concept of construction, the concept of function is also at the heart of this analytical strategy. Function is not to be confused with the intentions of an interlocutor or with the explicit goal stated in a source. It refers mostly to the discursive or ideological effects produced by groups of segments in the material. Here are some of the questions the researchers might have in mind to identify the function of a segment:

- What implicit effects do segments of a speech, an interview transcript or a document achieve?

- Do they participate in justifying actual gendered hierarchies?

- Do they undermine the authority of a received view?

- Do they enforce stereotypes?

- And so on.

VARIATION

Sometimes the function of an utterance is easily identifiable, sometimes not. In either case, 'functions are revealed through the study of variation' (Wetherell and Potter, 1988: 170). Discourse analysis through interpretative repertoires puts forth the idea that individuals produce multiple versions of what they talk about as they communicate. Variability is thus inherent in communication: 'Speakers give shifting, inconsistent and varied pictures of their social worlds' (Wetherell and Potter, 1988: 171). Consciously or not, we often tend to limit the analysis to the recurrent and coherent threads or portions in the material and discount the multiple, alternative, versions (Wilkinson, 2000). However, for discourse analysis through interpretative repertoires, variations are actually used as the analytical tool *par excellence* and a way to find the effects or functions of language in particular instances (Potter, 2012: 440; Wetherell and Potter, 1988: 171).

REPERTOIRE

The focus on variation, however, does not imply that regularities are silenced. The variations bring to light 'relatively internally consistent, bounded language units' that are called **interpretative repertoires** (Wetherell and Potter, 1988: 172). These are often shared by many participants or documents. They are characterized by particular language features such as styles, grammar, semantic networks, metaphors and figures of speech (Reynolds and Wetherell, 2003: 496). It is by mobilizing those interpretative repertoires that people build particular versions of their worlds.

Practically, the semantic condensation of a source using the approach of discursive analysis through interpretative repertoires proceeds in four steps as shown in Figure 7.4.

By following the logic of discourse analysis through interpretative repertoires, these steps will allow you to condense the essential content of each of your sources.

STEP 1 – READING AND QUESTIONING THE MATERIAL

The first analytical step is to read the document or transcription that we produced, several times, with open curiosity. The goal is to get to know the material and also, we suggest, to record:

- your general thoughts on the content of the document;

- the links to concepts and references known to you that might need to be revisited;

- your answers to questions about the factual aspects of the talk; and

- your preliminary thoughts about the formal aspects of the material.

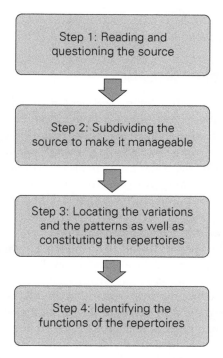

Figure 7.4 The four steps of semantic condensation using discourse analysis through interpretative repertoires

This step serves both to digest the material and to make explicit to yourself what it provokes in your analytical mind.

We read Parenti's speech at least five times. While doing so, we created a document in which we wrote about the four elements noted above. Table 7.1 contains a few excerpts of notes we produced at this first stage.

Table 7.1 Questioning grid for a first reading of the material

1. General thoughts on the content of the document	• 'The place of ethnicity is important in Parenti's cultural map. He emphasizes his Italian origins and the Old World urban village mentality he was raised in. There are a few mentions of associating with Jewish people and being mistaken for a Jewish man. The ethnicity of other characters in his narrative is also mentioned.'
2. Links to concepts and references	• 'The biographical sections of his speech evoke blue-collar masculinity with its respect for fighting and physical endurance to pain. See J.W. Messerschmidt 1993, for more on this issue.'
3. Answers to factual questions	• 'According to Wikipedia, Adlai Stevenson was the Governor of Illinois (1949-1953) and was nominated by the Democratic Party to be its candidate in the Presidential race of 1952.'
4. Preliminary thoughts about the formal aspects of the document	• 'Parenti's speech borrows from the lecture genre, explicitly using an analytical take on his experience (he wants to enlighten and impart knowledge to his audience) and the biopic genre (he displays his personal struggles and successes with relish).'

These four topics are tools to guide reflection on the content of the material and start generating avenues for analysis.

STEP 2 – SUBDIVIDING THE MATERIAL

Especially when faced with a lot of pertinent material, it might need to be subdivided to facilitate the analysis. A document can be divided and coded by topics, themes or narrative styles. This means that all the portions of a document coded under the same code will be gathered together. This step requires that we explicitly define the codes used (inclusion criteria) and apply the codes to the material. As the coding proceeds, the codes' definitions are refined and it might be necessary for the researcher to go back to portions of the document and recode them.

For Parenti's speech, we decided to proceed with codes that reflected a formal feature of the speech. Recall that, in step 1, while exploring the formal aspects of Parenti's speech, we were struck by the different voices that the speaker used to tell his story about how he became an activist. On the one hand, there is a biographical voice that builds the narrative of a kid growing up and becoming an activist. On the other hand, there is an analytical voice, one that reflects and comments on the 'raw' experience. As Figure 7.5 shows, we decided to divide the whole source along those two voices, formulating the hypothesis that segments of talk under each of them would exhibit different interpretative repertoires at work or maybe even become repertoires on their own.

But generally mine was a rather provincial existence. There was a candy store and a handball court and the backyards and the streets. I was a street kid. I hung around in the streets. I learned to fight. There were a lot of fist fights. We used to beat the brains out of each other. We had gangs, but they weren't with switchblades or anything serious usually, although there is a story or two there I could tell, but I don't want to start. It was very much like what Herbert Gans called the urban villagers. Gans did a study of an Italian-American neighborhood in North End Boston. And it's a very interesting theory, which is that in the midst of large, cosmopolitan cities you have these ethnic enclaves that are recreated sort of from the Old World, and where people live in a very kind of clustered way. Everyone knows each other, and if a strange face appeared, one might ask, "Who's that guy? We live on 118th Street. He's from 119th Street. What is he doing there?" You could walk pretty much freely down the streets, unless you were a kid, because there was the other gang who remembered how you beat up their guy. They might want to beat you up.

Experiential

Reflexive

Experiential

Figure 7.5   Example of subdivisions in the original document using experiential and reflexive voices

To do so, we used the qualitative data analysis software QDA Miner, but you can go through this step using your word processor or even a spreadsheet. We created two codes, one that we titled *experiential*, the other *reflexive*. We made sure to define them very clearly and list an example to make the definitions more concrete:

- Experiential voice: Each segment that narrates a state, an action or a course of events was coded under *experiential*. Most of these segments were told from the point of view of an active subject. For example: 'People sometimes say to me – they don't ask, they say – "You were a Red diaper baby, right?".'

- Reflexive voice: Each segment that explains or comments on the narration of a state, an action or a course of event was coded under *reflexive*. In these segments, the narrator is often generic or impersonal and the sentence construction is more often passive. For example: 'Money was a constant problem and a concern, which itself is a political lesson that one kind of learns, in this society, in one's gut really, not that much in your head.'

STEP 3 – LOCATING THE VARIATIONS AND THE PATTERNS AS WELL AS CONSTITUTING THE REPERTOIRES

The heart of this school of discourse analysis requires: (1) delving into the material with minutiae, searching for variations and patterns in order to generate ideas about potential repertoires; and (2) systematizing the definition and identifying the features of those interpretative repertoires. The two tasks accomplished in this step are listed separately for pedagogical reasons but, in practice, they occur simultaneously.

SEARCHING FOR VARIATIONS AND PATTERNS TO GENERATE REPERTOIRES

At this point in the analysis, the task is to read and reread the excerpts to look for variations, patterns and organizing features. This is a lengthy and hesitant process that works by trial and error as well as hunches. While reading the excerpts, the goal is to generate hypotheses for a repertoire and apply these burgeoning repertoires to the material, revising or abandoning them if the material does not back them up.

Recall that, in step 2, we subdivided Parenti's speech using the experiential or reflexive codes according to the voice that each segment expresses. In step 3, we start with all the segments of the speech coded under 'experiential'. We read them several times with the following questions in mind:

- What is Parenti accomplishing here?

- How is he crafting his social participation story?

- What actions is he achieving with his words?

These questions reflect an interest both in the content of the material and in its form. It quickly appeared to us that there are recurrent actions accomplished in these experiential segments. Table 7.2 shows the 12 initial interpretative repertoires that we identified in the experiential segments in Parenti's speech.

Table 7.2 Initial interpretative repertoires generated from the 'experiential' segments

Emphasizing fight or struggle	Discrediting powers
Invoking nature	Objectivizing his identity
Building connections to ethnic groups (racializing)	Claiming exaggeration
Constructing himself as underprivileged	Appealing to religion
Showing resourcefulness	Playing on contrasts
Depicting professionals (namely academics) as phony	Chastising the Right

The 12 repertoires were used as codes to label each 'experiential' segment. A few segments were coded under more than one code. Figure 7.6 shows an example of a segment being coded under two intertwined interpretative repertoires.

> But generally mine was a rather provincial existence. There was a candy store and a handball court and the backyards and the streets. I **was a street kid**. I hung around in the streets. I learned to fight. There were a lot of fist fights. We used to beat the brains out of each other. We had gangs, but they weren't with switchblades or anything serious usually, although there is a story or two there I could tell, but I don't want to start. It was very much like what Herbert Gans called the urban villagers.
>
> Constructing himself as underprivileged
> Emphasizing fight or struggle

Figure 7.6 Example of a double-coded segment where two interpretative repertoires are in play

We then searched and retrieved each segment coded under each of the 12 repertoires; this created a printout of the 7 'experiential' segments from Parenti's speech that were coded under 'Invoking nature' (Figure 7.7) and another printout with the 6 segments that were coded under 'Building connections to ethnic groups' etc.

Coses: [Invoking nature]

CASE: Case#1

> People sometimes say to me-they don't ask, they say – "You were a Red diaper baby, right?" I guess assuming that since I hold so fast to these views I must have got them through my mother's milk. And I say, "No, I'm not Red Diaper."

CASE: Case#2

> We were really poor. Money was a constant problem and a concern, which itself is a political lesson that one kind of learns, in this society, in one's gut really, not that much in your head.

Figure 7.7 Partial list of segments coded under the interpretative repertoire 'Invoking nature'

These segments were then read with one question in mind: does each segment really reflect the interpretative repertoire it is labeled under? This exercise demonstrated that some interpretative repertoires significantly overlapped with others. Therefore, the codes and the excerpts attached to them were merged together. At this stage, it also appeared that some of the interpretative repertoires identified were either rarely mobilized in the speech (e.g. claiming exaggeration) or too nebulous to have any analytical consistency (e.g. playing on contrasts). They were therefore abandoned. We ended up with the 6 repertoires shown in Table 7.3.

Table 7.3   Final interpretative repertoires generated from the 'experiential' segments

Emphasizing fight or struggle	Constructing himself as underprivileged
Invoking nature	Showing resourcefulness
Building connections to ethnic groups (racializing)	Discrediting powers

OPERATIONALLY DESCRIBING THE REPERTOIRES

When the repertoires have taken shape, we can then define them operationally. The goal is to describe the ways in which each repertoire is different from all the others. For example, different repertoires might be used in different sections of the source. Imagine a speech against fracking in a geographic area. It can open and end with a 'call for action repertoire' while the 'appeal to reason and science repertoire' can be found mostly in the body of the speech. There might be inconsistencies between the repertoires or one repertoire might be used as a disclaimer for another. Each repertoire must be defined and its characteristics identified. When proceeding with this characterization, it might become apparent that some rich repertoires present many facets or need to be divided into two different repertoires. In order to generate coherent and solid repertoires, all segments of the material associated with them need to have unity in substance or form and serve the same specific function.

After many trials, and with some hesitancy, we ended up with a definition for each of the 6 interpretative repertoires identified from the analysis of the 'experiential' excerpts in Parenti's allocution. For each one, in addition to a short description, we listed some excerpts belonging to the repertoire and wrote a short analytical memo on the possible functions or effects of the repertoire. You can find the whole list on the companion website https://study.sagepub.com/gaudetandrobert, but for the sake of economy we will show you only one example here.

Repertoire: Showing resourcefulness

Description: The narrative that Parenti builds pertaining to the way he became an activist is a story of effectiveness. It is a narrative of (partial) victories of agency. He is a doer. He gets things done and he has an impact.

Examples of excerpts included in this repertoire:

- 'I, with just three other people, organized the largest peace demonstration in New Haven up to that point. We had William Sloane Coffin speak, to whom I dedicated my first book, by the way. We got Arthur Miller to speak.'

- 'I remember Sandy Levinson saying to me, I went out and spoke at Ohio State, "Well, you know, these things can happen in places like" – he made a very brilliant analysis of why these things happen in places like Michigan, Madison, Berkeley. He said, "It can't happen at Ohio State." And I gave my talk. Four days later Ohio State blew open, and people were out on the streets fighting the cops.'

Analytical memo attached to the repertoire:

- This repertoire is characterized by the use of the first-person pronouns (I, we), active verbs and a tone of enthusiasm. Showing resourcefulness uses the proactive mode and more often than not relates to positive outcomes. It is not much to go on but it seems that this discursive action is given relief by narratives of the negative events that are told using a passive mode. For example: 'It was in Champaign-Urbana where my academic career pretty much ended, because I got beaten up by the police.' This important life event was suffered by him, he was the object rather than the subject of the action; the event is told in a way that downplays Parenti's part in his loss of employment. Losing his job was something that happened to him, not something that he did.

- Moreover, 'Showing resourcefulness' is all the more noteworthy in that the participant emphasizes, elsewhere in the narrative, his humble roots – something we capture in the repertoire 'Constructing himself as underprivileged'. Those two are linked to accomplish the same function of building agency.

So far, we have illustrated the two tasks involved in step 3 using only examples from our analysis of the 'experiential' segments of Parenti's speech. It is important to note that the same tasks were accomplished with the 'reflexive' segments as well (Table 7.4).

Table 7.4   Final interpretative repertoires generated from the 'reflexive' segments

Discrediting powers	
Invoking nature	Already found in 'experiential' segments
Building relations to ethnic groups (racializing)	
Theorizing his experience	
Individualizing/collectivizing	

The result of this step disproved, at least in part, our initial hypothesis that the biographical voice ('experiential') and the analytical voice ('reflexive') would lead to different repertoires. Indeed, many of the excerpts that were coded under 'reflexive' accomplished the same discursive actions as those excerpts coded under 'experiential'. These excerpts were therefore listed together no matter what voice they were initially associated with. The description, excerpts and analytical memos for the repertoire labeled 'Theorizing his experience' and 'Individualizing/collectivizing' can be found on the companion website https://study.sagepub.com/gaudetandrobert.

STEP 4 – IDENTIFYING THE FUNCTIONS OF THE REPERTOIRES

Variations and patterns are the pathways to identifying repertoires. But the vertical analysis does not stop there. The end goal of discursive analysis through interpretative repertoires is to reflect on the functions or effects produced by the mobilized repertoires. Hence, the final step of the vertical analysis of each document requires forming hypotheses about the discursive functions performed or social effects produced, at the local or societal level, by the repertoires. It is about systematizing our previous work. Indeed, in step 3, through our analytical memos attached to each repertoire, we began to single out the tentative functions that we associate with each repertoire generated from Parenti's speech. Table 7.5 synthesizes the reflections in the analytical memos produced during step 3.

From our analytical memos, it is clear that the functions accomplished by each repertoire are not disconnected from each other. Together, they produce cumulative and contrasting effects. Hence, it is worth thinking about the configurations of those repertoires and distinguishing what broader or compounded effects they might have. Like a puzzle for which there is no given final picture, this task proceeds by trial and error. Table 7.6 illustrates the three main functions or effects that we generated by comparing and linking the interpretative repertoires found in Parenti's speech that shared commonalities.

Many repertoires combine to establish a version of authenticity in activism and authenticity as a value in itself for activism. In this specific case, an authentic activist has personally experienced injustice and has been fundamentally shaped by this experience. The authentic activist shares bonds with other people who have experienced similar injustices. Contrary to people who put on a façade of being concerned with issues of justice, an authentic activist is deeply committed to fighting for justice despite the suffering it brings. Establishing a version or a degree of authenticity in activism might serve as a mechanism to sift the wheat from the chaff, or at least to make allies and identify people upon whom a cause can truly depend, the people who have a vocation, the pure, real, essential justice advocate.

While no repertoire in itself explicitly points to this effect, some of the repertoires weaved into the speech under study collectively lead to recognizing the benefits of liminality for activism, at least when one works for greater justice between people. The narrative bridges the working class and the Ivy League; the

Table 7.5 Final interpretative repertoires and their tentative functions generated from Parenti's speech

Emphasizing fight or struggle: The dichotomy *us versus them* found in this repertoire polarizes the narrative and builds social participation into an antagonist activity The emphasis on fight or struggle (physical and political) creates a biographically coherent line. Telling his story using the war repertoire gives his involvement seriousness, gravitas. He puts himself at risk for his beliefs. He is a true and persistent fighter	**Showing resourcefulness:** This repertoire is all the more noteworthy in that the participant constructs himself as underprivileged, as another repertoire testifies. Those two are linked to accomplish the same function of building agency
Invoking nature: The interspersed references to nature instil a feeling of genuineness, truthfulness and, we would venture, confidence, toward the interlocutor	**Discrediting powers:** This repertoire acts in tandem with previous repertoires, namely 'Invoking nature' and 'Constructing himself as underprivileged.' The latter two naturalize the justice-seeker vocation of the participant; they construct his authenticity. Along this line, depicting the powers as deceiving contributes to establishing a fundamental dichotomy in his narrative between the genuine and the pretend
Building connections to ethnic groups (racializing): Connections built to ethnic groups serve to appropriate the characteristics the interlocutor associates with them. The references to the Italian-Americans and the Latinos evoke images of hard-working immigrants, working-class solidarity and sensitivity of marginalized ethnic groups to unfairness or abuse of others. Reference to Jewish people serves to appropriate what the participant sees as political awareness and intelligence	**Theorizing experience:** References to social science concepts have the effect of connecting to his audience and lending credibility to his analysis of the situation of injustice in America and to his actions as an activist. It is also a testimony to the wide breadth of the world he inhabits: the ghetto and the ivory tower
Constructing himself as underprivileged: Putting forth the financial hardship and cultural deprivation that marked his early life contributes to branding him with the seal of authenticity: he suffered the economic inequalities he is now fighting and was affected by their very material and cultural consequences. In the same breath, emphasizing his humble origins has the effect of making his trajectory and achievements even more remarkable	**Individualizing/collectivizing:** Anchoring social change in individual consciousness and actions allows for the distribution of blame and worthiness. Some characters are praised, others are criticized. Playing on the continuum of individualization and collectivization reconciles the possibilities of making specific people into heroes while still acknowledging the force of the masses and of history

Table 7.6 Three effects generated by configurations of repertoires in Parenti's speech

Effect 1	Repertoires producing effect 1	Effect 2	Repertoires producing effect 2	Effect 3	Repertoires producing effect 3
Establishing a version of authenticity in activism	Constructing himself as underprivileged Invoking nature Emphasizing fight or struggle Building connections to ethnic groups (racializing) Discrediting powers	Constituting liminality as a tool for activism	Constructing himself as underprivileged Building connections to ethnic groups (racializing) Showing resourcefulness Theorizing his experience	Crystallizing the primacy of agency for social change	Showing resourcefulness Individualizing/collectivizing

Italian, Afro-American, Latino and Jewish communities; the arts world and the boxing gym. There is a unifying power in being a 'street kid' who quotes Gramsci. Navigating different segments of society is more than a feat in itself, it is a work tool. Laboring for justice requires liminal character that acts as a translator between separate worlds.

Finally, the function of the repertoire 'Individualizing/collectivizing' is reinforced by that of another repertoire, 'Showing resourcefulness'. Both repertoires work at instilling a reading of social change that is premised on individual actions that add up as collective actions. Both repertoires reproduce the primacy of the individual. We can even wonder whether the acknowledgment of collective power (e.g. there are no self-made people and each individual owes to the previous generations) serves as a disclaimer to the power of the individual agent.

The interrelated eight repertoires as well as the three configurations of repertoires identified in Parenti's speech are just stepping stones leading toward the final results of our research. They are unlikely to appear, as is, in the final research report. Indeed, they will evolve as the semantic condensation of the next source (and the next, and the next) progresses and as the horizontal analysis is performed (Figure 7.8).

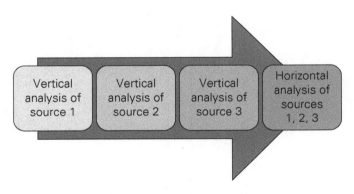

Figure 7.8   The dynamic between vertical and horizontal analysis

MIXED APPROACH INSPIRED BY GROUNDED THEORY AND NARRATIVE ANALYSIS

In their daily reality, most researchers construct their analytical strategies based on several approaches. The example of vertical analysis presented here shows how the analysis is tweaked based on field experience, readings and the epistemological perspective of the researcher as well as the contribution of two qualitative approaches.

Our example uses the coding techniques of Glaser and Strauss (1967), the founders of grounded theory, but the epistemological position is based more on the interpretation of Charmaz (2014), who adapted grounded theory. Epistemologically, it is situated in the constructionist stream, which is to say that social reality is thought to be partially constructed. This explains why subjective and historical chronologies are given equal weighting within an analysis.

The construction of the analytical approach rests on three components:

- the subjectivity of the actor;

- the narrativization process; and

- the socio-historic process within which the individual's trajectory occurs.

We are inspired by three conceptual frameworks: the socio-anthropological approach to life stories (Bertaux, 2010); narrative analysis (Demazière and Dubar, 1996) and the life-trajectory approach (Charbonneau, 2003). Thus, the socio-anthropological narrative analysis guides us in understanding the subjectivization process: how, through reflexivity, do people constitute themselves as social actors?

Obviously, language is very important, because we analyse the stories told by people. The way people craft their stories must therefore be approached as one having a hero, a plot, adventures and an ending. Finally, since we are interested in social processes that guide the trajectories of people's lives, the life-trajectory approach helps us to analyse the various temporalities (social, personal, professional) at different levels (micro, meso and macro). Power relationships are thus analysed in terms of an inter-scalar perspective.

Vertical analysis, especially semantic condensation, is crucial when analysing life stories because it is necessary to consider the source in its totality. An approach that is based only on grounded theory and coding would make the narrative thread disappear. In the coming pages we will illustrate the three steps of our strategy, mixing grounded theory and narrative analysis as illustrated in Figure 7.9.

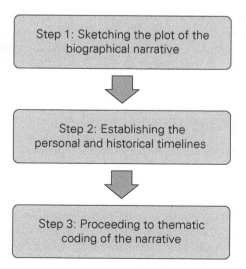

Figure 7.9 The three steps of semantic condensation using a mixed approach of grounded theory and narrative analysis

STEP 1 – SKETCHING THE PLOT OF THE BIOGRAPHICAL NARRATIVE

After reading Parenti's speech, we tried to identify the plot of his story. Each person presents themselves as the hero of their own life. The biographical narrative exposes us to the subject's reality and agency. As researchers, we do not try to determine whether his story is 'true' or 'false'. Focus is put on one's perception of one's life. Sometimes, the narrative might contradict other types of information. It has been said that documents or other types of data can help to triangulate information and the researcher needs to be aware of it. However, inconsistent elements will not change reality as it is perceived by the participant. This rewriting of Parenti's story leads us to identify themes such as group identification or the ambiguity of belonging.

> This document unfolds chronologically. Because of the format of the speech – an autobiography – there are few differences between the subjective time and the chronological time. However, people narrating their own histories around a specific topic will not necessarily start with chronological time. This is when the 'performance' of narration needs to be considered. For example, if an activist presents his or her story by explaining his first participation in a riot, this event might be a key element of his narration. It needs to be considered.

We always give a 'metaphoric' name to the participant, because the participant is the 'hero' of the story. In sociology, metaphors have great importance. They help to change the level of analysis, to move from the particular to the general (Busino, 2003). Weber's ideal types are complex metaphors. In this example, we would call Parenti the Idealistic Vagabond. First, we relate his narrative to a vagrant because Parenti has no mooring – no social identity to refer to as a social foundation. His story is about mobility: social mobility and professional nomadism.

CHARACTERISTICS OF THE 'HERO' AND THE PLOT

The Idealistic Vagabond

- **Group identification**

Events structuring Parenti's life relate to the experience of group identity. He talks about his belonging to a low-income, working-class, Italian American family but he does not identify himself with the low education of his family's environment. At the beginning of the speech, he talks about his experience at about 7–8 years old when he went to school with Bronx kids, 'very nice

Jew kids'. Later in the text, he comes back to this group identity. He talks about progressive Jews with whom people have mistaken him. He says, 'it's maybe because I read books and I write'. It is as though he identifies the intellectual sphere of his life with the Jewish identity. In other parts of his narration, he identifies with academia, the black community, the working class.

• **Ambiguity of belonging**

We would characterize the process of group identification as the intrigue of Parenti's narrative, and, moreover, we would qualify it as ambiguous. Throughout the text, Parenti talks about the notion of belonging. He starts his narrative by explaining that he used to belong to a section of 118th Street. Through all his fights, he shares his ambiguity about belonging. Moreover, this ambiguity is experienced as a duality: it's more about 'me' and 'them', than 'us' and 'them'.

• **Adventures: the fights**

Later, he talks about his battle for racial equality. He knew few African Americans – he did not belong to them, but he was part of the battle. The African American battle was part of the students' protests and the counterculture of the 1960s in the United States.

The other important stage of the story is about his fight in the academic world. He explains how he became disillusioned by academia. He thought he was part of this world. He completed his PhD, had a professor's position that could lead to a tenured job, had a rigorous work ethic. However, he discovered many discrepancies between what scholars said and did, or what they did not do to protect freedom of speech related to student activism.

• **The enemy: the system**

One of his main efforts was to explain how inequalities were created by a system. He discovered that his activism was related to Marxist claims. He wrote more than 20 books on activism, inequalities, class struggles.

• **Authentic self of the public intellectual**

Even though he felt excluded from academia, he worked as a 'public intellectual' presenting at conferences and writing papers. He explains how, with age, he became less radical. However, he struggled for his ideal of justice and equality. He never accepted being an instrument of the system in the way that many of his colleagues in academia did. That is why he is still perceived by the academic community as a radical.

STEP 2 – TIMELINES

Information regarding the context of production has been presented in the contextual condensation earlier in this chapter. We present here the elements of context we considered important in our analysis using a mix of grounded theory and narrative analysis.

LIFE CHRONOLOGY

The first step was to condense the information concerning 'objective' time, that is to say chronological time. We highlighted the key events in Parenti's life trajectory with particular attention to its path of social engagement since it is our main research goal. Using NVivo for the qualitative software analysis, we created nodes related to his biography (Figure 7.10). Because we are using a document and not an interview, information is missing. We identified important life events knowing that we would be completing information (dates) with other types of documents over time.

Figure 7.10   The life chronology of the participant

HISTORICAL TIMELINE

Because his activism trajectory is embedded in US social and political history, we added another timeline, this one related to socio-political history (Figure 7.11). In other research, we do not necessarily develop this type of timeline. But if we do, it is specific to the research topic. For example, we might build an 'organization' timeline or a 'public policy–labour law' timeline to create the history of a factory if we focus on the working experiences of low-wage earners in a specific area.

To better appreciate the context of the participant, we generally create three chronological timelines respecting three levels of analysis: micro (the level of individual experience), meso (the level of group and institutional experience) and macro (the socio-political and historic levels). In Parenti's speech, we focus on the micro and the macro, but we could have created a meso timeline analysis based on his participation in different organizations. The actual data did not give us the opportunity to do so.

Figure 7.11 The historical timeline of the participant's life story

STEP 3 – THEMATIC CODING

The last phase of the semantic condensation using the mixed approach of grounded theory and narrative analysis is directly inspired from grounded analysis. It first requires a layer of open condensation followed by a layer of directed condensation.

OPEN CONDENSATION

We created codes related to our first readings of the material and the sketching of the narrative. As shown in Figure 7.12, the node '1st categorization'

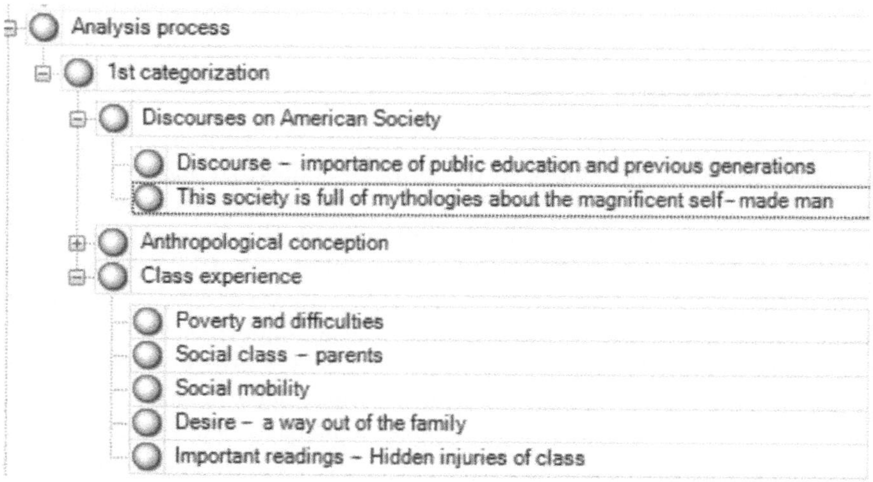

Figure 7.12 Excerpt from the open coding tree

contains all the codes we created during the semantic condensation. It shows the example of three open codes (i.e. codes created from inductive reading): Anthropological conception, Class experience, Discourses on American society. The node 'Class experiences' first emerged from the parts of the text where Parenti tells us about middle-class kids making fun of his accent. We also have an open code related to an illustration of his parents' social class habitus.

DIRECTED CONDENSATION

As mentioned earlier in the book (see Chapter 6), directed semantic condensation is related to a deductive process. As researchers working inductively, we slowly develop hypotheses and we need specific information to make sense of them.

For example, in the case of social participation, we had the hypothesis that organizations are vectors of social engagement. We then needed to code 'organization' for each group, institution, political party, and so forth, which Parenti brings up in his speech. This way, we create as many codes (under 'organization'; Figure 7.13) as there are organizations mentioned in Parenti's speech.

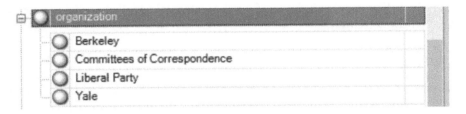

Figure 7.13   Excerpt from the directed coding tree

CHAPTER SUMMARY

This chapter taught you what the vertical analysis of each source entails. More precisely, you were introduced to the work of contextual and semantic condensation. While the former consists of identifying each source and documenting its context of production, the second pertains to diving into the content of the source. Two examples of semantic condensation were presented. The first one showed you, step by step, how to proceed to semantic condensation if you use discourse analysis through interpretative repertoires. The second one showed you how to proceed to the semantic condensation using our own mixed approach informed by grounded theory and narrative analysis. We also illustrated each of those steps using one source from our research project on social participation: the allocution of Michael Parenti on how he became an activist.

Your project checklist

Now that you are more familiar with the whole process of vertical analysis, you can:

✓ Go back to the readings you did on your chosen approach in order to see whether the analytical steps are laid out to accomplish the vertical analysis of each source.

✓ Perhaps consider other examples. Find additional methodological texts that illustrate the application of your chosen approach, starting with the list below as well as the references we introduced you to in Chapter 3 on the different qualitative approaches. This might be necessary to complement the texts you are already familiar with if they are not explicit enough as to the details of analysis. Indeed, some texts will explain the history and philosophy of an approach very well but will not be explicit as to the 'how' of the empirical analysis. You need to have a few good examples of texts that illustrate the application of your chosen approach(es) to empirical material.

✓ Adopt or create from the previous readings and examples a list of steps necessary to proceed to the contextual and semantic condensation of each source gathered or produced for your research project. Take time to define each step as if you were explaining it to somebody else. This will not only help you during your analysis, but also help you when writing the method section of your research protocol or your research report.

✓ Finally, take the plunge. Choose an empirical source from your material and open it up using the steps you listed earlier. The goal at this point is both to complete the vertical analysis of your first source and to tweak the way you go about doing the contextualizing and semantic condensation of your source. You want to make sure that you can learn from that first experience so as to facilitate, render explicit and systematize the vertical analysis of your second source and all the rest of them.

What you should read next

Butler-Kisber, Lynn. 2010. 'Phenomenological Inquiry', pp. 50–61 in *Qualitative Inquiry: Thematic, Narrative and Arts-Informed Perspectives*, ed. L. Butler-Kisber. Thousand Oaks, CA: Sage.

• If you are interested in the phenomenological approach, this book chapter explains and illustrates deftly the process one has to go through to accomplish the vertical analysis in phenomenology.

Kohler Riessman, Catherine. 1993. 'Practical Models', pp. 25–53 in *Narrative Analysis*, ed. C. Kohler Riessman. Newbury Park, CA: Sage.

- In this chapter of this very good and succinct book, Catherine Kohler Riessman illustrates three ways to proceed to the vertical analysis following the precepts of different schools of narrative analysis. This comparative chapter is very informative for those inclined toward narrative analysis. The three examples are published studies and can be read on their own for more details.

McMullen, Linda M. 2011. 'A Discursive Analysis of Teresa's Protocol: Enhancing Oneself, Diminishing Others', pp. 205–223 in *Five Ways of Doing Qualitative Analysis: Phenomenological Psychology, Grounded Theory, Discourse Analysis, Narrative Research, and Intuitive Inquiry*, ed. F. J. Wertz et al. New York: Guilford Press.

- In this book chapter, Linda McMullen takes the reader by the hand and shows how she proceeds to accomplish the vertical analysis of an interview.

Saldaña, Johnny. 2009. *The Coding Manual for Qualitative Researchers*. Thousand Oaks, CA: Sage.

- Without necessarily going all the way and following the whole process of grounded theory, many researchers analyse their material using a tool we owe to grounded theorists: coding. In this book, Johnny Saldaña will introduce you to all kinds of codes, and show you how to define and apply them. It is a great book to generate coding ideas for your own research.

Spector-Mersel, Gabriela. 2011. 'Mechanisms of Selection in Claiming Narrative Identities: A Model for Interpreting Narratives'. *Qualitative Inquiry* 17(2): 172–85.

- In this journal article, Gabriela Spector-Mersel explains a method to analyse biographical narrative. She applies it to an interview step by step.

Thai, Mai Thi Thanh, Li Choy Chong and Narendra M. Agrawal. 2012. 'Straussian Grounded-Theory Method: An Illustration'. The *Qualitative Report* 17(Art. 52): 1–55.

- This article illustrates in a meticulous way the application of grounded theory. The annexes attached to the article are especially enlightening.

8

HORIZONTAL ANALYSIS

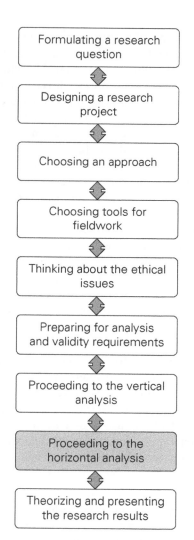

Figure 8.1   Where we are in the research process

IN THIS CHAPTER, YOU WILL LEARN:

- To define and distinguish horizontal from vertical analysis.
- To proceed to the horizontal analysis of several sources using two different analytical strategies: discourse analysis through interpretative repertoires and a mixed approach inspired by grounded theory and narrative analysis. An example will be provided from the research project on social participation introduced in the two previous chapters.

INTRODUCTION

In this chapter, we will illustrate how to proceed with the second layer of the palimpsest. The previous chapter was dedicated to the vertical analysis of each source, one at a time. We now explore ways to tackle all of the empirical material generated or gathered for a particular project. It is called the horizontal analysis: that is, the comparison of the vertical analysis of each of the sources between themselves in order to generate an iterative interpretation of the whole material. This process could rightly be called transversal semantic condensation of your empirical material. Indeed, you will see that it captures many of the analytical steps that you were introduced to during the semantic condensation part of the vertical analysis. We will continue the work started in the previous chapter and demonstrate horizontal analysis using the same two analytical strategies: (1) discourse analysis through interpretative repertoires; and (2) a mixed approach inspired by grounded theory and narrative analysis. We will also continue to illustrate the horizontal analysis by using sources from the social participation research that we used earlier (see Chapters 6 and 7). Recall that the impetus of this project is that, in a context of general disengagement from civic life experienced in many Western countries, we want to understand the meaning of social participation. Hence, we targeted North American participants from different generations who were significantly involved in their communities in different decades (from the 1960s onward). Since horizontal analysis requires comparing many sources, beyond the allocution of Parenti used in the previous chapter, we will refer to speeches and interviews conducted with other participants. In the section pertaining to discourse analysis through interpretative repertoires, we will work from the transcript of an interview conducted with Jodi, a communication specialist who is also an activist. In the section pertaining to the mixed approach inspired by grounded theory and narrative analysis, we will use the material produced with two other participants in addition to Parenti and Jodi.

> To help you follow this chapter, we recommend that you pause and take a moment to read the interview with Jodi on the companion website https://study.sagepub.com/gaudetandrobert.

As the horizontal analysis proceeds, you will notice that the initial research question becomes more present in the mind of the researcher. It is by systematically comparing the vertical analysis of each source and abstracting from the specific and individual patterns that we uncover in the material that we can slowly generate an answer to our question. However, in the type of iterative research process that we suggest here, the initial research question might very well need to be tweaked and rewritten to do justice to the analysis of the material. Coherence and flexibility are key.

HORIZONTAL ANALYSIS USING DISCOURSE ANALYSIS THROUGH INTERPRETATIVE REPERTOIRES

Going from vertical analysis to horizontal analysis requires switching mindset. Rather than uncovering the specificities of each source and appreciating the discursive effects that they each perform, it is now time to take a step back and look at your sources as a collective. As a whole, what do they accomplish? What kind of world do they create? What topic do they bring to life and how?

To develop this broader picture and proceed to the horizontal analysis, discourse analysis through interpretative repertoires requires us to take four steps, as shown in Figure 8.2.

As we said earlier, to illustrate these four steps we will use Parenti's allocution as well as an interview with a Canadian communication specialist we will call Jodi. This middle-aged woman is an experienced activist involved in politics and women's rights issues. She was raised in an immigrant family.

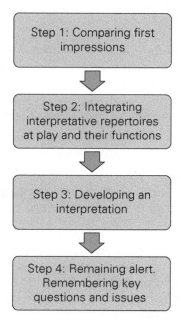

Figure 8.2 The four steps of horizontal analysis using discourse analysis through interpretative repertoires

STEP 1 – COMPARING FIRST IMPRESSIONS

The comparison between the results of the vertical analysis of each document requires the creation of a grid to record our 'notes to ourselves'. You might remember the table we created as part of the vertical analysis of each source and called a questioning grid for a first reading of the material (see Table 7.1). Very similar to this grid, the new grid we recommend you create is organized around three topics. It is depicted in Table 8.1.

Table 8.1   Questioning grid for comparing first impressions of the sources

1. General thoughts from comparing the content of the sources: What do they have in common? What distinguishes them?	•
2. Links to concepts and references: As a whole, what concepts, theories and specific references do they echo, question, call upon?	•
3. Preliminary thoughts about the formal aspects of the sources: What do they have in common? What distinguishes them?	•

This grid serves as an important work tool to make decisions about the next stages of material production and analysis.

> Remember that we suggest you intersperse periods dedicated to producing or gathering your material with periods dedicated to analysing it. Doing so will allow your material and analysis to guide you for the next round. This iterative process will strengthen the internal coherence of your research and results.

The comparative questioning grid is also a document where interpretative thoughts and lines of inquiries are very likely to emerge. These are precious and will be used and developed in the theorizing phase of the analysis. Here are some excerpts of the notes we jotted down when comparing our impressions from Parenti's speech and Jodi's interview after the vertical analysis of each one was completed:

(a) General thoughts from comparing the content of the sources

- 'One of the organizing categories in Jodi's interview is that of paid/unpaid activism and eventually "free" time. She explains feeling an urgency to go back to her own writing and music. She cannot be lost in her work anymore. It seems that, contrary to Parenti, she actively works at defining a space for herself outside her paid/unpaid activism, something that was not present in the speech of Parenti, who seems content with having "activist" as his main status. Three lines of questioning follow that observation: 1) Would it be useful to distinguish participants along a continuum of involvement? Possibly even rework the sampling for the next phase of material production?

2) Is this rapport to self and time a gendered issue? Could it be that some women segment their lives more clearly, that the public/private division is a key defining category of self, whereas men more readily define themselves primarily through the public aspect of their lives? 3) Is this observation the product of the type of material?'

- 'Both Parenti and Jodi have a critical perspective on social change. While Parenti's seems closer to orthodox critical theory where gender power is often silenced, Jodi is more influenced by critical feminist theories. This comparison brings up two avenues for the next material production phase: 1) We should make sure to have, in our sample, speech and interviews from people from a more conservative political persuasion as well as from people who are not explicitly politicized. Ensuring that we can compare understandings of social participation among politicized people, both left and right, and other less politicized people would allow us to abstract commonalities related to social participation in general, not just explicit political social participation of left wing activists. 2) ...'

(b) Links to concepts and references

- 'The comparison between Parenti's speech and Jodi's interview brings up the possible benefit of going back to Goffman's work on status and, more generally, identity theories. Being an activist seems, in part at least, to be related to definition of self and performance of self.'

(c) Thoughts about the formal aspects of the sources

- 'Despite being thought out and written in advance, Parenti's speech is a performance and a dialogue tailored for an expected audience and a live audience (as we saw when he is interacting with attendants). As Jodi's interview shows us, an interview conducted in private is also a performance and a dialogue. Here are some very explicit quotes from Jodi's interview that illustrate what we mean:

  o Interviewer: And you said you had three women. Were there some men in your ... Jodi: Yeah, I know. It's funny. Like, when I said "women", I thought, "Oh, she's going to pick up on that."
  o So I would say people call, instead of friends call. And I don't mean to correct your wording. But, like, people call me a lot.

Jodi is aware of being on the spot; she is aware of provoking reactions in the interviewer. For example, she makes a disclaimer to manage her projected identity. In this sense, an interview is really a performance for an audience, like a speech. There is this sensitivity to being coherent with her politics in the way she speaks about all aspects of her life. Maybe it is an effect of her strength in communication, her interest for writing and her sensitivity to words? However, both types of material (speech and interview) partake of the same nature: both are producing a representation of self. It therefore seems legitimate to continue with a mixed corpus of speeches and interviews.'

These general thoughts are a source of methodological notes, those with implications for the rest of the fieldwork and the write-up of the methods section of the final report. They are also a source of analytical notes, those that are likely to be revisited as avenues to document, or discard, as the theorization builds up.

STEP 2 – INTEGRATING THE INTERPRETATIVE REPERTOIRES AT PLAY AND THEIR FUNCTIONS

The vertical analysis of the two sources (Parenti's speech and Jodi's interview) was conducted completely independently. While the vertical analysis of Jodi's interview was occurring, no attempt was made to homogenize the repertoires found in this source with those found in Parenti's speech earlier. Table 8.2 lists, side by side, in no particular order, the repertoires for each participant and their tentative functions.

At the horizontal analysis stage, the task is to compare, fuse, rename, redefine the interpretative repertoires. It is about merging different sources into one. This task involves both rationalizing and refining the results produced in the vertical analysis of each source. This comparative work has to be remade anew after each source has been through the vertical analysis phase. It is to be expected that there will not be a perfect match between the repertoires of one source and the repertoires of another. In fact, it is often far from the case, as shown in Table 8.2. However, little by little, as the horizontal analysis progresses with additional sources, clusters of repertoires will emerge as key to integrating the material. Of course, other repertoires will remain on the periphery. A perfect integration of the repertoires from all the sources into a neat bundle would likely be artificial, constrained, and do violence to the thickness and idiosyncrasies of each source, as well as the inductive process itself.

By comparing the two sources we have vertically analysed so far and displayed in Table 8.2, we can see a series of parallel repertoires:

- Both participants connect their social participation to the marginality they experienced at some point in their life or the marginality they still experience (Parenti: 'Constructing himself as underprivileged'; Jodi: 'Building experiential legitimacy'; 'Distinguishing between activism and volunteering'). From these accounts, social participation is not like any other activity; one does not get into social participation on the basis of pure interest. Social participation is made here into the organic product of experienced injustice. Not only does this repertoire build a sense of genuineness in social participation, but it also marks the participants as resilient, if not heroic. It also likely serves as the basis to distinguish activism from volunteering. On the same note, these corresponding repertoires in Parenti's and Jodi's

Table 8.2 List of Parenti's and Jodi's repertoires and their tentative functions

Parenti's repertoires: definition and tentative functions	Jodi's repertoires: definition and tentative functions
Emphasizing fight or struggle: The dichotomy *us versus them* found in this repertoire polarizes the narrative and builds social participation into an antagonist activity The emphasis on fight or struggle (physical and political) creates a biographically coherent line. Telling his story using the war repertoire gives his involvement seriousness, gravitas. He puts himself at risk for his beliefs. He is a true and persistent fighter **Building connections to ethnic groups (racializing):** Connections built with ethnic groups serve to appropriate the characteristics the interlocutor associates with them. The references to the Italian Americans and the Latinos evoke images of hard-working immigrants, working-class solidarity and sensitivity of marginalized ethnic groups to unfairness or abuse of others. Reference to Jewish people serves to appropriate what the participant see as political awareness and intelligence **Constructing himself as underprivileged:** Putting forth the financial hardship and cultural deprivation that marked his early life contributes to branding him with the seal of authenticity: he suffered the economic inequalities he is now fighting and was affected by its very material and cultural consequences. In the same breath, emphasizing his humble origins has the effect of making his trajectory and achievements even more remarkable **Individualizing/collectivizing:** Anchoring social change in individual consciousness and actions allows for the distribution of blame and worthiness. Some characters are praised, others are criticized. Playing on the continuum of individualization and collectivization reconciles the possibilities of making specific people into heroes while still acknowledging the force of the masses and of history	**Distinguishing the 'center' from the 'ground':** This repertoire is couched in terms of an opposition between the site of power and the site of power effects. This dichotomy between the top and the ground reinforces the idea that power (or, at least, decisions) is concentrated in a specific place, a possession in the hands of a few, and suffered by people on the ground. It reinforces the idea that the center is disconnected, separated from the base. But the same repertoire also resists this idea by underlining the interest and importance of being involved on the ground, counterbalancing the power (at the top) **Building connectedness about social problems:** This repertoire links social problems (women's issues, racism, student movement, labor issues, environmentalism, human rights and poverty) together. Their distinct character is only superficial for we are faced with a common cause: capitalism. It is not so much that her involvement is scattered but rather multiple, always related to a common source and therefore, coherent **Conflating underclass and awareness:** The association between working/underclass neighborhoods and awareness inverts the classist hierarchy. By emphasizing the authenticity and depth of the working/underclass, she creates them as conscious social actors, not sleepy, hidden, passive. They are portrayed as being aware of the serious social problems that run through our society **Building experiential legitimacy:** It displays the instances where she is being short-changed if not victimized in many aspects of her life: race, class and gender. It also includes the instances where she proactively chose to be on the minority's side: physically, geographically and politically. Emphasizing one's marginality builds experiential legitimacy by opposition to scholarly legitimacy

(Continued)

Table 8.2 (Continued)

Parenti's repertoires: definition and tentative functions	Jodi's repertoires: definition and tentative functions
Invoking nature: The interspersed references to nature instil a feeling of genuineness, truthfulness and, we would venture, confidence, toward the interlocutor	**Distinguishing theory and practice:** It opposes practice and theory. It is built around bodily metaphors. For example: seeing 'was just made clear' and coming face to face. It reflects the idea of an embodied knowledge as opposed to an abstract one such as 'understanding academically'. It values experience over knowledge, action over analysis. This repertoire echoes the importance of authenticity and the process of engagement. Once it is lived, experienced, it can be advocated, it can become a cause and one can be a legitimate spokesperson about a problem
Discrediting powers: 'Discrediting powers' acts in tandem with previous repertoires, namely 'Invoking nature' and 'Depicting himself as underprivileged'. The latter two naturalize the justice-seeker vocation of the participant, they construct his authenticity. Along this line, depicting the powers as deceiving contributes to establishing the fundamental dichotomy in his narrative between the genuine and the false	**Distinguishing between activism and volunteering:** This repertoire generates a hierarchy connecting political and apolitical involvement. The first is framed as activism whereas the second is framed as volunteering. The latter does not require 'an analysis'. Volunteering means accomplishing discrete tasks that appeal to one's strengths (fund raising, for her mother) or one's interests (kids, for parents) and are not political commitments to long-term social change. Jodi mostly uses the word 'volunteering' when talking about other people's involvement. When she talks about her own involvement the terms used are 'community development', 'public awareness' and 'political work'. This type of participation is clearly valued whereas volunteering is less so
Showing resourcefulness: 'Showing resourcefulness' is all the more noteworthy in that the participant constructs himself as underprivileged – as another repertoire testifies. Those two are linked to accomplish the same function of building agency	**Showing the cost she pays as an activist:** This repertoire presents the border between paid and unpaid work as porous. By blending in this way paid and unpaid work, she displays her dedication: the salary is a bonus. This way of downplaying the role of a salary adds to the rigor often associated with serious activism. An activist has to pay the price of his or her involvement, live by his or her principles, lead by example, etc. If not, she loses her status, prestige, power to influence and credibility. She also shows that activism involves all spheres of life: free time, work, social interests, neighborhood you choose to live in, and social circles. There is something enveloping and, maybe, invasive about activism

Parenti's repertoires: definition and tentative functions	Jodi's repertoires: definition and tentative functions
Theorizing experience: References to social science concepts have the effect of connecting to his audience and lending credibility to his analysis of the situation of injustice in America and to his actions as an activist. It is also a testimony to the wide breadth of the world he inhabits	**Working out one's identity:** This repertoire produces activism as a form of identity work. Being engaged in a cause is identifying one's core beliefs and principles and negotiating this identity when the circumstances demand it. This repertoire emphasizes the desire for a unity between beliefs and actions and a profound imbalance and active search, re-evaluation of alliances and self-questioning when those do not match. Activism is also a quest for self
	Emphasizing the importance of the collective: This repertoire brings out the value of the collective in activism. Being part of a community is not just a state of being, it requires involvement, showing up, caring, coming together. Being 'reaffirmed' in the 'power of mobilization' and 'connected with one another and working toward the common goal or common interest' is the symbolic salary of activism. This repertoire shows that activism is also about confirming one's belief about political systems and the human species. It also makes activism magnanimous. It is for the greater good, not just a selfish pursuit
	Gendering the intellectual and the emotional: In this repertoire, a men/brain versus women/heart dichotomy is generated. She identifies women with emotional support, and men with colder, intellectual role models. In doing so, she lends life to a stereotype that places her, as she is well aware, in contradiction with her feminist stance. But she is also putting in place the conditions needed in order to influence someone like younger women activists. Influencing someone is not just a rational exercise; it is a relational and identity issue
	Typifying an activist trajectory and normalizing her withdrawal from activism: She recalls her 20s as a 'blur' during which she was 'consumed' by activity, whereas now, in her 40s, she is significantly more selective. This repertoire is not just describing a particular story that went from intense involvement to 'lack of follow-through'. It is creating a normalization effect. The reference to a collective entity ('classical stories about activist burnout', 'a lot of younger activists', 'a lot of activists', 'we all do that') characterized Jodi's slow withdrawal from activism as part of a typical activist career. Moreover, this repertoire also merges activist career and identity quest

accounts contribute to creating the effects identified in the vertical analysis of Parenti ('Establishing a version of authenticity in activism') and for Jodi ('Building experiential legitimacy').

- Interestingly, in both cases we find repertoires that promote the qualities of marginalized groups and invert the traditional hierarchy of values in Western societies (Parenti: 'Building connections to ethnic groups'; Jodi: 'Conflating underclass and awareness'). Social participation is not just about getting involved, it is seen as a way to redress or propose an alternative to the actual political order.

- In both accounts, we also find a polarized definition of power (Parenti: 'Emphasizing power or struggle'; Jodi: 'Distinguishing the center from the ground' and 'Building connectedness about social problems'). In both cases, there is an antagonistic approach to social change; fighting is an essential activity and a metaphor for social participation.

- Power is very much anchored in individual actors that need to change their understanding and behavior. Indeed, both Parenti and Jodi are involved in public awareness, trying to change individuals' consciences (Parenti: 'Individualizing/collectivizing'; Jodi: 'Working out one's identity' and 'Emphasizing the importance of the collective'). While they have a macro theory on social problems, they still have a basic humanistic approach. As an effect, people have to be changed before structure can change in turn, and this individual change has costs that one has to pay (Parenti: 'Emphasizing fight or struggle'; Jodi: 'Showing the cost she pays as an activist'). This view responsibilizes individuals into agreeing to be changed or changing themselves; that is, developing awareness of the power structures that produce inequality.

- Finally, a common thread between both series of interpretative repertoires is this continuum found in the stories of social participation between individual development and the desire to participate in a collective endeavor (Parenti: 'Individualizing/collectivizing'; Jodi: 'Working out one's identity' and 'Emphasizing the importance of the collective').

On the basis of these first observations of similarities between the two participants, we suggest in Table 8.3 a first merging of repertoires.

This partial merging of repertoires between our first two sources leaves a few repertoires and functions generated in the vertical analysis stage of Parenti and Jodi's accounts that are still unique to those two sources. For Parenti, those repertoires are:

- 'Invoking nature'
- 'Showing resourcefulness'
- 'Discrediting powers'
- 'Theorizing experience'.

And the function is:

- 'Constituting liminality as the mean for activism'.

Table 8.3 List of common repertoires

Common repertoires	Results of the fusion of these repertoires for each participant
• Building experiential legitimacy	• Parenti: 'Constructing himself as underprivileged' • Jodi: 'Building experiential legitimacy'; 'Distinguishing theory and practice'; 'Distinguishing between activism and volunteering'
• Reversing the traditional hierarchy of worth	• Parenti: 'Building connections to ethnic groups' • Jodi: 'Conflating underclass and awareness'
• Fighting for power or social change	• Parenti: 'Emphasizing power or struggle' • Jodi: 'Distinguishing the center from the ground', 'Building connectedness about social problems' and 'Centralizing power'
• Basing social change on individuals' transformation	• Parenti: 'Individualizing/collectivizing', 'Emphasizing fight or struggle', 'Crystallizing the primacy of agency for social change' • Jodi: 'Working out one's identity', 'Emphasizing the importance of the collective' and 'Showing the cost she pays as an activist'
• Working for self and working for others	• Parenti: 'Individualizing/collectivizing' • Jodi: 'Working out one's identity' and 'Emphasizing the importance of the collective'; 'Activism as the pursuit of self and of the collective'

In the case of Jodi, they are:

• 'Gendering the intellectual and the emotional'

• 'Typifying an activist trajectory and normalizing her withdrawal from activism'.

Again, this is not a cause for alarm because these repertoires and effects may very well be merged with repertoires and effects from additional sources later on when the next sources are integrated into the horizontal analysis (Figure 8.3).

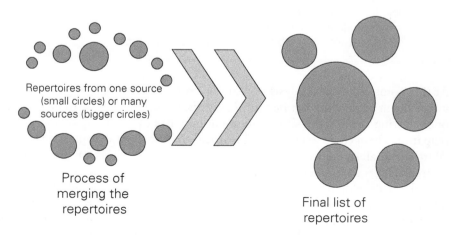

Repertoires from one source (small circles) or many sources (bigger circles)

Process of merging the repertoires

Final list of repertoires

Figure 8.3 The process of integrating repertoires

STEP 3 – DEVELOPING AN INTERPRETATION

From the repertoires we have generated and fused, here is the start of a conceptual reflection that would need to be pursued further and linked with knowledge already produced on social participation. Compatible with the precepts of discourse analysis through interpretative repertoires, the interpretation borrows a Foucauldian approach and emphasizes performativity, that is the social that is produced through the narrative.

Social participation involves the formation of an activist subject, somebody who experienced injustice, realized it, was capable of articulating it and had the impetus to become an agent for social change. If not asceticism, social participation involves costs for the participants: there is a feeling of strangeness, in-between-ness, or liminality to cope with. The activist subject is a being that is caught between many mental universes or communities that are not fully compatible (e.g. childhood milieu vs. chosen path). Moreover, the activist subject works at telling his or her stories following the language and precepts defended in his or her activist career. Coherence between the expressed worldview and the explicit analysis of one's own life is expected in order to be seen as credible. Both the experienced injustices and the costs paid for the social participation have the effect of placing the social participants along a continuum of legitimacy and merit.

We could tentatively suggest that the activist subject that Parenti embodies in his narrative is significantly different from the activist subject embodied in Jodi's narrative. The first puts forth an ethic of service, serving the groups and causes that need to be served. The second is constructed in an ethic of self-care that is expressed by the emphasis on the pursuit of self-discovery emerging from Jodi's narrative. We are skating on very thin ice here but we can certainly suggest the working hypothesis according to which the activist subject, while maintaining a core of common dimensions, also presents specific historical configurations that reflect the broader discourses of an era.

At this point, with the analysis of material from only two participants whose involvement spans different historical periods, we still have little to be capable of answering the initial research question: how has the meaning of social participation changed in relation to historical and structural transformations? With the analysis of further material, we might be capable of discerning a clearer change in the pattern of repertoires used over time. If so, we will be capable of developing a theorization in accordance with our initial research question. If not, we will tweak our initial research question to render justice to what the material allowed us to uncover. Remember: an iterative research process is, by definition, dynamic and requires constant adjustments.

STEP 4 – REMAINING ALERT. REMEMBERING KEY QUESTIONS AND ISSUES

The common repertoires and functions generated in the horizontal analysis, and those that are unique to each source that we still keep alongside, are fuel to feed the production of a theorization of the phenomenon under study. This theorization is crafted at the intersection of the repertoires and the background knowledge, sensitizing concepts and theoretical inclinations of the researcher.

To increase the strength and credibility of the analysis, here are some guidelines that the analysis might need to implement as desirable criteria:

1. **Documentation of the procedures followed in order to be capable of describing them in detail.** This is part of a wider concern for validity. By reading the research report, the reader must have enough information to judge the researcher's interpretations. As we will discuss in the next chapter, transparency of analysis is key (Jorgensen and Phillips, 2002: 125–6).

2. **Coherence between the interpretation developed and the assumptions and techniques as the basis of the analytical strategy.** For example, discursive analysis through interpretative repertoires assumes that language is performative and aims at uncovering discursive functions or effects that are produced, consciously or unconsciously, by people when they speak and write. The interpretation of the sources must hence keep that in mind and not fall unduly into ascribing intentions to the participants of the study.

3. **Development of the interpretation to the point where the researcher succeeds in providing a new or richer understanding, or at least suggesting new dimensions to the phenomena under study.** As the horizontal analysis progresses, the interpretation the researcher develops will gain in abstraction. The goal is not just to describe what is present in the material, but to develop a new understanding of a phenomenon, including the need to tweak the initial research question to ensure the best fit with what the material can offer.

4. **Interpretation phrased in terms of discursive effects.** The analysis does not focus on the psychological motivations of one or the other participant to use such and such repertoires, but rather on the social consequences of the use of those repertoires.

The process of theorization will be covered in the next chapter, but the guidelines above should sensitize you to the importance of making notes of your decisions and the provenance of your insights.

HORIZONTAL ANALYSIS USING A MIXED APPROACH INSPIRED BY GROUNDED THEORY AND NARRATIVE ANALYSIS

As with discourse analysis through interpretative repertoires, for a mixed approach inspired by grounded theory and narrative analysis, horizontal analysis basically consists of a systematic comparison of data. We compare semantic condensations from the vertical analysis of each source and we recreate a semantic condensation from this comparison. The objective of this process is to question the material to identify accurately common grounds between sources and specific characteristics of each individual source. The horizontal analysis layer invites us to take a step back from our material and return to the literature review as well as the conceptual and theoretical framework previously developed.

In this example, rooted in grounded theory and narrative analysis, we present the development of semantic condensation based on a multiple case sampling. In grounded theory, theoretical sampling is a key component of research design. Thus, it is difficult to construct a complete horizontal semantic condensation with only two cases (i.e. Jodi and Parenti). In the example that follows, we relied on 4 sources, but for the complete horizontal analysis using our mixed approach, we relied on 14 sources including Parenti's speech and Jodi's interview. The criteria for the theoretical sampling were:

1. Extended experiences of social and/or political participation in Canada or in the United States.

2. Decades where participants stated their involvement (1960s onward).

3. Gender.

4. Ethnicity.

We recruited as many women as men and tried to derive one half of the sample from the majority and the other half from a visible ethnic minority. We also made sure that participants started their involvement in the five decades under study (1960s onward). Our sample is small, but it was enough to lead to the saturation of the main category emerging from the data: the sequencing of the social and political participation process.

STEP 1 – CONSTRUCTING A TRANSVERSAL SEMANTIC CONDENSATION

Because we are interested in the process of social and political participation, we coded the sequences of the process. When does it start? Why? Who or what triggers the initial participation? What is the context? For what cause is the participant pleading? For each source, we condensed the relevant information and refined the definition of the code used. Figure 8.4 shows the chart that represents three nodes, after four sources.

The vertical analysis led us to identify the 'turning point' of the social and political participation of each participant. To identify it, we asked: at what point did their life narrative reveal a higher intensity of participation? What oriented their life course toward a new goal or a new existential quest?

After rereading each source, we identified an event or a situation that induced social and political participation. For one participant, the decision of

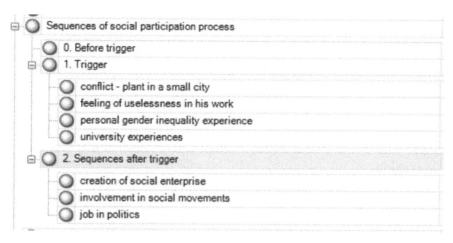

Figure 8.4 The coding of the process under study

an international company to construct a small plant on the bank of his hometown's main river led him to organize a protest and propelled him to act as a leader of environmental groups. For the second participant, a feeling of uselessness while working in a large law firm led him to become involved in his childhood neighborhood. He decided to organize basketball games as an after-school activity for young black males. His volunteering was so popular and appreciated by the kids that he quit his job to establish a social enterprise where he helped basketball coaches to become life coaches. For Parenti, we identified his university experiences of protesting for greater rights as a key element. For Jodi, we coded a personal experience of gender inequality as a trigger for her later involvement.

Identifying these common events, situations and/or states of mind automatically led us to construct a transversal semantic condensation. In other words, we tried to classify social phenomena having common characteristics. This intellectual and logical task is common in social sciences, for example the classification of social categories such as ethnic groups, age groups and gender groups. A major task of social scientists is to describe the social boundaries of groups. In natural science, categories such as species, proteins or chemical elements all respond to the imperative of classification. We need to distinguish one element from another. We also need to identify the characteristics of a category to be able to identify singular elements. This generalization process opens onto conceptualization.

This type of classification process can seem similar to a thematic analysis (i.e. what we did in the vertical analysis), which is to apply a descriptive 'tag' to a phenomenon. In the horizontal analysis process, analysis goes deeper. We are in search of a 'textual expression' that goes beyond the description of the data. This search for the rigorous, creative and 'textual expression' anchored in the data is the quest of all analytical processes. It will change through time.

Below, we illustrate the first steps of the horizontal analysis. We used the term 'trigger' to condense and illustrate a key moment in the narrative of participants, knowing that it will change through our conceptualization. By identifying a segment of the life course, we start to categorize life sequences – it is not a simple tagging of a theme. The idea of 'trigger' leads us to understand the temporality of the process: there is a before and an after the trigger. It might seem a small addition but it leads to the structuring of the three nodes you can see in Figure 8.5. This new idea will also influence our further reading of the data because we will try to understand what comes before and after Time 1 (the trigger).

In the example, we recategorized and reconceptualized the sequence 'After trigger' with information found within the material. We observed that the participants changed their professional occupations soon after the trigger. This might have been because the obstacle obliged them to be more reflective regarding their professional identity (we create the in-progress professional identity concept). We also noted the idea of innovation, because they all tried to change something in their community or in the form of their social and political engagement.

- 2. Sequences after trigger - creative process
  - 1. job change
    - creation of social enterprise
    - job in politics
    - self-employed
  - innovation
    - creation of social enterprise
    - involvement in social movements
  - new professional identity

Figure 8.5 The reconceptualization of the category 'after trigger'

STEP 2 – MEMOING

A memo is a note to oneself related to intuitions, theoretical and empirical readings, methodological choices or any decisions or insights related to the study. Memoing should start during the research design but it is especially important while analysing the data. Because horizontal analysis is a rich stage for the definition of categorizations or codes, memoing is more intense. Here are four examples of memos:

Memo 1 – Trigger?
The term 'trigger', as defined in the dictionary, means 'a device used to release or activate a mechanism'. This textual and intuitional expression is not accurate enough to group and explain the four codes because the term 'trigger' refers to 'an explosion', a sudden event. In the four cases, it is much more a 'lived experience' than a specific event, especially in the case of the interviewee feeling useless in his job.

Memo 2 – Test
Returning to French theory, we read François Dubet's book on social experience (1995). For him, individual experience is a preferred operator to understand contemporary phenomena rather than focusing on groups, classes or other social categories. More recently, Danilo Martuccelli (2006) rethought this notion though the concept of 'hurdle' (in French, *épreuve*). Because we anchored our study in a sociological perspective, the notion of hurdle has a specific meaning. It is a way to study social phenomena through a particular lens. Martuccelli argues that in pluralistic and individualized societies, it is difficult to understand the new forms of social categories and social boundaries. Thus, to produce useful descriptions, we need to follow individuals' trajectory in order to understand how they experience these social obstacles. This theoretical influence is similar to Dewey's pragmatism – understanding society through social problems or experiences – with the difference that Martuccelli's lens is a social and historical process and not just a 'problem'.

Memo 3 – etic vs. emic (a)
After referring to my readings and memoing on the idea of a trigger, social experience and hurdle, we decided to rename the category 'challenge' and we will try to identify, based on the data, the characteristics that make the observed phenomenon a 'social challenge' in the lived experience of each interviewee.

Memo 4 – etic vs. emic (b)
The social challenge is an etic perspective – our perspective as informed researchers – and the emic perspective is the perspective of the participants.

With our horizontal analysis, we try, in a way, to join those etic and emic perspectives.

STEP 3 – BACK AND FORTH BETWEEN VERTICAL AND HORIZONTAL ANALYSES

Working with our theoretical memos on social challenge, we will go back to the 14 vertical analyses to 'test' or work deductively with our hypothesis. Can the intrigue we previously identified be related to a social challenge? Because we already condensed the information of each source, we do not really need to read them all again; we have a good understanding and we have the relevant information to test our working hypothesis. The time we have put into our vertical analysis pays off at this stage.

This step includes questioning the influences of the socio-demographics of each category. With the help of qualitative analysis software, this becomes very easy. We can search our database of sources to see if there are differences among gender, age or geographic location for categories, themes or simple semantic condensation codes. It makes the process of testing hypotheses easy because those that are unsupported by the material can be readily discarded.

STEP 4 – BACK TO THE RESEARCH QUESTION

Periodically, throughout the horizontal analysis process, returning to the research question is necessary. At the beginning of the process, the research question was focused on the general process of social and political participation. However, even with only four cases analysed and the memos, we can slightly redirect the research question onto the more specific relationships among the social engagements resulting from a social challenge. The question could now be: how did socially engaged individuals navigate their personal challenges? This approach would lead us to analyse how the personal lives of socially engaged people are related to their acts of participation. We could also ask a more theoretical question: how do people become socially engaged in a society that becomes increasingly individualized? This would lead us to explain how social processes push people to develop their uniqueness. In the individuation process, cultural norms and economic struggles constrain individuals toward singularity and uniqueness as an employee, a consumer or a 'happy' family member. It is now difficult to understand social categories based on classic boundaries such as class, ethnicity or gender resources. However, when individuals lose their jobs, experience inequalities or stigmatization, they understand that they are powerless in the face of these social relationships. Those are not singular problems. The individuals experience society in their singular lives.

The horizontal analysis steps have been exemplified with 4 cases out of 14. For the next 10 sources, we will go through these steps again. Our research question might be tweaked but the analysis will end when the answer to our research question crystallizes. This means that it will end when we obtain a saturation of important categories, such as those of challenge or creative process, and we are able to explain the relationship between categories and the research question.

These two examples show how different analyses can occur even though they derive from the same empirical material.

CHAPTER SUMMARY

This chapter described the second layer of the palimpsest: that is, the steps necessary to complete the horizontal analysis of your sources. This process requires an in-depth comparison between the analysis results you produced during the previous phase: the vertical analysis. The goal is to integrate those vertical analysis results into a coherent whole. We presented two examples of horizontal analysis. The first one showed you, step by step, how to proceed to the horizontal analysis of your sources if you use discourse analysis through interpretative repertoires. We illustrated this process by integrating the vertical analysis results generated from Parenti's allocution with the vertical analysis results generated from an interview with Jodi. The second one showed you how to proceed to the horizontal analysis of your sources using our own mixed approach informed by grounded theory and narrative analysis. We illustrated this process using Parenti's allocution, Jodi's interview as well as 2 other sources from the 14 we generated for our social participation project. We also shared with you the thoughts this horizontal analysis generated regarding our initial research question.

Your project checklist

It is time for you to experiment with horizontal analysis of your sources. For this, you will need to:

✓ Complete independently the vertical analysis of at least two of your sources.

✓ Go back to the readings you did on your chosen approach in order to see whether the analytical steps are laid out explicitly to accomplish the horizontal analysis.

✓ Go back to the additional methodological texts you found that specifically illustrate the application of your chosen approach. The list below might help. Unfortunately, methodological texts are sometimes not very explicit when it comes to the analytical process as a whole. This is even more so for horizontal analysis. Take your inspiration from what we showed you in this chapter.

✓ Use this chapter and your previous readings to adopt or create the list of steps necessary to proceed to a horizontal analysis of the sources gathered or produced for your research project. Here again, take time to define each step as if you were explaining it to somebody else. This work will not only help you during your analysis, but also help you when the time comes to write the method section of your research protocol or report.

✓ Finally, test the process. Try to follow the route you designed to integrate the vertical analysis results from two sources produced for your project. The goal at this point is both to complete the horizontal analysis of a few sources and to tweak this horizontal analysis process. You want to make sure you can learn from that first experience so as to facilitate, render explicit and systematize the horizontal analysis of all your sources.

What you should read next

Frank, Arthur. 1995. *The Wounded Storyteller: Body, Illness, and Ethics.* Chicago: Chicago University Press.

- This sociology of health book illustrates the results of the horizontal analysis of tens of interviews with sick people using narrative analysis. The horizontal analysis presented takes the form of a typology. It bridges the phase of horizontal analysis, covered in this chapter, and theorization by typology that will be introduced in the next chapter.

Miles, Matthew B. and A. Michael Huberman. 1994. *Qualitative Data Analysis: An Expanded Sourcebook.* London: Sage. And the more recent version: Miles, Matthew B., A. Michael Huberman and Johnny Saldaña. 2013. *Qualitative Data Analysis: A Sourcebook of New Methods.* Thousand Oaks, CA: Sage.

- This book is a classic in qualitative research. While heavily influenced by grounded theory, it is also a great source of inspiration for other traditions on how to develop ways of comparing different sources, both intra- and inter-site. The authors are firm believers in the saying 'you can only analyse what you can display', hence their focus on using graphs, charts, figures, matrices.

Wetherell, Margaret and Jonathan Potter. 1986. *Mapping the Language of Racism: Discourse and the Legitimation of Exploitation.* New York: Columbia University Press.

- This monograph is a complete example of a research report produced using discourse analysis through interpretative repertoires. Even if it does not explicitly detail the process of horizontal analysis, you will be capable of appreciating it when reading the results of the rigorous analysis of more than 80 interviews conducted with white European New Zealanders on their rapport with the indigenous Maori people.

Want more support and inspiration? The online resources are here to help! Get to grips with key terms using **glossary flashcards**, see methods in action with a **library of SAGE cases and journal articles**, and follow analysis step-by-step with full transcripts of the sources discussed in the book.

9

THEORIZING AND PRESENTING THE RESULTS

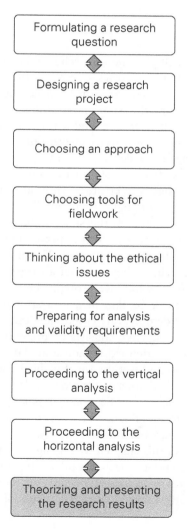

Figure 9.1 Where we are in the research process

IN THIS CHAPTER, YOU WILL LEARN:

- To familiarize yourself with a few mechanisms to theorize the research results you generated at the vertical and horizontal stages of the analysis: classification by typology, making use of contrasting characters, and establishing a dialogue between the empirical material and the concepts present in the literature.
- To recognize and avoid some common mistakes that we tend to commit in qualitative research: under-analysis through summarizing, over-quotation or isolated quote, taking sides, false survey and spotting features.
- To enhance the quality of your research by emphasizing reflexivity, that is by making your decisions transparent, using and discussing counter-examples and explicitly voicing the limits of your research.

INTRODUCTION

Any analytical strategy will give the researcher some guidelines as to the steps to undertake the vertical analysis (one source at a time, Chapter 7) and, hopefully, the horizontal analysis (comparison between sources, Chapter 8) of the empirical material. However, the next analytical layer of our palimpsest, theorization, is a less documented process and a result more nebulous to achieve. The theorizing stratum must allow us to answer our evolving research question. As such, it should bring us to develop an interpretation based on empirical evidence. This answer, because it rests on rich qualitative material, will have many nuances. The challenge is to create a synthesis of the most important elements of response, that is to make them intelligible, while conserving the richness of the empirical material. At this stage of the research process, the work consists of presenting our interpretation and persuading the reader of its power. This task means overcoming three challenges. The first requires condensing the information so that it reaches a high level of abstraction. The second involves documenting the process by which we brought the information to this level of abstraction. The proof must be laid in a journal article, a dissertation or a research report. We must demonstrate empirically the theoretical elements that we rely upon. The third challenge consists of presenting all that, skillfully, in writing. The accuracy of written expression and clarity in the presentation of the results are thus essential objectives for this third layer of analysis.

In the first half of this chapter, we explore tools to help us when theorizing and presenting research results: classification by typology, bringing out contrasting characters and establishing a dialogue to enrich concepts. These are not the only ways to achieve theorization but they certainly are a good point of departure. Then, in the second half of this chapter, we highlight some 'dos and don'ts' when theorizing as well as presenting research results. We start by listing and showing examples of some mistakes to avoid and conclude the chapter by discussing reflexivity, a principle that greatly contributes to the quality of good research.

CLASSIFICATION BY TYPOLOGY

Whatever the approach used in qualitative methodology, the researcher's work consists of producing an interpretation that makes sense for someone who has not seen or experienced the singular phenomenon under study. Making a phenomenon intelligible requires that you identify relationships or structuring connections. In natural as well as social sciences, phenomena are made intelligible through inductive classification. We also label this exercise of classification of abstract relationships: typology (Schnapper, 2005). In the French sociological tradition, this type of inductive classification of complex links is specific to the historical social sciences (Passeron, 2006).

For example, if we want to understand the influence of power relationships on practices of social engagement, we will have to classify the power relationships that we identify in the material. The first reflex of a less experienced researcher would be to analyse the relationships that have been established based on the social positions of individuals, but this exercise would not correspond to the analysis of abstract relationships. Rather, this would be a classification of social characters (Martuccelli, 2005). For example, interviews could be classified based on the socio-economic origins of the interviewees or their professional roles as is done in a statistical analysis that connects dependent and independent variables. The analysis of abstract relationships deals with the relationships of social actors, as well as social and cultural norms. We could identify the connections between the social representation of power held by people or organizations and their practices and then understand how their social positions influence these relations.

In the following sections, we present four forms of typology:

1. descriptive typology;

2. conceptual typology;

3. mapping; and

4. ideal type.

DESCRIPTIVE TYPOLOGY

The descriptive typology is a stage in the third level of analysis rather than a research result. Indeed, the exercise of classifying the relationships according to criteria of internal similarities and external differences is a constant exercise at this stage of the analysis. This classification is carried out inductively by aggregating the analytical relationships developed as the analysis proceeds around 'core units of meaning' (Coenen-Huther, 2006). This type of aggregation necessarily leads us to drop those elements that 'make less sense' with regard to the selected analytical core. There is therefore a certain loss of material that should not be ignored during the rest of the analysis.

For example, in conducting a study on the involvement of high school students in the student council, we identified two types of actors who encouraged them to run for school elections and get involved: (1) interpersonal agents and (2) institutional agents. During the interviews, the students named the people who had encouraged them to get involved when they entered high school. We grouped them according to the types of relationships they had with the participants. The interpersonal agents had horizontal relations with the participants and were members of their personal and family networks. Institutional agents had hierarchical relations and had an educational role within the school.

We quickly identified a subcategory within the group of institutional agents. We found adults who went beyond the normal agreed-upon limits of their professional 'role' by engaging in a horizontal relationship with the young people. Because of the nature of their social status within the educational institution and the type of relationship with the young people, this phenomenon led us to propose a new social category: vocational agents. Thus by combining the characteristics of agents who encouraged young people to become involved, we came to identify some social relationships at the core of the mobilization process as shown in Table 9.1.

Table 9.1   Descriptive typology

Interpersonal agent	Peers (brothers, sisters, friends)
	Significant adults (father, mother, extended family)
Institutional agent	Professor, educator, coach, instructor
Vocational agent	Professor or some other professional who inspires and has a horizontal relationship with a young person
Unclassifiable	Hero, inspiring public personality

We grouped into the category 'unclassifiable' the references to those inspiring people who played an important role in the process of mobilization. In order to not eliminate material that does not 'fit' our interpretive model, it is important to create this type of category. It is necessary to be as methodical with regard to the material cast aside as the material retained for the interpretation phase. The risk of eliminating from the empirical corpus data which does not 'coherently' fit into the theoretical stratum of analysis must be avoided at all costs. This procedure would be equivalent to presenting the 'enlightened' opinions of the researcher rather than constructing an argument anchored in the empirical material. Thus, the quality and rigor of research depend on the rigorous classification of elements cast aside during the process. First, to forget this material creates a problem of transparency of the data, which is one of the criteria of validity within qualitative research. Second, data that resists the interpretive model can often act as a significant interpretive lever. 'Contrasting cases' – the existence of atypical information – obliges us to refine our interpretation.

CONCEPTUAL TYPOLOGY

Abstract typology is constructed from interpretations or work hypotheses developed by the researcher through the vertical and horizontal analysis strata. If we return to the research example inspired by grounded theory principles (Chapters 7 and 8), our research question 'How do individuals become involved?' leads us to interpretive insights on forms of participation. Based on our material and the plots of the interviewees' narratives, we developed the hypothesis that (1) the visibility of the involvement and (2) the degree of institutionalization of the involvement are the two abstract relationships that allow us to better distinguish forms of participation.

The vertical and horizontal analyses led us to concentrate the units of meaning around the emerging category of visibility. The third stratum of analysis allows us to distinguish between the criteria of inclusion and exclusion within this category. We must return to our analyses, our units of meaning and our narratives in order to refine the distinctions that we can develop between visible and invisible participation based on the empirical data. This theoretical analysis leads us to define criteria of internal resemblance among visible practices of engagement and, in opposition, to define the criteria of external differences which, in this case, are grouped under the label 'invisible participation'. Table 9.2 illustrates these results.

Table 9.2   Conceptual typology

Visible participation	Invisible participation
Social participation mainly takes place outside the household	Social participation takes place inside and/or outside the household
The narrative showcases a desire to share a problem	The narrative centers on a logic of attention to The Other
The participation narrative is driven by a need to recognize a cause, an interest, a group	The participation narrative is driven by a logic of authenticity and the recognition of self
The participation is focused on impacting institutional positions	The participation of the actors is focused on personal interactions
The participation involves strangers	The participation does not necessarily involve strangers

The other important characteristic that distinguishes the different practices of participation of our participants is the social 'form' in which the engagement practices occur. The scientific literature in political sociology distinguishes among institutional forms of participation; groups recognized by peers that exist over the long term; and 'informal' forms of participation – those which are sporadic. Throughout the interviews, we see these two types of forms. There are people like Parenti, who belong to formal organizations (unions, movements, organizations). These social institutions can have different orientations (anarchists or others), but they exist over a long period and are recognized by people from outside the group. However, in the case of Jodi, we can see practices that are formal and informal. She is involved with a political party, but she dedicates a lot of time to women from her neighborhood who are experiencing financial and emotional difficulties. Thus, her social participation is informal.

We returned to the teachings of Georges Simmel (1896) regarding the idea of social form in an attempt to identify the characteristics of forms of participation. Simmel first identifies the form 'institution' based on its permanence in time. It is thus easy for us to identify the permanence of certain organizations that people participated in. There are institutions that transcend a physical location: unions, the feminist social movement, the student movement, the Communist Party, the Church. There are organizations that are anchored in historical and geographical permanence: the US Congress in Washington, the Parliament of Canada, the University of Montreal or of Wisconsin. Table 9.3 systematizes the differentiation criteria between the two forms of participation.

Table 9.3   Institutional forms of participation

Institutional forms of participation	Non-institutional forms of participation
Participation within an organization that has an historical permanence	Participation within an ephemeral organization
Participation within an organization that is geographically situated	Participation can involve a de-territorialized network
Participation within an organization recognized by the public	Participation within an organization not recognized by the public
Participation within an organization that has a collective mission	Participation not necessarily within an organization or a network having a collective mission, because participation can be seen as a 'lifestyle'

MAPPING

Mapping consists of situating the cases under study (documents, interviews, analytical categories, etc.) within a spatial typology under construction (Demazière, 2013). This mapping is also an intermediate stage of the analysis. That is to say, it will not necessarily be part of the report. Rather, it allows us to think about hypotheses, to question boundary cases and to grasp the nuances that a typology 'by nodes' can erase.

If we go back to the conceptual typology presented above, two rapports to participation lead us to create two axes along which to locate the commitment of the interviewees. But as we mentioned, it is necessary to return to the material in order to refine our analysis. That is when mapping can be useful.

Mapping (see Figure 9.2) allows us to situate our cases (in this case the participants) to identify the 'unclassifiable'. We use the two analytical relationships, formal–informal and visibility–invisibility, to form a plan. Whenever we try to situate the narrative of a participant we question his or her relationship to the institutions and the visibility of his or her participation. And we question our typology in the following way: Does it help to answer our research question? Does the interpretation help us to make intelligible the phenomena that we have observed? Does the typology adequately account for the object studied or is it subject to too much distortion at the time of case mapping? If we return to the first chapter of this book, we exemplify here a deductive operation. We 'test' the interpretations arising from abduction and induction.

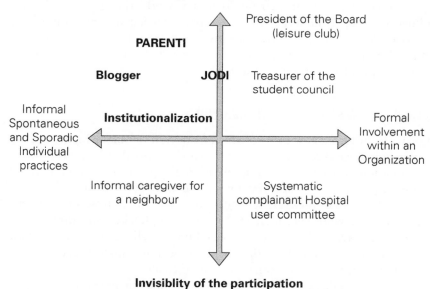

Figure 9.2 Mapping different participants along their practices of participation

THE IDEAL TYPE

The 'ideal type' is part of a Weberian tradition. For Weber, the researcher can use an ideal construct, a construct built from his or her observations to give shape to the analysis. If we go back to the mix of grounded theory analysis and narrative analysis presented in Chapters 7 and 8, we can identify five categories of participants based on the typology of our cases. In the figure, we presented the mapping of each case that we ordered along their inclusion in and exclusion from different categories (formal–visibility; formal–invisibility; informal–visibility and informal–invisibility).

In the presentation of our data, we would only use the ideal types to explain our analysis. For example, we would explain that the category of the 'good neighbor' represents those people who frequently participate by donating time to their immediate social circles, but not through organizations. We would list the characteristics of the 'good neighbor': a woman in her late 40s whose children are in high school and who lives in a working-class area. The ideal type thus allows us to understand a social phenomenon.

In the analysis, we came across as many men as women, but since the number is not relevant, we want to describe what seems most significant. It is often women who occupy care-giving positions in their paid work activities or women who received the services of professionals or organizations. For example, in our sample, we had a homeless woman involved in a collective for social housing, but who saw herself as a 'good neighbor' because her participation consisted mainly of helping young street girls, directing them toward resources and key people.

To answer our research question, we would therefore present the ideal types we constructed through our typology work: the 'good neighbor', the 'influencer', the 'volunteer', the 'cyberspace participant' and the 'dropout' (inactive). We would present a narrative built from the events and practices gathered in the material for participants associated with each ideal type. Here is an example of the dropout ideal type.

EXAMPLE OF AN IDEAL TYPE: THE DROPOUT

In order to fit into a new area to which he moved to pursue higher education, Martin volunteered to coach a hockey team, a sport that he played for many years in a junior league, the last level before the professional one. This volunteering experience also allowed him to further develop in a domain that touches on his area of expertise: education. His intention was to meet adults of his own age who were interested in coaching hockey and thinking about educational practices for a sport that he knows well. He knows the world of hockey but he does not know the people of his municipality very well and he is experiencing, for the first time, the role of coach.

He soon realizes that he is violating an implicit norm: he is training a team of young boys without being a parent himself. Several members of the group question his motivations: might he be a pedophile? To remove any suspicions, his girlfriend supports him and participates in most of the practices. He explained, in his own words, that if '[I] had been single, I probably would have been accused of being a pedophile … you name it. But at the very least … I know that there are some who … there is always … in that environment, you always feel you were being watched'.

Being a coach demands many volunteering hours per week and requires that you show up at the arena very early on weekend mornings. It is therefore not a flexible and sporadic commitment. The involvement is significant, since in Quebec and in Canada hockey is the 'national' sport and it is taken very seriously, even among young children. Although the participation of Martin is extremely demanding, the parents of the players do not recognize this. They have trouble trusting him. They challenge his ways of doing things as well as his decisions. Paradoxically, when they learn that he has an expertise in education, they have even more doubts about his skills:

> But I have been reproached with many things because everyone was asking me 'what are you doing?' And knowing that I was that [a teacher] ... I remember one parent saying 'and on top of all that he's a teacher and he does that!' Yes [laughing!] ... I'm thinking of one parent in particular who was very intrusive. She always wanted to interfere with everything. Control everything. I like, brushed her with the back of my hand. So then she goes off to complain.

The experience is difficult. Martin says he received verbal and physical threats. What was wrong? How was it that his volunteering, which was meant to better connect him to people in his new environment, only served to further isolate him? Martin has trouble comprehending the situation.

His explanation points to the fact that he does not belong to the group that controlled the organization:

> I know the term: nepotism – is that what it was? When we mean: the friend of a friend. But, I ... I wasn't the friend of a friend. I was someone who showed up just like that and offered his service, I wasn't close enough to the core, if you like, and so I was less protected.

We explain this phenomenon by the fact that Martin did not know the informal rules of the milieu, he was an outsider. Recent studies emphasize that the absence of participation results more from practices at the mesosocial scale: the organizations, the networks and groups rather than purposes: causes, political ideas.

In the case of the practice of a very conservative sport, people constantly reminded him of his differences: an adult of 40 who was still studying, a coach who was not a parent, someone who came from another city. His over-qualifications in the areas of education and hockey even seemed to work against him. He might have represented a threat to the established order of the organization. It is an organization that is often controlled by the same families or lineage. Hockey is 'a family affair'. The fathers dream of professional careers for their sons. Hockey, which, as adults, they generally no longer play, remains their daily subject of conversation, their mode of socializing. Every day they discuss player trades, the antics of one or another player, listen to radio phone-in shows and watch sports broadcasts.

Even though he shares the same language, the same ethnic origin and the same culture of hockey, Martin carries a special status: he is a mature university student, he does not work full time and he has no children. These are all characteristics that distinguish him from most other adult volunteers or adults, who, as parents, visit the arena. Not everyone can volunteer in this milieu. To participate socially, he must still conform to the norms of the group. It is difficult to get involved without having already woven bonds of trust with the local people. It has cost Martin to learn this. The people in the organization do not protect him, he has no influence on the decisions taken by the organization;

he is rejected. Thus, an unequal relationship exists between him and *them* – those he identifies as the core people. These people who have been around for years and who have children on a city hockey team; people who understand the ways of being and of doing.

This experience is so difficult that he and his partner decide to leave the area and completely give up on social participation activities: 'we were involved, we tried things out, you know, we tried to see … to integrate in this milieu … It gets you more frustrated. You give time, and you get the feeling they are laughing in your face.' He became a dropout.

The case of Martin is particularly interesting because it shows the difficulty of being accepted by a group. He had no experience of formal participation and he seemed helpless in the face of the power games and group norms: How to oppose group practices without being rejected? How to create a bond of confidence? We can imagine the difficulty that some minority groups might have in penetrating very homogeneous volunteer associations.

Martin's experience does not seem that unusual. In many militant groups and organizations, political or social, a small number of people control the destinies of these organizations and thus limit the participation of new people who have not mastered the implicit norms of the group. The organizational cultures, more so than causes (to borrow the vocabulary of Hirschmann), are often the reason for quitting. Indeed, when one can neither express oneself nor prove one's loyalty, one opts for the exit: one becomes a dropout.

BRINGING OUT CONTRASTING CHARACTERS

While typologies can help situate participants in relation to one another along a conceptual continuum, bringing out the contrasting characters a participant puts forth in his or her narrative is a way to portray the dynamism and multiplicity among each source.

We saw in the previous chapters that in order to create hypothetical propositions, it can be fruitful to actively look for contrasts in the material. While some analytical strategies rest on analysing variability, such as discourse analysis through interpretative repertoires, others are not explicitly built around this analytical task. Contrasting excerpts so as to identify the actions the participant is pursuing in his or her speech, interview or text (in the case of documents) as well as the characters the participant puts in play in his or her narrative can be an effective way to identify analytical avenues. In order to illustrate the power of contrasts and characters to feed the theorization process, we will use some excerpts from Parenti's speech.

When expressing ourselves, we do not always appear clear, coherent, stable. We seem to contradict ourselves; we test one version of ourselves out loud and then switch to another. That is what performing oneself entails. We are not always neatly rehearsed, in character. We are multiple and hesitant, even when writing. Rather than seeing these contrasts as an indicator of a lack of sincerity, we can use them as an anchor for our analysis and generate hypotheses as to what action is accomplished with these different characters. Look at the following excerpts:

> And there are other times when we so focus on the individual accomplishment that we overlook this collective effort and the social context that it takes place in. All individual human endeavor is also a collective social endeavor.

> I remember Sandy Levinson saying to me, I went out and spoke at Ohio State, 'Well, you know, these things [massive mobilizations and protests] can happen in places like' – he made a very brilliant analysis of why these things happen in places like Michigan, Madison, Berkeley. He said, 'It can't happen at Ohio State.' And I gave my talk. Four days later Ohio State blew open, and people were out on the streets fighting the cops.

The experience of activism is expressed, if not justified, by a vision of how social change unfolds. From the beginning of his speech, Parenti underlined the forces of history, the power of the collective and the shaping influence of context. However, while he openly identifies with the political left and shares a structural understanding of the world, there is little structural determinism in his narrative. The power of individual agency is clearly stated, as we see in the second excerpt above. Moreover, the ruling powers he is talking about are more often than not individualized if not personalized:

> [T]hose who are dedicated to making the world safe for inequality.

> [T]hose who want to use the world's land, labor, technology, natural resources, and markets for a capital accumulation process that increasingly enriches the few as opposed to those who want to use these things for collective betterment for the well-being of the many.

> We do have evidence of people who have never had an interior dialogue. They're all in power right now.

The powers he targets are embodied in a series of people, not structural powers. In fact, in the overall speech there is no mention of structure. There are, however, two mentions of the 'system':

> And then I began to question the system that produced these leaders.

> And what the system does is, they attack ad hominem. They attack the protesters. So they make the protester the issue rather than the things we're protesting.

In the last instance, the system is an aggregate of identifiable individuals: 'they'. It is not an abstract force acting through people. Such a view of social change, so strongly anchored in individual consciousness and actions, allows for the distribution of blame and worthiness – something that is quite pervasive in the speech. We caricature a bit, but in the narrative of how Parenti became an activist there are good guys and bad guys, there are the fighter and his enemy, there are authentic justice seekers and pseudo justice seekers who are on the side of power when it suits their interests. Some characters are praised, others are criticized. There is a strong moral tone to this life story.

Playing on the continuum of individualization and collectivization reconciles the possibilities of making specific people into heroes, while still acknowledging the force of the history and structure in the background. In this case at least, the historical and structural views of social change, according to which individual endeavors are necessarily also collective achievements, almost act as forms of disclaimer: they are mentioned and soon forgotten, so as to leave the stage to the individual characters mobilized in Parenti's narrative.

As contrasts are gathered in this way, we see that participants rely on many characters to put their stories together. They can alternate between the individual hero and the bearer of structural determinants; the black sheep and the authority figure; the justice seeker and the victim; and so on. Being aware of this multiplicity of characters and looking for scenes and patterns which define when a participant relies on such and such a character to tell his or her story is a way to create a textured view of the social participation a story tells. Documenting the multiplicity of characters mobilized by participants is also a way to create a configuration of social participation narratives and make sense of the evolving career of social participation for each research participant over time and era. Hence, a social participation career that is spurred by a sense of victimization and that is aimed at addressing an individual harm, and told mainly from the points of view of a cast of characters such as the sufferer, the wounded, the underdog, might have a different trajectory and form than a career that is spurred by a justice-seeking mission (to repair a collective harm) and mainly told from the points of view of another cast of characters such as the missionary and the crusader. Looking for contrasts and characters is thus a way to render justice to the internal dynamic of the single social participation trajectory, but also to identify the social scripts, dominant and marginal, that a cultural group or an era relies on to make sense of social participation.

ESTABLISHING A DIALOGUE TO ENRICH CONCEPTS

The end product of inductive qualitative research can take the form of rich concepts to fully grasp people's experience. Concepts are by definition abstract entities referring to complex practice, ideas or processes. They are used to distinguish some practices, ideas and processes from others. In order to be useful analytically, they need to be operationalized. That is, their dimensions and components have to be laid out. Hence, crafting rich concepts is not just a tool to help us theorize our material, it is also a research outcome that can be, in itself, a contribution. To do so, a dialogue between the material and the existing concepts found in the literature on the topic can help the researcher to theorize.

For example, when talking about her experience in the women's and union's movements, Jodi makes a distinction between being a volunteer and being an activist. The contrast that she lays out can contribute to substantiate this conceptual difference and, therefore, add nuance to the answer to our research question: how forms of engagements change in relation to historical and structural transformations (see Chapter 6 for the synthesis of our initial research project).

Some empirical studies use general categories to refer to social participation such as social involvement, community engagement, volunteering and activism indiscriminately (Binder and Blankenberg, 2016). Others distinguish volunteering from activism (Gilster, 2012).

For the benefit of this example, we will limit ourselves to conceptualizing the difference between volunteering and activism using Jodi's interview and Gilster's (2012) study. For a final research report, though, all the empirical material pertaining to volunteering and activism found in our sources as well as the totality of our literature review on the topic would be brought to contribute.

Jodi, who was involved in a political party and community initiatives, distinguishes between activism and volunteering on the basis of the nature of the involvement. While she sees herself as an activist, she presents her mother as a volunteer:

> Interviewer: But what is the role of government, the type of help that a government gives to a citizen?
>
> Jodi: I would imagine it would be a hard question for people who don't work in politics or think about politics. Like even my mom who is this volunteer extraordinaire person which you're going to ask me about anyway, like I imagine there are a lot of volunteers who just don't think about those levels. My mom doesn't have any analysis whatsoever.

And

> And people like my mom make choices about her volunteer time that have nothing to do with political analysis. You know, and I ask her questions, mostly teasing her, like, 'Well why are you involved with the CIBC Run for the Cure for breast cancer, but I never hear you talk about the amount of funding that isn't given to women's health?' Like, why don't we talk about why we need to do private fundraising for women's cancer? You know? Anyway.

Jodi sees volunteering as being associated primarily with formal organizations. She lists her mother's involvement on different boards, a professional association and, more and more, with charity organizations such as the Osteoporosis Society and the Cancer Society.

Jodi defines volunteering as providing a service. She notices that, over her volunteering career, her mother has specialized and developed an expertise she offers and that takes precedence over the cause she embraces:

> I think the other shift that happened too for her was over time as a volunteer she began to notice a particular strength in fund-raising, and so I thought of her in one of your other questions because she gets approached a lot by groups to come into a fund-raising campaign. Like she over time has become really good at it, so sometimes I don't think she picks a project based on the organization but on the job.

She goes further in suggesting that this service dimension of volunteering can take the form of discreet and measurable tasks, the completion of which is rewarding in itself:

> Like I think she also enjoys putting together a whole fund-raising event. She loves from start to finish, and she likes I think – I understand this about her. It's such an obvious goal, right? So I think for her what's really tidy and clean about it is you decide how much you want to raise. You go raise it. You can measure it. She likes that sort of stuff.

While she acknowledges that she sometimes has short-term and measurable tasks to achieve, Jodi also mentions the long haul and the diffuse measure of success that come with her form of social participation:

> So when that person said 'Will you come and work on developing the communication strategy for our new project on women's rights?' You know, I guess I sort of always look at something of what change is possible if we accomplish those goals. So it could be big, measureless, immeasurable change, or just very concrete change, right? I mean, part of working in public awareness is that you never really know your success. But, you know, I often say if we've changed one mind, we've done good work, you know? It's about changing attitudes and minds instead of numeric totals.

Moreover, while talking about people's lifestyle, Jodi, who does not have children, also brings up the very important issues of motivation and awareness:

> And we know that once you're a parent, you start to kind of pay attention to stuff like, 'oh, there should be a stop sign there', or 'God, that arena is falling apart, we should do something about that', or 'better food at my kid's school', or whatever how people think about it. But I never think about those things, because it doesn't come to mind. They think about that sort of stuff. Or you heard all the stories lately about the recall of toys. Yeah, so there's just a whole other world of [inaudible] that I don't belong to, but I think it must have a lot to do with the choices they make about their volunteer time. So, you know, they're selling chocolate covered almonds and stuff. And that's volunteer work, right?

This reflection ties in with the target of action and highlights the relationship a volunteer has with the potential beneficiaries of the service offered. One can postulate that volunteers' experience might differ whether they are sporadically involved in selling chocolate-covered almonds for raising money to repair the arena where their kids play or whether they are involved at the foodbank to deliver meals on wheels to underprivileged seniors whom they do not know.

Now, let us see if and how Jodi's conceptualization is supported and can enrich the literature. In her quantitative study, Gilster posits that there is indeed a difference between activism and volunteering:

> Activists seek to create change at the neighborhood, community, or global level. Activists view the social structure as a target of intervention, not a framework within which to work. Musick and Wilson (2008) suggest that activism is differentiated by *collective action* for a *collective good* ... Volunteers, on the other hand, seek to provide services through formal organizations ... Research supports the conventional wisdom that activists are oriented towards politics and social change, whereas volunteers are oriented towards providing services – volunteers distance themselves from the political connotations of activism (e.g., Eliasoph, 1988; Wuthnow, 1991). Certainly, the line between activism and volunteerism is blurred: often activists do volunteer work and volunteers become activists. (2012: 770–1, emphasis in the original)

She sets out to document this difference by measuring empirically the type and level of psychological well-being and social connectedness that both activists and volunteers experience from their social participation. In order to differentiate operationally the two groups, she uses the answers to a few questions about people's participation in community projects and in any group that took local action for reform. Those who answered those questions positively are labeled activists. The researcher also asks about a number of organizations to which people might have given their time as well as how many hours they have given. Those who have given at least one hour to a formal organization are labeled volunteers. After analysing the answers to a comprehensive survey, Gilster confirms that there is indeed a difference between the activist and volunteer experience. While the former leads to empowerment, the latter brings people to experience less hopelessness. Both lead to an increase in social ties (Gilster, 2012: 779).

Far from being complete, the dialogue we created between the conceptualization of activism and volunteering taken from Jodi's own worldview and one journal article already feeds a more sophisticated proposition to operationalize those concepts, as shown in Table 9.4.

There is no doubt that this operationalization table is too schematic and that it crystallizes issues that are much more fluid in real life. However, it captures the gist of what we mean by creating a dialogue between the empirical material and the literature to enrich concepts. This is one of the possible ways to initiate the theorization process.

Table 9.4   An enriched view of the conceptual distinction between activism and volunteering

Dimensions	Components	Concepts	
		Activism	Volunteering
Aim	Timeframe of the goal	Creating political and social change or reform at any level	Providing a service
	Measure of success	Mostly long term	Mostly short term
		Mostly diffuse	Measurable
Target of action	Relationship to the potential beneficiaries of service	Collective good	Individual well-being
		Mostly unknown to the participant	Can be known to the participant
Intermediary		Work through community groups or projects	Work through formal organizations
Outcome		Empowerment and increase in social ties	Decrease in hopelessness and increase in social ties

We covered here some of the tools used to theorize and present results, whether it is a typology, an analysis of contrasting characters or a direct dialogue between the material and existing concepts. We cannot be exhaustive on this issue; the options are numerous. However, we would like to bring your attention to some pitfalls to avoid when theorizing and presenting your research results.

ENSURING THE QUALITY OF THE STUDY

In this second part of the chapter, we will emphasize, on the one hand, mistakes to avoid when conducting your analysis and theorization, and, on the other hand, a principle to adopt to increase the quality of your research.

MISTAKES TO AVOID

In their perceptive text, Antaki and colleagues (2003) point to a list of analytical shortcomings found in studies using discourse analysis. We believe that five of those weaknesses apply more broadly to qualitative research, no matter what analytical strategy one chooses:

- Under-analysis through summarizing.

- Under-analysis through over-quotation or isolated quote.

- Under-analysis through taking sides.

- Under-analysis through false survey.

- Under-analysis through spotting features.

To structure our discussion about mistakes to avoid, we will refer to these five elements and amalgamate them with mistakes other authors have identified, as well as our own interpretation and examples.

UNDER-ANALYSIS THROUGH SUMMARIZING

Any analytical strategy will require the researcher to condense, at one point or another, the material. Whether it is through identifying themes, or codes or narrative structures or discursive features, all analytical strategies will require the researcher to identify and extract elements from the chaos of the rich material. This analytical step results in a reduction of the complexity of the material to clusters that make the material manageable for the rest of the analysis. However, as mentioned earlier (see Chapter 6), stopping the analysis there is insufficient. Listing the themes within the material and summarizing the participants' opinions about them, or else describing the narrative structures of the various sources, are only preparatory steps that must be followed to facilitate the analytical unpacking of those clusters of information. As Dumez (2012) accurately points out, in all study there is a necessary tension between the participants' (emic) and researchers' (etic) perspectives. It is from this tension that the interpretation emerges. Ending the analytical process at the summarizing phase can be the result of an underdeveloped conceptual model. It can happen if a shortcut to the fieldwork was taken early in the research process at the expense of reading and developing a conceptualization of the research object. This is what Burman (2004) calls 'under-analysis' through not having a question. An interpretation is a dialogue that the researcher creates between, on the one hand, the literature review and the conceptualization of the research object and, on the other hand, the material. To generate a rich interpretation, a researcher must nourish him- or herself with existing studies of the topic and a thorough reflection upon the main concepts and axioms at the basis of the empirical study. Without these, the researcher is mute in front of the material because there are no partners (previous authors and theoreticians) to engage in dialogue about the material.

UNDER-ANALYSIS THROUGH OVER-QUOTATION OR ISOLATED QUOTATION

'Don't state, demonstrate' is an old and wise maxim in research. It is not enough for the researcher to have a creative interpretation to offer, the interpretation must also be thoroughly grounded in the material. Some interpret this imperative as a command to quote participants at length, barely linking the multiple quotes with an interpretative sentence from the researcher. Quoting participants to a point where we have exhausted all the instances of an experience found within the material is bound to confuse rather than enlighten the reader. It is difficult but necessary to find the right balance between stating, that is proposing an interpretation, and demonstrating, that is grounding the interpretation in the empirical material. Moreover, for projects following mostly an inductive logic, the material should not be used just to support already existing theoretical assertions. It should be the reverse: the material should be the main source of theorization, supported by the literature.

Jodi has experienced minority statuses throughout her life. She has experienced the difficulty of being a woman: 'So you're judged and treated unjustly as a woman all the time ... Like, as an independent, self-efficient woman dealing with mortgage brokers and financial agencies and mechanics and the world, I feel that every day.' She also experienced what she calls 'injustice by osmosis': 'so much of the racism experienced by my family, my dad and my mom individually as well as my brother, feels like mine.' In her youth, being a supporter of the Quebec francophone province while living in an anglophone province was not easy: 'I was a psycho separatist in Regina, had no ally, no ally ... I did feel very alienated.' And, because she values the underclass, she chooses to live in poor neighborhoods. In brief, she experienced, willingly or not, many layers of marginality. This lived experience builds what we might call 'experiential legitimacy' as an activist. She has not just been sensitized to those causes through school, books or volunteer work; she has experienced, in her flesh, powerlessness. For someone advocating for social change in grassroots movements, this type of legitimacy is probably particularly prized. This ties in with the literature on positive marginality where marginality is redefined and used as a source of strength (Unger, 2000) and symbolic capital.

Under-analysis can also occur at the other end of the spectrum. In this case, it is not through a large number of quotes that under-analysis occurs, but by overreliance on one chosen quote. Building one's whole argument around a key quote from the participants can be tempting. This is especially the case when the statement encapsulates the participant's explanation of the phenomenon under study. For example, in his speech on how he became an activist, Parenti states:

> But I can sum it in one word, and that's dogs. That is, my grandfather had a brown dog and he named him Brownie. My uncle Nick got a white dog, big, fluffy, white dog, and he named him Whitey. And we got a dog that had spots on it, and everybody called him Spotty. And that was the level of imagination in my family. And that's when I knew I had to get the hell out and go to school.

We might want to isolate this quote as the principal basis of an argument according to which Parenti's social mobility and later activism were the products of a strong personal reaction to a family deprived of economic and social capital. In a way, this would mean over-analysing one assertion from the whole material. As attractive as that might be, singling out such an excerpt would not do justice to the richness of the material. Later in the speech, Parenti explained how history and social context shaped his social trajectory. Hence, one selected quote from the material cannot bear the whole weight of a conclusion. Moreover, the analysis requires more than proposing and explaining using the argument: 'It is true, the participants said it.' By doing so, the researcher essentially delegates the analytical work to the participants.

UNDER-ANALYSIS THROUGH TAKING SIDES

While there is undeniably a moral component to any study, producing knowl-edge is not about judging a phenomenon, a practice or a people. It is about providing a comprehensive account or an explanation for them. For example, our analysis of social participation could be centered on denouncing the lack of political awareness of participants who volunteer and promoting the political engagement of participants involved in activism. Our report would not result in an analysis so much as an evaluation of people's attitudes. As individuals, researchers favor some behaviors, ideas and rationales over others. However, promoting them as the organizing principles for the presentation of their analysis amounts to taking sides. That being said, researchers can conclude their reports with recommendations for action and policy changes. Indeed, many justify doing research for the purpose of possible social and political developments in the long term. However, to maximize the possibilities for such developments, a researcher might aim at uncovering a dynamic or mechanism relating to the phenomenon being studied. For example, a study might attempt to uncover the key elements in the trajectory of volunteers versus those in the trajectory of activists. Another possibility would be identifying and documenting the worldviews promoted in volunteer and activist cultures. The goal of the analysis is to provide a solid explanation of a phenomenon, rather than promote a particular view or a course of action by siding with some participants at the expense of others.

UNDER-ANALYSIS THROUGH FALSE SURVEY

Quantifying is prescribed by some analytical strategies often associated with qualitative research, namely content analysis. In such a case, though, it is more appropriate to present such an analysis as part of a quantitative or mixed research design. However, even if we opt for a qualitative approach to study situations, phenomena or worldviews in depth, our positivist culture with its preference for quantification (see Chapter 1) is still often our default position. Especially when we are inexperienced and uncertain as to our analytical strat-egy, the reflex might be to hierarchize the themes, codes, narrative features or interpretative repertoires found in the material on the basis of the frequency with which they appear. Here is an example:

> The code we titled 'trigger' was used twice more often and for much longer segments in the account of women participants than in men's. This might result in women having a more tumultuous social participation career as well as being more articulate on their reasons to get involved.

If the analysis stops at this type of assessment, the analysis basically takes the form of a quantitative summary interpreted through folk wisdom. This false survey misses the point of qualitative analysis. First, qualitative analysis is inter-ested in variety. Repetitions or commonalities in the material are certainly interesting, but not to the detriment of the outliers and differences as was shown previously. Outliers and differences need to be taken into account as well. Second, frequency is not necessarily an indicator of importance. Finally, determining what is frequent or rare in the material can lead to the implicit assumption that it is appropriate to statistically generalize the findings to a larger population. This would be a mistake, since qualitative studies are often based on small, purposeful samples. We have to keep our counting reflexes in check.

UNDER-ANALYSIS THROUGH SPOTTING FEATURES

Paying attention to the specificity of the language in use is a requirement in many schools of discourse analysis and narrative analysis as well as in many mixed analytical strategies, such as the one we demonstrated in Chapters 7 and 8. This close attention to discursive features such as metaphors, metonymy, the use of the pronoun 'we' by an individual or the use of the passive form (Parenti: 'Money was a constant problem and a concern') can help us uncover many analytical avenues. However, the identification of these discursive features still needs to be interpreted. In her book on narrative in social science research, Czarniawska warns us: 'Many young scholars, fascinated by the presence of stories, proceed to do studies that show this presence ... many [studies] are of the "Look, Ma, there is a narrative" type' (2004: 40–1). Explaining the role performed by these stories, the discursive contexts in which they are used and the consequences they have is needed to make sense of them. Of course, this advice is relevant to any discursive feature.

Being told what to avoid might help guide your analysis. But beyond and above escaping these pitfalls, we would like to conclude this chapter with a final word of advice on the importance of practicing reflexivity as a guide throughout your analysis.

THE QUALITY OF A GOOD ANALYSIS: REFLEXIVITY

The most important skill to cultivate as a researcher is reflexivity: a capacity to see oneself think, being aware of the way the mind works to assemble pieces of the empirical puzzle, the will to ask questions to test our developing ideas. Being a witness to the way we analyse the material is useful in at least two important ways. First, it feeds the analysis, helping it mature. Second, it is a key contributing factor for a more solid study. A reflexive piece of analysis is characterized by three interrelated characteristics: the transparency of the analytical process; the will to acknowledge and discuss counter-examples; and the capacity to articulate and discuss the limits of one's research.

TRANSPARENCY

The researcher needs to make explicit to a third party the steps taken, the dilemma pondered, the choices made all along the analytical process. For example, when proceeding to the vertical layer of discourse analysis through the interpretative repertoires of Parenti's talk, we mentioned the initial choice made to subdivide the material into two voices, the reflexive and the experiential. The logic was not only to make the material more manageable, but also to serve our intuition that those two voices would mobilize different sets of repertoires. When completing the vertical analysis, we mentioned that our intuition was not verified and that both voices mobilized, partly, the same repertoires. This is a banal example of transparency that allows the reader to assess the care invested in the analysis and evaluate the rationale that governed the analytical decisions. Ideally, we should aim at offering the reader a solid analysis that resembles the experience of having a meal in a good restaurant: not only is the food delicious, but also the chef comes to your table to explain how the ingredients were selected, how the herbs were blended, as well as the complementarity of the main and side dishes. Being made aware of what goes into the preparation of a creation adds to the enjoyment and appreciation of the results.

USING AND DISCUSSING COUNTER-EXAMPLES

In our experience, no matter how small the number of sources in a research project, there will be contradictions between the interpretations developed and some portions of the material. It is difficult to craft analytical assertions that apply equally to all the sources under study. For example, in our research on social participation we see a pattern emerge among our participants that links personal experiences of injustice to their involvement in the social and political spheres. However, two of our participants do not conform to this pattern. In their accounts, there is no mention of having experienced a form of injustice before joining their respective social justice organizations. Rather than silencing these counter-examples, we can transform them into analytical leverage. For example, while they may not have mentioned experiencing injustices personally, do these two participants mention having witnessed injustices in their close circles? Do their accounts emphasize a political struggle that was occurring, in the public sphere, at the time of their involvement? Could it be that they have a keen sensitivity to injustice, a capacity to identify it and with those suffering from it, that is enough to trigger a desire to get involved? We could be tempted to see counter-examples as obstacles. However, actively searching for them in our material and using them to develop better interpretations is a great way to strengthen our conclusions. For example, our discursive analysis of Parenti's speech suggests that it rests on individualist values and promotes the primacy of individual will for social change. In our analysis, we could have been tempted to ignore or downplay the segments where he acknowledges the force of history and structure as a driving force for change, since they seem to contradict our initial statement on the importance of individual will. Rather, by asking questions as to the relationship between the segments that promote individual versus collective values, we came to the conclusion that the latter serve as a disclaimer to the former, actually giving them more relief. How demonstration will succeed in convincing the reader is another story, but using counter-examples to improve upon the analysis is undeniably a reflex worth developing. When we cannot find a way to develop interpretations that encompass all the cases under study, it is good practice to mention it, reflecting out loud as to why this is the case. Discussing counter-examples is a sign of rigor on the part of the researcher. It adds credibility to a study. It shows that the interpretations developed were not forced at all cost upon the material.

VOICING THE LIMITS OF THE RESEARCH

Explicitly stating the limits of the study improves the quality of a manuscript. But let us be clear as to what we mean by limits here. Too often, we read research reports that include a methodological section or a portion of the conclusion devoted to the limits of the study written in a self-deprecative manner. Indeed, an author will note that since he or she has not conducted a survey on a wider sample, the results cannot be generalized to a broader population of activists. Or because the author interviewed only activists taking part in official social justice organizations, the research does not relate to people who offer their time to babysit their neighbors' kids or shop for some elderly neighbors. These are not the sorts of limits we have in mind. They are methodological decisions that have been, hopefully, carefully considered in the methods section of the report. Voicing the limits of the research does not mean apologizing for not having undertaken a study different from the one we chose to do. We are talking about acknowledging the shortcomings in the study we did choose to undertake. For example, an upper middle-class apolitical researcher might want to discuss the influences of his or her class and political background on the interviews conducted with underprivileged youths about their political involvement. How did these characteristics impact the type and quality of material the researcher produced? What was the quality of the rapport? How did power relations play out during the interviews? What topics were left out or difficult to discuss? The limits we are referring to here are issues internal to the chosen research project that should be explicitly reflected upon for the benefit of your audience.

CHAPTER SUMMARY

In this final chapter, we delved into the process of theorization and introduced you to different ways of producing typologies. We also discussed the potential of exploring the diversity of characters among your sources and a process to develop a dialogue between your empirical material and concepts, as they are defined in the literature, in order to enrich them. Moreover, common mistakes in theorizing were discussed: under-analysis through summarizing, over-quotation or isolated quote, taking sides, false survey and spotting features. Finally, we emphasized reflexivity, the capacity to articulate your own decisions. This capacity strengthens your study and translates into transparency in research, especially a will to openly discuss counter-examples as well as research limits.

Your project checklist

Now that you are more familiar with the process of theorization, you can:

✓   Choose a few empirical studies on your topic that share a similar approach to yours and read them closely to identify what theorization mechanisms are at play in those texts. How does the author go from describing empirical research results to interpreting them? What are the theorization mechanisms, explicit or implicit, used (typologies, dialogues between material and concepts, etc.)? Can you think of a way to develop the interpretation some more? How would you have proceeded?

✓ Using the same empirical studies, read their interpretation section carefully and analyse this section. How is it written? What is the structure of this section? How is the empirical material brought into this section, if at all? Do you see any of the mistakes we discussed in this chapter? Others? Could these mistakes be avoided? Are they compensated by strengths in the interpretation?

✓ Using the same empirical studies again, identify the strategies they use to convince you of their results and interpretation. What criteria do they use to claim the quality of their results and interpretation? Do they mention the limits of their study? If so, what do they mention and how do they address or explain those limits? How would you have proceeded?

✓ Finally, use a portion of the horizontal analysis you generated previously (in Chapter 8, when comparing two of your sources) and try to develop a typology, a map, to bring out the contrasting characters; if it applies, try to generate a dialogue between your empirical results and key concepts in the literature. The goal at this point is to try out the possibilities we listed here and evaluate whether they are helpful to develop your own theorization of the phenomena you study. Whether you rely on the theorization mechanisms we suggest here or those that you uncovered in the empirical studies you analysed in the exercises above, you are now better equipped to go beyond mere description, get creative and discipline your interpretative imagination toward developing a substantive interpretation of your chosen phenomenon.

What you should read next

Alasuutari, Pertti. 1996. 'Theorizing in Qualitative Research: A Cultural Studies Perspective'. *Qualitative Inquiry* 2(4): 371–84.

- In this article, Alasuutari explains the goal of social sciences, more specifically cultural studies, to produce theories of a middle-range level that explain a specific phenomenon. Using the analogy of the hourglass and detailed examples from the fieldwork he conducted with working-class men who are also regulars in pubs, he explains how he proceeded to generate interpretation to make sense of the texture of the society he studied.

Silverman, David. 2005a. 'Quality in Qualitative Research', pp. 209–26 in *Doing Qualitative Research: A Practical Handbook*, ed. D. Silverman. Thousand Oaks, CA: Sage.

- Silverman, an important reference in qualitative research, presents in this chapter a no-nonsense guide to increase the validity of research and the reliability of an interpretation. He gives many concrete examples for each criterion he suggests. The chapter is particularly interesting for researchers working with interviews.

Timmermans, Stefan and Iddo Tavory. 2012. 'Theory Construction in Qualitative Research: From Grounded Theory to Abductive Analysis'. *Sociological Theory* 30(3): 167–86.

- This journal article shows convincingly the fruitfulness of abduction and the importance of exploiting anomalies and novelties in your analysis to go beyond mere description or your substantive findings and, rather, to produce theory. We recommend you read this article, especially if you adopt grounded theory or a simpler type of analysis inspired by it, such as qualitative content analysis or thematic analysis. However, this article is a worthwhile read no matter what approach you use.

Trent, Allen and Jeasik Cho. 2015. 'Interpretation Strategies: Appropriate Concepts', pp. 639–57 in *The Oxford Handbook of Qualitative Research*, ed. P. Leavy. Oxford: Oxford University Press.

- This chapter explains thoroughly, but in an accessible manner, what interpretation means, a process to follow to achieve interpretation and the role of the researcher in such an endeavor. The authors capture their suggestions to generate a good interpretation under the acronym TRAVEL (Transparency, Reflexivity, Analysis, Validity, Evidence and Literature).

Wolcott, Harry F. 2009. *Writing Up Qualitative Research*. Newbury Park, CA: Sage.

- In this book you will find a wealth of tips and suggestions on how to tackle the writing of your research report or thesis, from time management to structure, from editing your own writing to keeping up the motivation. Whether one has trouble getting the writing done or not, this is a good resource and an inspiring read.

Want more support and inspiration? The online resources are here to help! Get to grips with key terms using **glossary flashcards**, see methods in action with a **library of SAGE cases and journal articles**, and follow analysis step-by-step with full transcripts of the sources discussed in the book.

GLOSSARY

Term	Definition
Abduction	The mental process in which we imagine our problem and its possible answers. An inference to the best explanation.
Cell sampling	The sampling is based on the choice categories, but they can overlap.
Comprehensive approach	A social science perspective that believes in the importance of interpreting reality from the lived experience of subjects and human praxis.
Concept	According to the *Merriam-Webster Dictionary*, it is an 'abstract or generic idea generalized from particular instances'.
Constructionist epistemology	Based on the belief that reality is partially socially constructed and our knowledge of it is a construction between the researcher and reality.
Constructivist epistemology	Based on the belief that reality is totally socially constructed and our knowledge of it needs to take this into account.
Constructivist ontology	Based on the belief that reality is totally or partially socially constructed.
Covert observation	Refers to situations in which researchers divulge the least information possible about their identity and goals as researchers.
Critical realist epistemology or critical realist or critical realism	Based on the belief that an objective reality exists outside of us, but the different types of apprehension of reality we have through our senses, our cognitive schemes and our knowledge are socially constructed.
Deduction	A logical operation based on universal premises from which we deduce specific information.
Diachronic or diachronically	Relating to a phenomenon over a period of time.
Disclosed observation or disclosure	Refers to a situation where the researcher chooses to clearly reveal his identity and research purpose and deal with participants' reactivity upfront. In this case, the researcher tries to develop trust and stay in the milieu long enough to 'blend in'.

Discourse	We translated a definition of the *Larousse Dictionary* that explains the common use of this term and helps to understand Foucault's perspective on discourse: a set of statements bound together by a specific and consistent logic, made up of rules and laws which do not necessarily belong to a natural language, and which provide information about material or ideal objects.
Emic	Refers to the perspective of the participants.
Empirical	We use this term to refer to the concrete manifestations of reality, manifestations that can be grasped by the senses. In this context, the term 'empirical' is opposed to theoretical or conceptual. When we refer to an empirical study, we mean that it is built on the analysis of research material, in any form, and is not limited to a conceptual text.
Epistemology	Is 'the study ... of the nature and grounds of knowledge, especially with reference to its limits and validity' (www.merriam-webster.com/dictionary/epistemology).
Etic	Refers to the perspective of the researcher.
Generalization	The process by which researchers expand the relevance of empirical observations to a larger group of people, situations or phenomena that have not been empirically observed. The process of going from the particular to the general, the concrete to the abstract.
Hegemonic discourse	The dominating discourse in a cultural realm.
Horizontal analysis	Comparative analysis of multiple sources, whether an observation period, an interview or a document. The goal is to identify the commonalities and differences in the entire empirical material.
Hypothesis	A tentative explanation of a scientific problem.
Hypothetico-deduction	The model according to which a researcher first needs to create a hypothesis, then to put this hypothesis to test using research material, to conclude by accepting or rejecting the hypothesis. Hypothetico-deduction is a model different from induction and abduction.
Induction	The model according to which a researcher generates a broad comprehension, or a theory from the ground up, that is based first and foremost on the empirical material gathered or produced.
Institution	We support the definition of institution as a custom or tradition that has existed for a long time and is accepted as an important part of a particular society (*Cambridge Advanced Learner's Dictionary & Thesaurus* © Cambridge University Press).

Interpretation (and interpretive understanding)	We support the definition of interpretation (and interpretive understanding) as a method that stresses the importance of understanding intentional human action. Semantically, any account is an interpretation. What distinguishes the interpretive paradigm from other movements is the recognition that any statement about the social world is necessarily relative to any other (*Collins Dictionary of Sociology*, 3rd edition. © HarperCollins Publishers 2000).
Interpretative repertoires	Following Wetherell and Potter (1988: 172), we define interpretative repertoires as 'relatively internally consistent, bounded language units'. These are often shared by many participants or documents. They are characterized by particular language features such as semantic networks and figures of speech.
Iterative process	Iteration is the act of repeating a sequence in a process. An iterative process is to repeat sequences of decisions and analytical objectives with the aim of approaching a desired goal.
Localized knowledge	Knowledge that does not aspire to be universal, but rather contextual to a time and a place and situated.
Logical positivism	Philosophical school that emphasizes the utmost importance of verificationism. According to this school, only what can be verified empirically can qualify as scientific knowledge.
Metaphysics	In Greek, *meta* means beyond. Metaphysics means beyond physical reality. It is also a branch of philosophy – the inquiry of things beyond scientific knowledge, such as the existence of God.
Methodological approach	Coherent ensemble of concepts, premises and guidelines that directs researchers' investigation of the world. A methodological approach is informed by ontological and epistemological positions (upstream), and is embodied in the choice of research tools (downstream).
Methods	A set of tools to grasp elements of reality.
Narrative	The subjective temporal thread that a person uses to order a sequence of events and share their experience.
Ontology	A discussion or a reflection 'about the nature of being or the kinds of things that have existence' (www.merriam-webster.com/dictionary/ontology).
Operationalization	Analytical process that consists of taking a complex concept apart to identify its dimensions, components and, sometimes, indicators to make the concept observable empirically.

Positivist epistemology	Epistemology based on the belief that knowledge is produced by the identification of natural law based on objectivity.
Practice	Practices refer to the actions taken by people. For Bourdieu (1980), a social practice is objective and subjective. It is an action structured by social norms and constraints, and it is subjective because it is also a set of actions that a person may want to adopt to position themselves.
Procedural ethics	Ethics designating values codified in laws, codes or rules.
Purposive sampling	In opposition to random sampling, a sampling based on the informative value of sources.
Quota sampling	Sampling based on a minimum of cases to explore.
Realist ontology	Based on the belief that reality exists outside the observer.
Reflexivity	The capacity to see oneself think. Being aware of the way the mind works to assemble pieces of the empirical puzzle and cultivating the ability to describe this process.
Representation	A social representation is 'a mental state or concept regarded as corresponding to a thing perceived' (*Oxford English Dictionary Online*, n.d.). Representations are not unrelated to discourse. The distinction is that a social representation indicates a particular object – for example, the social representation of alcohol – while a discourse indicates a historical process wherein a more global vision of a phenomenon develops.
Research design	Represents the architecture of a research inquiry. Its intent is to draw coherent relations between the research question, the research problem, the epistemological perspective, the theoretical framework and the methods.
Rigor	Rigor in research, as in common life, is 'the quality of being extremely thorough and careful' (https://en.oxforddictionaries.com/definition/rigour).
Sample, sampling	Using explicit criteria and rationale, sampling consists of selecting items (whether participants, observation sites, documents) from a larger group of such items. The result of this selection is called a sample.
Scientific knowledge	Knowledge constructed by researchers who challenge interpretation of reality based on empirical observations and logical claims.

Scientific paradigms	For Thomas Kuhn, a scientific paradigm is a set of concepts and rules adopted by scientists in a specific period of time. A scientific paradigm can change over time depending on new findings.
Semantic	Refers to the study of meanings of words or of signs.
Situation	A social interaction embedded in time and space.
Snowball sampling	A sampling method based on referrals from participants to the inquiry, generating other participants.
Statistical generalization	The process by which researchers build their sample following the principle of statistical representativity on certain criteria so that the results from this sample can be applied to a larger group. To proceed to statistical generalization, the research would need to have a sample that represents, in miniature, the main characteristics of the population this sample is taken from.
Stratified sampling	The sampling based on a number of respondents per category to compare.
Subjectively, subjectivity	Reality and experience as they are mediated through human consciousness.
Synchronic, Synchronically	Relating to an event in a limited period of time.
Theoretical analysis	Also called analytic generalization, it refers to the research phase where one has to link a case (or empiric data) to theories or concepts.
Theoretical generalization	The process by which researchers build their sample based on diversity of situations, profiles, experiences, with no preoccupation for the proportion of those existing in a larger group, to ensure that the analysis will yield a rich analysis: that is, an analysis where all the dimensions of the created concepts are present. As opposed to statistical generalization, theoretical generalization depends on the capacity of the concepts derived from a study to explain similar phenomena.
Theoretical sampling	Sampling is done throughout the fieldwork and the analysis depending on the saturation of categories of analysis.
Transferability	Transferability refers to the degree to which results can be generalized to other contexts.

Triangulation	Principle according to which the data gathered or produced needs to be verified or complemented to ensure the most accurate description of a reality.
Universal	A term that can be applied to all situations in the same circumstance. The law of gravity is universal because it can be applied to all objects on planet Earth.
Validity	A quality criterion in qualitative methods, it means that the knowledge produced is based on transparent empirical facts and that the interpretation is coherent.
Verbatim	Transcription word for word of an oral communication whether it is a speech, a conversation or an interview.
Verisimilitude	The property of being credible, convincing, realist, believable.
Vertical analysis	Analysis of a source, whether an observation period, an interview or a document, on its own, as a whole. The goal is to get to the core of this one source.

BIBLIOGRAPHY

Abrams, Laura. S. 2010. 'Sampling "Hard to Reach" Populations in Qualitative Research: The Case of Incarcerated Youth'. *Qualitative Social Work* 9(4): 536–50. doi: 10.1177/1473325010367821.

Adams, Jill. 2009. 'The Civil Restraining Order Application Process: Textually Mediated Institutional Case Management'. *Ethnography* 10(2): 185–211.

Alasuutari, Pertti. 1995a. 'Narrativity', pp. 70–84 in *Researching Culture: Qualitative Method and Cultural Studies*, ed. P. Alasuutari. London: Sage.

Alasuutari, Pertti. 1995b. *Researching Culture: Qualitative Method and Cultural Studies*. London: Sage.

Alasuutari, Pertti. 1995c. 'The Factist Perspective', pp. 47–62 in *Researching Culture: Qualitative Method and Cultural Studies*, ed. P. Alasuutari. London: Sage.

Alasuutari, Pertti. 1996. 'Theorizing in Qualitative Research: A Cultural Studies Perspective'. *Qualitative Inquiry* 2(4): 371–84.

Aluwihare-Samaranayake, Dilmi. 2012. 'Ethics in Qualitative Research: A View of the Participants' and Researchers' World from a Critical Standpoint'. *International Journal of Qualitative Methods – ARCHIVE* 11(2): 64–81.

Alvesson, Mats. 2002. 'Taking Language Seriously', pp. 63–89 in *Postmodernism and Social Research*, ed. M. Alvesson. Buckingham: Open University Press.

Alvesson, Mats. 2011. 'Rethinking Interviews: New Metaphors for Interviews', pp. 75–104 in *Interpreting Interviews*, ed. M. Alvesson. London: Sage.

Alvesson, Mats and Dan Karreman. 2011. *Qualitative Research and Theory Development: Mystery as Method*. Thousand Oaks, CA: Sage.

Andrews, Tom. 2012. 'What Is Social Constructionism?'. *Grounded Theory Review* 11(1) (http://groundedtheoryreview.com/2012/06/01/what-is-social-constructionism/).

Angrosino, Michael. 2003. 'L'Arche: The Phenomenology of Christian Counterculturalism'. *Qualitative Inquiry* 9(6): 934–54.

Antaki, Charles, Michael Billig, Derek Edwards and Jonathan Potter. 2003. 'Discourse Analysis Means Doing Analysis: A Critique of Six Analytic Shortcomings'. *Discourse Analysis Online* 1(1).

Arborio, Anne-Marie and Pierre Fournier. 1999. *L'enquête et ses méthodes. L'observation directe*. [Research Inquiry and Its Methods. Direct Observation]. Paris: Nathan Université.

Atkinson, Paul and Amanda Coffey. 1997. 'Analysing Documentary Realities', pp. 45–62 in *Qualitative Research: Theory, Method and Practice*, ed. D. Silverman. London: Sage.

Atkinson, Paul, Amanda Coffey, Sara Delamont, John Lofland and Lyn H. Lofland. 2001. 'Introduction to Part One', pp. 8–11 in *Handbook of Ethnography*, ed. P. Atkinson et al. London: Sage.

Atkinson, Paul, Sara Delamont and Martyn Hammersley. 1988. 'Qualitative Research Traditions: A British Response to Jacob'. *Review of Educational Research* 58(2): 231–50.

Bachelard, Gaston. 1999. *La formation de l'esprit scientifique* [Formation of the Scientific Mind]. Paris: Librairie philosophique Vrin (1st edition, 1938).

Becker, Howard S. 1963. *Outsiders: Studies in the Sociology of Deviance*. New York: Free Press.

Berger, Peter L. and Thomas Luckmann. 1966. *The Social Construction of Reality: A Treatise in the Sociology of Knowledge*. Garden City, NY: Anchor Books.

Bertaux, Daniel. 2010. *Le récit de vie – L'enquête et ses méthodes* [Life Narrative: Research Inquiry and Its Methods]. 3rd edition. Paris: Armand Colin.

Bhaskar, Roy. A. 1975/1997. *A Realist Theory of Science*. London: Verso.

Binder, Martin and Ann-Kathrin Blankenberg. 2016. 'Environmental Concerns, Volunteering and Subjective Well-Being: Antecedents and Outcomes of Environmental Activism in Germany'. *Ecological Economics* 124: 1–16. doi: 10.1016/j.ecolecon.2016.01.009.

Birch, Maxine and Tina Miller. 2000. 'Inviting Intimacy: The Interview as Therapeutic Opportunity'. *International Journal of Social Research Methodology* 3(3): 189–202.

Blanchet, Alain. 1987. 'Interviewer', pp. 81–126 in *Les Techniques d'enquête en sciences sociales. Observer, interviewer, questionner* [Research Techniques in Social Sciences. Observations, interviews and surveys], ed. A. Blanchet. Paris: Dunod.

Blanchet, Alain. 1989. 'Les relances de l'interviewer dans l'entretien de recherche. Leurs effets sur la modalisation et la déictisation du discours de l'interviewé' [The effect of the interviewer's prompts on the interviewee's discourse]. *L'année psychologique* 89(3): 367–91.

Blumer, Herbert. 1954. 'What Is Wrong with Social Theory?' *American Sociological Review* 18: 3–10.

Blumer, Herbert. 1969. *Symbolic Interactionism: Perspective and Method*. Englewood Cliffs, NJ: Prentice Hall.

Bourdieu, Pierre. 1980. *Le sens pratique* [Outline of a Theory of Practice]. Paris: Éditions de Minuit.

Bourdieu, Pierre, Jean-Claude Chamboredon and Jean-Claude Passeron. 1983. *Le métier de sociologue* [The Craft of Sociology]. Paris: Mouton.

Bowen, Glenn A. 2009. 'Document Analysis as a Qualitative Research Method'. *Qualitative Research Journal* 9(2): 27–40.

Brown, Sheila. 2006. 'The Criminology of Hybrids: Rethinking Crime and Law in Technosocial Networks'. *Theoretical Criminology* 10(2): 223–44.

Bruner, Jerome. 1987. 'Life as Narrative'. *Social Research* 54(1): 11–32.

Bruner, Jerome. 1991. 'The Narrative Construction of Reality'. *Critical Inquiry* 18(1): 1–21.

Bruner, Jerome. 2002. 'The Narrative Creation of Self', pp. 63–87 in *Making Stories: Law, Literature, Life*, ed. J. Bruner. Cambridge, MA: Harvard University Press.

Bryant, Anthony and Kathy Charmaz. 2007. 'Grounded Theory in Historical Perspective: An Epistemological Account', pp. 31–57 in *The Sage Handbook of Grounded Theory*, ed. A. Bryant and K. Charmaz. Thousand Oaks, CA: Sage.

Bülow, Pia H. 2004. 'Sharing Experiences of Contested Illness by Storytelling'. *Discourse & Society* 15(1): 33–53.

Burke, Shani and Simon Goodman. 2012. '"Bring Back Hitler's Gas Chambers": Asylum Seeking, Nazis and Facebook – A Discursive Analysis'. *Discourse & Society* 23(1): 19–33. doi: 10.1177/0957926511431036.

Burman, Erica. 2004. 'Discourse Analysis Means Analysing Discourse: Some Comments on Antaki, Billig, Edward and Potter "Discourse Analysis Means Doing Analysis: A Critique of Six Analytic Shortcomings"'. *Discourse Analysis Online* 1(1).

Burri, Regula Valérie. 2012. 'Visual Rationalities: Towards a Sociology of Images'. *Current Sociology* 60(1): 45–60. doi: 10.1177/0011392111426647.

Busino, Giovanni. 2003. 'La place de la métaphore en sociologie' [Metaphor's Role in Sociology]. *Revue européenne des sciences sociales* No. XLI–126: 91–101. doi: 10.4000/ress.539.

Butler-Kisber, Lynn. 2010. 'Phenomenological Inquiry', pp. 50–61 in *Qualitative Inquiry: Thematic, Narrative and Arts-Informed Perspectives*, ed. L. Butler-Kisber. Thousand Oaks, CA: Sage.

Campbell, Marie and Frances Gregor. 2002. *Mapping Social Relations: A Primer in Doing Institutional Ethnography*. Aurora, ON: Garamond Press.

Campenhoudt, Luc Van and Raymond Quivy. 2011. *Manuel de recherche en sciences sociales* [Research Handbook of Social Science]. 4th edition. Paris: Dunod.

Carabine, Jean. 2001. 'Unmarried Motherhood 1830–1990: A Genealogical Analysis', pp. 267–310 in *Discourse as Data: A Guide for Analysis*, ed. M. Wetherell et al. London: Sage and The Open University Press.

Carrabine, Eamonn. 2012. 'Just Images'. *British Journal of Criminology* 52(3): 463–89. doi: 10.1093/bjc/azr089.

Cellard, André. 1997. 'L'analyse documentaire' [Document Analysis], pp. 275–96 in *La Recherche qualitative. Enjeux épistémologiques et méthodologiques* [Qualitative Research. Epistemological and Methodological Issues], ed. J. Poupart et al. Montreal: Centre international de criminologie comparée.

Charbonneau, Johanne. 2003. *Adolescentes et mères* [Teenagers and Mothers]. Saint-Nicolas: Presses de l'Université Laval.

Charmaz, Kathy. 2000. 'Grounded Theory Objectivist and Constructivist Method', pp. 509–35 in *Handbook of Qualitative Research*, ed. N. Denzin and Y. Lincoln. Thousand Oaks, CA: Sage.

Charmaz, Kathy. 2014. *Constructing Grounded Theory*. 2nd edition. Thousand Oaks, CA: Sage.

Clarke, Adele E. 2005. *Situational Analysis: Grounded Theory after the Postmodern Turn*. Thousand Oaks, CA: Sage.

Coenen-Huther, Jacques. 2006. 'Compréhension sociologique et démarches typologiques' [Sociological Understanding and Typologies]. *Revue européenne des sciences sociales* No. XLIV–135: 195–205. doi: 10.4000/ress.272.

Collins Discovery Encyclopedia. 2005. London: HarperCollins.

Cooper, Geoff, Nicola Green, Kate Burningham, David Evans and Tim Jackson. 2012. 'Unravelling the Threads: Discourses of Sustainability and Consumption in an Online Forum'. *Environmental Communication* 6(1): 101–18. doi: 10.1080/17524032.2011.642080.

Corbin, Juliet and Anselm Strauss. 1990. 'Grounded Theory Research: Procedures, Canons, and Evaluative Criteria'. *Qualitative Sociology* 13(1): 3–21.

Creef, Elena Tajima. 2002. 'Discovering My Mother as the Other in the Saturday Evening Post', pp. 73–89 in *The Qualitative Inquiry Reader*, edited by N. K. Denzin and Y. S. Lincoln. Thousand Oaks, CA: Sage.

Creswell, John W. 2012. *Qualitative Inquiry and Research Design: Choosing among Five Approaches*. Thousand Oaks, CA: Sage.

Czarniawska, Barbara. 2004. *Narratives in Social Science Research*. London: Sage.

Daunais, Jean-Paul. 1992. 'L'entretien Non Directif' [Non-directive Interviews], pp. 273–93 in *Recherche sociale. De la problématique à la collecte de données* [Social Research. From Modelization to Data Gathering], ed. B. Gauthier. Sainte-Foy: PUQ.

De Fina, Anna and Alexandra Georgakopoulou. 2008. 'Analysing Narratives as Practices'. *Qualitative Research* 8(3): 379–87.

Della Porta, Donatella. 2013. *Can Democracy Be Saved? Participation, Deliberation and Social Movements*. Cambridge: Polity Press.

Demazière, Didier. 2013. 'Typologie et description. À propos de l'intelligibilité des expériences vécues' [Typologies and Description. Understanding the Lived Experience]. *Sociologie* 4(3): 333–47.

Demazière, Didier and Claude Dubar. 1996. *Analyser les entretiens biographiques. L'exemple des récits d'insertion* [Analysing Biographical Interviews. An Example of Social Insertion Narratives], Essais et recherches en sciences humaines [Essays and Research in Human Sciences]. Paris: Nathan.

de Montigny, Gerald. 2014. 'Doing Child Protection Work', pp. 173–94 in *Incorporating Texts into Institutional Ethnographies*, ed. D. E. Smith and S. M. Turner. Toronto: University of Toronto Press.

Deslauriers, Jean-Pierre and Robert Mayer. 2000. 'L'observation directe' [Direct Observation], pp. 135–57 in *Méthodologie de la recherche pour intervenants sociaux* [Research Methods for Social Services Professionals], ed. R. Mayer et al. Montreal: Gaétan Morin.

Diamond, Timothy. 1992. *Making Gray Gold: Narratives of Nursing Home Care*. Chicago: University of Chicago Press.

Dictionnaire Larousse en ligne (www.larousse.fr/dictionnaires/francais/discours/25859?q=discours#25733). Retrieved June 6, 2017.

Dilthey, Wilhelm. 1942. *Introduction à l'étude des sciences humaines. Essai sur le fondement qu'on pourrait donner à l'étude de la société et de l'histoire.* [Introduction to Human Sciences Study. Essay on the Principles of Studying Society and History]. Paris: Presses Universitaires de France.

Dubet, François. 1995. *Sociologie de l'expérience* [Sociology of Experience]. Paris: Seuil.

Dumez, Hervé. 2012. 'Qu'est-ce que l'abduction, et en quoi peut-elle avoir un rapport avec la recherche qualitative?' [What is Abduction? How It Is

Related to Qualitative Research]. *Le Libellio d'AEGIS,* 8(3): 3-9. http://lelibellio.com/wp-content/uploads/2013/02/DOSSIER-Abduction.pdf.

Durkheim, Emile. 2013. *Le suicide* [Suicide]. Paris: Presses Universitaires de France (1st edition, 1897).

Elder-Vass, Dave. 2012. 'Towards a Realist Social Constructionism'. *Sociologia, Problemas E Práticas,* 70: 9–24.

Eliasoph, Nina. 1998. *Avoiding Politics: How Americans Produce Apathy in Everyday Life.* Cambridge: Cambridge University Press.

Ellis, Carolyn and Jerry Rawicki. 2013. 'Collaborative Witnessing of Survival During the Holocaust: An Exemplar of Relational Autoethnography'. *Qualitative Inquiry* 19(5): 366–80. doi: 10.1177/1077800413479562.

Esterberg, Kristin G. 2002. *Qualitative Methods in Social Research.* Boston, MA: McGraw-Hill.

Fairclough, Norman. 1995. *Critical Discourse Analysis: The Critical Study of Language.* London: Longman.

Fairclough, Norman. 2001. 'Critical Discourse Analysis as a Method in Social Scientific Research', pp. 121–38 in *Methods of Critical Discourse Analysis,* ed. R. Wodak and M. Meyer. Thousand Oaks, CA: Sage.

Farge, A. 1989. *Le goût de l'archive* [Allure of the Archives]. Paris: Seuil.

Festinger, Leon, Henry W. Riecken and Stanley Schachter. 1956. *When Prophecy Fails.* Minneapolis: University of Minnesota Press.

Finley, Nancy J. 2010. 'Skating Femininity: Gender Maneuvering in Women's Roller Derby'. *Journal of Contemporary Ethnography* 39(4): 359–87.

Flick, Uwe. 2006. 'Focus Groups', pp. 189–203 in *An Introduction to Qualitative Research,* ed. U. Flick. London: Sage.

Fontan, Jean-Marc and Isabel Heck. 2017. 'Parole d'exclués: croisement des savoirs, des pouvoirs et des pratiques au sein de l'incubateur universitaire. Parole d'exclués' [Exclusion: Cross-fertilization of Ideas, Powers and Practices within the University Incubator. Testimonies of marginalized people]. *Éducation et socialisation. Les Cahiers du CERFEE,* no. 45 (septembre): http://edso.revues.org/. doi:10.4000/edso.2540.

Fontana, Andrea. 2001. 'Postmodern Trends in Interviewing', pp. 161–75 in *Handbook of Interview Research,* ed. J. F. Gubrium and J. A. Holstein. Thousand Oaks, CA: Sage.

Fontana, Andrea and James H. Frey. 2005. 'The Interview: From Neutral Stance to Political Involvement', pp. 695–727 in *The Sage Handbook of Qualitative Research,* ed. N. K. Denzin and Y. S. Lincoln. Thousand Oaks, CA: Sage.

Foucault, Michel. 1971. *L'ordre du discours* [The Discourse on Language]. Paris: Gallimard.

Fouche, Fidéla. 1993. 'Phenomenological Theory of Human Science', pp. 111–44 in *Conceptions of Social Inquiry,* HSRC Series in Methodology, ed. J. Snyman. Pretoria: HSRC.

Frank, Arthur. 1995. *The Wounded Storyteller: Body, Illness, and Ethics.* Chicago: Chicago University Press.

Gee, James Paul. 2005. *An Introduction to Discourse Analysis: Theory and Method.* New York: Routledge.

Geertz, Clifford. 1973. *The Interpretation of Cultures: Selected Essays.* New York: Basic Books.

Gilster, Megan E. 2012. 'Comparing Neighborhood-Focused Activism and Volunteerism: Psychological Well-Being and Social Connectedness'. *Journal of Community Psychology* 40(7): 769–84. doi: 10.1002/jcop.20528.

Giorgi, Amadeo. 1985. *Phenomenology and Psychological Research*. Pittsburgh: Duquesne University Press.

Glaser, Barney G. 1978. *Theoretical Sensitivity: Advances in the Methodology of Grounded Theory*. Mill Valley, CA: Sociology Press.

Glaser, Barney G. and Anselm L. Strauss. 1965/1970. *Awareness of Dying*. Chicago: Aldine.

Glaser, Barney G. and Anselm L. Strauss. 1967. *The Discovery of Grounded Theory*. New York: Aldine.

Glaser, Barney G. and Anselm L. Strauss. 1968. *Time for Dying*. Chicago: Aldine.

Glaser, Barney G. and Anselm L. Strauss. 1971. *Status Passage*. London: Routledge & Kegan Paul.

Goffman, Erving. 1961. *Asylums: Essays on the Social Situation of Mental Patients and Other Inmates*. New York: Anchor Books.

Green, Helen. 2014. 'Use of Theoretical and Conceptual Frameworks in Qualitative Research'. *Nurse Researcher* 21(6): 34–8.

Greenwood, Davydd J. and Morten Levin. 2005. 'Reform of the Social Sciences and of Universities Through Action Research', pp. 43–64 in *The Sage Handbook of Qualitative Research*, ed. N. Denzin and Y. S. Lincoln. Thousand Oaks, CA: Sage.

Greimas, Algirdas Julien. 1966/1983. *Structural Semantics: An Attempt at a Method*. Lincoln: University of Nebraska Press.

Groenewald, Thomas. 2004. 'A Phenomenological Research Design Illustrated'. *International Journal of Qualitative Methods* 3(1): Art. 4.

Guba, Egon. G. and Yvonna S. Lincoln. 2004. 'Competing Paradigms in Qualitative Research: Theories and Issues', pp. 17–38 in *Approaches to Qualitative Research: A Reader on Theory and Practice*, ed. S. Hesse-Beiber and P. Leary. New York: Oxford University Press.

Gubrium, Jaber F. and James A. Holstein (eds). 2001. *Handbook of Interview Research*. Thousand Oaks, CA: Sage.

Halse, Christine and Honey, Anne. 2007. 'Rethinking Ethics Review as Institutional Discourse'. *Qualitative Inquiry,* 13(3): 336–52.

Harvey, Lee. 2011. 'Will Wright: Sixguns and Society', in *Critical Social Research*, ed. L. Harvey. London: Unwin Hyman (available at qualityresearchinternational. com/csr).

Heidegger, Martin. 1927/1962. *Being and Time*. San Francisco: Harper & Row.

Herman, Luc and Bart Vervaeck. 2005. *Handbook of Narrative Analysis*. Lincoln: University of Nebraska Press.

Hine, Christine. 2007. 'Multi-Sited Ethnography as a Middle Range Methodology for Contemporary STS'. *Science, Technology & Human Values* 32(6): 652–71. doi: 10.1177/0162243907303598.

Hirsch, Paul M. 1986. 'From Ambushes to Golden Parachutes: Corporate Takeovers as an Instance of Cultural Framing and Institutional Integration'. *American Journal of Sociology* 91: 800–37.

Hsu, Wendy F. 2014. 'Digital Ethnography toward Augmented Empiricism: A New Methodological Framework'. *Journal of Digital Humanities* 3(1) (http://journalofdigitalhumanities.org/3-1/digital-ethnography-toward-augmented-empiricism-by-wendy-hsu/). Retrieved June 15, 2014.

Jacob, Evelyn. 1987. 'Qualitative Research Traditions: A Review'. *Review of Educational Research* 57(1): 1–50.

James, Nalita and Hugh Busher. 2012. 'Internet Interviewing', pp. 177–92 in *The Sage Handbook of Interview Research: The Complexity of the Craft*, ed. J. F. Gubrium et al. Thousand Oaks, CA: Sage.

Jefferson, Gail. 2004. 'Glossary of Transcript Symbols with an Introduction', pp. 13–31 in *Conversation Analysis: Studies from the First Generation*, ed. G. Lerner. Amsterdam: John Benjamin.

Jorgensen, Marianne and Louise Phillips. 2002. *Discourse Analysis as Theory and Method*. London: Sage.

Kandel, Liliane. 1972. 'Réflexion sur l'entretien, notamment non directif et sur les études d'opinion' [Reflecting on Interviews. Non-directive Interviews and Surveys]. *Épistémologie sociologique* 13: 25–46.

Kindon, Sara, Rachel Pain and Mike Kesby. 2007. *Participatory Action Research Approaches and Methods: Connecting People, Participation and Place*. London: Routledge.

Kohler Riessman, Catherine. 1990. 'Strategic Uses of Narrative in the Presentation of Self and Illness: A Research Note'. *Social Science and Medicine* 30(11): 1195–200.

Kohler Riessman, Catherine. 1993. 'Practical Models', pp. 25–53 in *Narrative Analysis*, ed. C. Kohler Riessman. Newbury Park, CA: Sage.

Kohler Riessman, Catherine. 2008. *Narrative Methods for the Human Sciences*. Thousand Oaks, CA: Sage.

Kools, Susan. 2008. 'From Heritage to Postmodern Grounded Theorizing: Forty Years of Grounded Theory', pp. 73–86 in *Studies in Symbolic Interaction* Vol. 32, ed. N. K. Denzin et al. Bingley: Emerald.

Labov, William and Joshua Waletzky. 1967. 'Narrative Analysis', pp. 12–44 in *Essays on the Verbal and Visual Arts*, ed. J. Helm. Seattle: University of Washington Press.

Lapadat, Judith C. 2000. 'Problematizing Transcription: Purpose, Paradigm and Quality'. *International Journal of Social Research Methodology* 3(3): 203–19.

Laperrière, Anne. 2003. 'L'Observation directe' [Direct Observation], pp. 269–91 in *Recherche sociale. De la problématique à la collecte de données* [Social Research. From Modelization to Data Gathering], ed. B. Gauthier. Sainte-Foy: PUQ.

Larsen, Mike and Kevin Walby (eds). 2012. *Brokering Access: Power, Politics and Freedom of Information Process in Canada*. Vancouver: University of British Columbia Press.

Latour, Bruno. 1999. 'Circulating Reference: Sampling the Soil in the Amazon Forest', pp. 24–79 in *Pandora's Hope: Essays on the Reality of Science Studies*, ed. B. Latour. Cambridge, MA: Harvard University Press.

Latour, Bruno. 2005. *La Science en action. Introduction à la sociologie des sciences* [Science in Action]. Paris: Éditions La Découverte.

Latour, Bruno and Steve Woolgar. 1979/1996. *Laboratory Life: The Social Construction of Scientific Facts*. Beverly Hills, CA: Sage.

Lefrançois, David, Marc-André Éthier and Stéfanie Demers. 2009. 'Justice sociale et réforme scolaire au Québec. Le cas du programme d'Histoire et éducation à la citoyenneté' [Social Justice and Educational Reform in Quebec. The Case of the Curriculum of History and Citizenship Education]. *Éthique publique* 11(1): 72–85.

Lévi-Strauss, Claude. 1963/1999. *Structural Anthropology*, trans. C. J. and B. G. Schoepf. New York: Basic Books.

Lincoln, Yvonna and Gaile Cannella. 2009. 'Ethics and the Broader Rethinking/ Reconceptualization of Research as Construct'. *Cultural Studies: Critical Methodologies* 9(2): 273–85.

Lofland, John, David A. Snow, Leon Anderson and Lyn H. Lofland. 2006. *Analyzing Social Settings: A Guide to Qualitative Observation and Analysis*. Belmont, CA: Wadsworth/Thomson Learning.

Los, Maria. 2006. 'Looking into the Future: Surveillance, Globalization and the Totalitarian Potential', pp. 69–94 in *Theorizing Surveillance: The Panopticon and Beyond*, ed. D. Lyon. Cullompton: Willan.

Loseke, Donileen R. and Spencer E. Cahill. 1999. 'Reflections on Classifying Ethnographic Reflections at the Millennium's Turn'. *Journal of Contemporary Ethnography* 28(5): 437–41. doi: 10.1177/089124199129023514.

Madison, Soyini. 2005. *Critical Ethnography: Methods, Ethics and Performance*. Thousand Oaks, CA: Sage.

Malinowski, Bronislaw. 1922/1966. *Argonauts of the Western Pacific: An Account of Native Enterprise and Adventure in the Archipelagoes of Melanesian New Guinea*. London: Routledge.

Mallozzi, Christine A. 2009. 'Voicing the Interview: A Researcher's Exploration on a Platform of Empathy'. *Qualitative Inquiry* 15(6): 1042–60.

Marcus, George E. 1995. 'Ethnography in/of the World System: The Emergence of Multi-Sited Ethnography'. *Annual Review of Anthropology* 24(1): 95–117. doi: 10.1146/annurev.an.24.100195.000523.

Marcus, George E., Tom Boellstorff and Bonni Nardi. 2012. *Ethnography and Virtual Worlds: A Handbook of Method*. Princeton, NJ: Princeton University Press.

Marquart, James. 2003. 'Doing Research in Prison', pp. 383–93 in *Qualitative Approaches to Criminal Justice: Perspectives from the Field*, ed. M. R. Pogrebin. Thousand Oaks, CA: Sage.

Marshall, Catherine and Gretchen B. Rossman. 2006. *Designing Qualitative Research*. Thousand Oaks, CA: Sage.

Martineau, Stéphane. 2005. ' L'observation en situation: enjeux, possibilités et limites. L'instrumentation dans la collecte des données: choix et pertinence' [Situated Observations: Issues, Possibilities and Limits. Instruments in Data Collection: Choice and Relevance], pp. 5–17 in *Actes du Colloque de l'Association pour la Recherche Qualitative (ARQ)*, Hors-Série numéro 2, ed. C. Royer et al. Trois-Rivières: UQTR.

Martuccelli, Danilo. 2005. 'Les trois voies de l'individu sociologique' [The Three Roads of the Sociological Individual]. *Revue électronique des sciences humaines et sociales.* EspacesTemps.net (www.espacestemps.net/articles/trois-voies-individu-sociologique/), June 8.

Martuccelli, Danilo. 2006. 'Forgé par l'épreuve' [Forged through Adversity]. *L'individu dans la France contemporaine* [The Individual in Contemporary France]. Paris: Armand Colin.

Maxwell, Joseph. 2013. *Qualitative Research Design: An Interactive Approach.* Thousand Oaks, CA: Sage.

Mayer, Robert and Marie-Christine Saint-Jacques. 2000. 'L'Entrevue de recherche' [The Research Interview], pp. 115–33 in *Méthodologie de recherche pour intervenants sociaux*, Research Methods for Social Services Professionals] ed. R. Mayer and F. Ouellet. Montreal: Gaétan Morin.

McGraw-Hill Dictionary of Scientific & Technical Terms. 2003. New York: McGraw-Hill.

McMullen, Linda, M. 2011. 'A Discursive Analysis of Teresa's Protocol: Enhancing Oneself, Diminishing Others', pp. 205–23 in *Five Ways of Doing Qualitative Analysis: Phenomenological Psychology, Grounded Theory, Discourse Analysis, Narrative Research, and Intuitive Inquiry*, ed. F. J. Wertz et al. New York: Guilford Press.

Mead, George Herbert. 1934/1963. *Mind, Self, and Society.* Chicago: University of Chicago Press.

Merleau-Ponty, Maurice. 1945/2012. *Phenomenology of Perception*, trans. D. A. Landes. New York: Routledge.

Merriam-Webster Online (https://www.merriam-webster.com/dictionary). Retrieved June 6, 2017.

Merton, Robert K. 1968. *Social Theory and Social Structure*, Enlarged edition. New York: Free Press.

Messerschmidt, James W. 1993. *Masculinities and Crime: Critique and Reconceptualization of Theory.* Lanham, MD: Rowman & Littlefield.

Michelat, Guy. 1975. 'Sur l'utilisation de l'entretien non directif en sociologie' [The Use of Non-directive Interviews in Sociology]. *Revue française de sociologie* XVI: 229–47.

Miles, Matthew. B. and A. Michael Huberman. 1984. *Qualitative Data Analysis: A Sourcebook of New Methods.* London: Sage.

Miles, Matthew. B. and A. Michael Huberman. 1994. *Qualitative Data Analysis: An Expanded Sourcebook.* London: Sage.

Miles, Matthew B., A. Michael Huberman and Johnny Saldaña. 2013. *Qualitative Data Analysis: A Sourcebook of New Methods.* Thousand Oaks, CA: Sage.

Mishler, Elliot G. 1986. *Research Interviewing: Context and Narrative.* Cambridge, MA: Harvard University Press.

Mol, Annemarie. 2002. 'Cutting Surgeons, Walking Patients: Some Complexities Involved in Comparing', pp. 228–57 in *Complexities*, ed. J. Law and A. Mol. Durham, NC: Duke University Press.

Monceau, Gilles and Marguerite Soulière. 2017. 'Mener la recherche avec les sujets concernés: comment et pour quels résultats?' [Conducting Research with the Concerned Subjects: How and for Which Results?]. *Éducation et socialisation* 45 (septembre): http://edso.revues.org/2525. doi:10.4000/edso.2525.

Moore, Robert J., E. Hankinson Gathman and Nicolas Ducheneaut. 2009. 'From 3D Space to Third Place: The Social Life of Small Virtual Spaces'. *Human Organization* 68(2): 230–40.

Moustakas, Clark. 1994. *Phenomenological Research Methods*. Thousand Oaks, CA: Sage.

Munhall, Patricia L. 2007. 'A Phenomenological Method', pp. 145–210 in *Nursing Research: A Qualitative Perspective*, ed. P. L. Munhall. Sudbury, MA: Jones and Bartlett.

Murthy, Dhiraj. 2008. 'Digital Ethnography: An Examination of the Use of New Technologies for Social Research'. *Sociology* 42(5): 837–55. doi: 10.1177/0038038508094565.

Musick, Marc A. and John Wilson. 2008. *Volunteers: A Social Profile*. Bloomington, IN: Indiana University Press.

Ocejo, Richard E. and Stéphane Tonnelat. 2014. 'Subway Diaries: How People Experience and Practice Riding the Train'. *Ethnography* 15(4): 493–515. doi: 10.1177/1466138113491171.

Ochoa, Alberto, Julio Ponce, Rubén Jaramillo, Francisco Ornelas, Alberto Hernández, Daniel Azpeitia, Arturo Elias and Arturo Hernández. 2011. 'Analysis of Cyber-Bullying in a Virtual Social Networking', pp. 229–34 in *11th International Conference on Hybrid Intelligent Systems*. Malacca, Malaysia.

Oliver, Carolyn. 2011. 'Critical Realist Grounded Theory: A New Approach for Social Work Research'. *British Journal of Social Work* 42(2): 371–87. doi: 10.1093/bjsw/bcr064.

O'Reilly, Karen. 2005. *Ethnographic Methods*. London: Routledge.

O'Toole, Paddy and Prisca Were. 2008. 'Observing Places: Using Space and Material Culture in Qualitative Research'. *Qualitative Research* 8(5): 616–34.

Oxford English Dictionary Online (https://en.oxforddictionaries.com/definition/representation). Retrieved June 6, 2017.

Paillé, Pierre. 1994. 'L'analyse par théorisation ancrée' [Grounded Theory Analysis]. *Cahiers de recherche sociologique* 23: 147–81.

Paillé, Pierre and Alex Mucchielli. 2003. 'L'analyse thématique' [Thematic Analysis], pp. 123–45 in *L'analyse qualitative en sciences sociales et humaines* [Qualitative Research in Social and Human Sciences], ed. P. Paillé and A. Mucchielli. Paris: Armand Colin.

Paillé, Pierre and Alex Mucchielli. 2010. *L'analyse qualitative en sciences sociales et humaines* [Qualitative Analysis in Social and Human Sciences]. Paris: Armand Colin.

Parazelli, Michel. 2002. *La rue attractive. Parcours et pratiques identitaires des jeunes de la rue* [Attractiveness of the Street. Paths and Identity of Street Youth], Collection Problèmes sociaux & interventions sociales, 5. Sainte-Foy: Presses de l'Université du Québec.

Pascale, Céline-Marie. 2011. *Cartographies of Knowledge: Exploring Qualitative Epistemologies*. Thousand Oaks, CA: Sage.

Passeron, Jean-Claude. 2001. 'La forme des preuves dans les sciences historiques' [Proofs in Historical Sciences]. *Revue européenne des Sciences Sociales* 39(120): 31–76.

Passeron, Jean-Claude. 2006. *Le raisonnement sociologique* [Sociological Reasoning]. Paris: Albin Michel.

Peled-Elhanan, Nurit. 2010. 'Legitimation of Massacres in Israeli School History Books'. *Discourse & Society* 21(4): 377–404.

Peretz, Henri. 1998. *Les méthodes en sociologie. L'observation* [Sociological Methods. The Observation]. Paris: La Découverte.

Perreault, Isabelle and Marie-Claude Thifault. 2016. *Récits inachevés : réflexions sur la recherche qualitative en sciences sociales.* [Unfinished Narratives. Reflecting on Qualitative Research in Social Sciences] Ottawa: Presses de l'Université d'Ottawa.

Peterson, Eric E. and Kristin M. Langellier. 2006. 'The Performance Turn in Narrative Studies'. *Narrative Inquiry* 16(1): 173–80.

Phillips, Nelson and Cynthia Hardy. 2002. 'The Varieties of Discourse Analysis', pp. 18–39 in *Discourse Analysis: Investigating Processes of Social Construction*, Qualitative Research Methods Series, ed. N. Phillips and C. Hardy. Thousand Oaks, CA: Sage.

Pinnegar, Stefinee and Gary D. Daynes. 2007. 'Locating Narrative Inquiry Historically: Thematics in the Turn to Narrative', pp. 3–34 in *Handbook of Narrative Inquiry: Mapping a Methodology*, ed. J. D. Clandinin. Thousand Oaks, CA: Sage.

Pires, Alvaro. 1997. 'De quelques enjeux épistémologiques d'une méthodologie générale pour les sciences sociales' [Epistemological Challenges for a General Methodology for Social Sciences], pp. 113–69 in *La recherche qualitative. Enjeux épistémologiques et méthodologiques* [Qualitative Research. Epistemological and Methodological Issues], ed. J. Poupart et al. Montreal: Centre international de criminologie comparée.

Potter, Jonathan. 2012. 'Re-Reading Discourse and Social Psychology: Transforming Social Psychology'. *British Journal of Social Psychology* 51(3): 436–55.

Poupart, Jean. 1993. 'Discours et débats autour de la scientificité des entretiens de recherche' [Debates on the Scientificity of Research Interviews]. *Sociologie et sociétés* XXV(2): 93–110.

Prelli, Lawrence J. and Terri S. Winters. 2009. 'Rhetorical Features of Green Evangelicalism'. *Environmental Communication: A Journal of Nature and Culture* 3(2): 224–43.

Prior, Lindsay. 2003. *Using Documents in Social Research*. Thousand Oaks, CA: Sage.

Prior, Lindsay. 2004a. 'Following in Foucault's Footsteps: Text and Context in Qualitative Research', pp. 317–33 in *Approaches to Qualitative Research: A Reader on Theory and Practice*, ed. S. Hesse-Biber and P. Leary. New York: Oxford University Press.

Prior, Lindsay. 2004b. 'Documents', pp. 345–60 in *Qualitative Research Practice*, ed. C. Seale et al. London: Sage.

Prior, Lindsay. 2008. 'Repositioning Documents in Social Research'. *Sociology* 42(5): 821–36. doi: 10.1177/0038038508094564.

Propp, Vladimir. 1968. *Morphology of the Folktale*. Austin: University of Texas Press.

Prus, Robert. 2003. 'Policy as a Collective Venture: A Symbolic Interactionist Approach to the Study of Organizational Directives'. *International Journal of Sociology and Social Policy* 23(6/7): 13–60.

Reynolds, Jill and Margaret Wetherell. 2003. 'The Discursive Climate of Singleness: The Consequences for Women's Negotiation of a Single Identity'. *Feminism & Psychology* 13(4): 489–510.

Richards, Lyn and Morse, Janice M. 2012. *README FIRST for a User's Guide to Qualitative Methods* (3rd edition), London: Sage.

Robert, Dominique and Shaul Shenhav. 2014. 'Fundamental Assumptions in Narrative Analysis: Mapping the Variety in Narrative Research'. *Qualitative Report* 19(38): 1–17.

Robinson, Oliver C. 2014. 'Sampling in Interview-Based Qualitative Research: A Theoretical and Practical Guide'. *Qualitative Research in Psychology* 11(1): 25–41. doi: 10.1080/14780887.2013.801543.

Rosenfeld Halverson, Erica, Michelle Bass and David Woods. 2012. 'The Process of Creation: A Novel Methodology for Analyzing Multimodal Data'. *Qualitative Report* 17: 1–27.

Roulston, Kathryn. 2011. 'Working through Challenges in Doing Interview Research'. *International Journal of Qualitative Methods* 10(4): 348–66.

Roy, Subhadip and Pratyush Banerjęe. 2012. 'Finding a Way out of the Ethnographic Paradigm Jungle'. *Qualitative Report* 17(Art. 61): 1–20.

Said, Edward. 2000. 'Invention, Memory, and Place'. *Critical Inquiry* 26(2): 175–92.

Saldaña, Johnny. 2009. *The Coding Manual for Qualitative Researchers.* Thousand Oaks, CA: Sage.

Sanjari, Mahnaz, Fatemeh Bahramnezhad, Fatemeh Khoshnava Fomani, Mahnaz Shoghi and Mohammad Ali Cheraghi. 2014. 'Ethical Challenges of Researchers in Qualitative Studies: The Necessity to Develop a Specific Guideline'. *Journal of Medical Ethics and History of Medicine* 7: August (www.ncbi.nlm.nih.gov/pmc/articles/PMC4263394/).

Savoie-Zajc, Lorraine. 2003. 'L'entrevue semi-dirigée' [Non-directive Interviews], pp. 263–285 in *Recherche sociale. De la problématique à la collecte des données* [Social Research. From Modelization to Data Gathering], ed. B. Gauthier. Sainte-Foy: Presses de l'Université du Québec.

Schnapper, Dominique. 1999. *La compréhension sociologique.* [Sociological Understanding] Paris: Presses Universitaires de France.

Schnapper, Dominique. 2005. *La compréhension sociologique. Démarche de l'analyse typologique* [Sociological Understanding. The Typological Analysis Process], Édition revue et augmentée. Paris: Presses Universitaires de France.

Schutz, Alfred. 1973. *Structures of the Life-World.* Evanston, IL: Northwestern University Press.

Schwartz-Shea, Peregrine and Dvora Yanow. 2012. *Interpretive Research Design: Concepts and Processes.* London: Routledge.

Serres, Michel. 1995. *Conversations on Science, Culture and Time with Bruno Latour*, trans. R. Lapidus. Ann Arbor, MI: University of Michigan Press.

Shaffir, William. 1999. 'Doing Ethnography: Reflections on Finding Your Way'. *Journal of Contemporary Ethnography* 28(6): 676–86. doi: 10.1177/089124199028006009.

Silverman, David. 2005a. 'Quality in Qualitative Research', pp. 209–26 in *Doing Qualitative Research: A Practical Handbook*, ed. D. Silverman. Thousand Oaks, CA: Sage.

Silverman, David. 2005b. *Doing Qualitative Research: A Practical Handbook*. Thousand Oaks, CA: Sage.

Silverman, David. 2013. 'Innumerable Inscrutable Habits: Why Unremarkable Things Matter', pp. 1–30 in *A Very Short, Fairly Interesting and Reasonably Cheap Book about Qualitative Research*, ed. D. Silverman. London: Sage.

Simmel, Georges. 1896. 'Comment les formes sociales se maintiennent' [How Social Forms Persist]. *L'Année sociologique (1896/1897–1924/1925)* 1: 71–109.

Smith, Dorothy E. 2002. 'Institutional Ethnography', pp. 17–52 in *Qualitative Research in Action*, ed. T. May. London: Sage.

Spector-Mersel, Gabriela. 2010. 'Narrative Research: Time for a Paradigm'. *Narrative Inquiry* 20(1): 204–24.

Spector-Mersel, Gabriela. 2011. 'Mechanisms of Selection in Claiming Narrative Identities: A Model for Interpreting Narratives'. *Qualitative Inquiry* 17(2): 172–85.

Spencer, Jonathan. 2001. 'Ethnography after Postmodernism', pp. 443–51 in *Handbook of Ethnography*, ed. P. Atkinson et al. London: Sage.

Spradley, James. 1979. *The Ethnographic Interview*. New York: Holt, Rinehart and Winston.

Springgay, Stephanie, Rita L. Irwin and Sylvia Wilson Kind. 2005. 'A/R/Tography as Living Inquiry through Art and Text'. *Qualitative Inquiry* 11(6): 897–912. doi: 10.1177/1077800405280696.

Stake, Robert E. 1995. *Qualitative Inquiry and Research Design: Choosing among Five Approaches*. Thousand Oaks, CA: Sage.

Starkey, Ken and Andrew Crane. 2003. 'Toward Green Narrative: Management and the Evolutionary Epic'. *Academy of Management Review* 28(2): 220–37.

Strauss, Anselm L. and Juliet M. Corbin. 1990. *Basics of Qualitative Research: Grounded Theory Procedures and Techniques*. Newbury Park, CA: Sage.

TCPS 2. 2014. *Tri-Council Policy Statement: Ethical Conduct for Research Involving Humans*, Latest edition (www.pre.ethics.gc.ca/eng/policy-politique/initiatives/tcps2-eptc2/Default/).

Thai, Mai Thi Thanh, Li Choy Chong and Narendra M. Agrawal. 2012. 'Straussian Grounded-Theory Method: An Illustration'. *Qualitative Report* 17(Art. 52): 1–55.

Timmermans, Stefan and Iddo Tavory. 2012. 'Theory Construction in Qualitative Research: From Grounded Theory to Abductive Analysis'. *Sociological Theory* 30(3): 167–86. doi: 10.1177/0735275112457914.

Tracy, Sarah J. 2010. 'Qualitative Quality: Eight "Big-Tent" Criteria for Excellent Qualitative Research'. *Qualitative Inquiry* 16(10): 837–51. doi: 10.1177/1077800410383121.

Trent, Allen and Jeasik Cho. 2015. 'Interpretation Strategies: Appropriate Concepts', pp. 639–57 in *The Oxford Handbook of Qualitative Research*, ed. P. Leavy. Oxford: Oxford University Press.

Unger, R. K. 2000. 'Outsiders Inside: Positive Marginality and Social Change'. *Journal of Social Issues* 56(1): 163–79.

Vachon, Marie-Lyne. 2008. 'La construction de l'idée politique de la présomp-
    tion d'innocence. Le cas de l'ADN dans la justice criminelle' [Construction
    of the Political Idea of the Presumption of Innocence. The Case of the DNA
    in Criminal Justice]. Masters thesis, University of Ottawa.
Van den Hoonaard, W. 2001. 'Is Research-Ethics Review a Moral Panic?',
    *Canadian Review of Sociology and Anthropology/Revue canadienne de
    sociologie et d'anthropologie*, 38(1): 19–36.
Van den Hoonaard, W. 2002. *Walking the Tightrope: Ethical Issues for
    Qualitative Researchers*. Toronto: University of Toronto Press.
van Dijk, Teun A. (ed.). 1985. *Handbook of Discourse Analysis*, Vol. 4.
    London: Academic Press.
van Manen, Max. 1990. *Researching Lived Experience: Human Science for an
    Action Sensitive Pedagogy*. New York: State University of New York Press.
Wacquant, Loic. 2004. *Body and Soul: Notebooks of an Apprentice Boxer*.
    Oxford: Oxford University Press.
Wang, Caroline C. and Mary Ann Burris. 1994. 'Empowerment through Photo
    Novella: Portraits of Participation'. *Health Education & Behavior* 21(2): 171–86.
Wang, Yong and Carl Roberts. 2005. 'Actantial Analysis: Greimas's Structural
    Approach to the Analysis of Self-Narratives'. *Narrative Inquiry* 15(3): 51–74.
Warren, Carol A. B. 2012. 'Interviewing as Social Interaction', pp. 129–142 in
    The Sage Handbook of Interview Research: The Complexity of the Craft,
    ed. J. F. Gubrium et al. Thousand Oaks, CA: Sage.
Watson, Rod. 1997. 'Ethnomethodology and Textual Analysis', pp. 80–98 in
    Qualitative Research: Theory, Method and Practice, ed. D. Silverman.
    London: Sage.
Wertz, Frederick J., Kathy Charmaz, Linda M. McMullen, Ruthellen Josselson,
    Rosemarie Anderson and Emalinda McSpadden. 2011. *Five Ways of Doing
    Qualitative Analysis: Phenomenological Psychology, Grounded Theory,
    Discourse Analysis, Narrative Research, and Intuitive Inquiry*. New York:
    Guilford Press.
Werunga, Jane, Sheryl Reimer-Kirkham and Carol Ewashen. 2016. 'A
    Decolonizing Methodology for Health Research on Female Genital
    Cutting'. *Advances in Nursing Science* 39(2): 150–64. doi: 10.1097/
    ANS.0000000000000121.
Westheimer, Joel, and Joseph Kahne. 2004. 'What kind of citizen? The politics
    of educating for democracy'. *American Educational Research Journal* 41
    (2): 237–69.
Wetherell, Margaret and Jonathan Potter. 1986. *Mapping the Language of
    Racism: Discourse and the Legitimation of Exploitation*. New York:
    Columbia University Press.
Wetherell, Margaret and Jonathan Potter. 1988. 'Discourse Analysis and the
    Identification of Interpretative Repertoires', pp. 168–83 in *Analysing
    Everyday Explanation: A Casebook of Methods*, ed. C. Antaki. London:
    Sage.
Whyte, William Foote. 1956. *Street Corner Society: The Social Structure of an
    Italian Slum*. Chicago: University of Chicago Press.

Wilkinson, Sue. 2000. 'Women with Breast Cancer Talking Causes: Comparing Content, Biographical and Discursive Analyses'. *Feminism & Psychology* 10(4): 431–60.

Wodak, Ruth. 2002. 'What CDA Is About – A Summary of Its History, Important Concept and Its Developments', pp. 1–13 in *Methods of Critical Discourse Analysis*, ed. R. Wodak and M. Meyer. Thousand Oaks, CA: Sage.

Wolcott, Harry F. 1990. *Writing Up Qualitative Research*. Newbury Park, CA: Sage.

Woodgate, Roberta L., Melanie Zurba and Pauline Tennent. 2017. 'Worth a Thousand Words? Advantages, Challenges and Opportunities in Working with Photovoice as a Qualitative Research Method with Youth and Their Families'. *Forum Qualitative Sozialforschung/Forum: Qualitative Social Research* 18(1): Art. 2.

Wright, Will. 1975. *Sixguns and Society: A Structural Study of the Western*. Berkeley: University of California Press.

Wright Mills, Charles. 1959. *The Sociological Imagination*. New York: Oxford University Press.

Wuthnow, Robert. (1991). *Acts of Compassion: Caring for Others and Helping Ourselves*. Princeton, NJ: Princeton University Press.

Yodanis, Carrie. 2006. 'A Place in Town: Doing Class in a Coffee Shop'. *Journal of Contemporary Ethnography* 35(3): 341–66.

INDEX

Page numbers in **bold** indicate an entry in the glossary, f denotes figure and t denotes table